THE ARTHUR MILLER TAPES

Christopher Bigsby and Arthur Miller shared a regular correspondence which stretched over nearly three decades of friendship. Their interaction and collaboration included a unique series of recorded interviews which now bring fresh and surprising perspectives to the life, thought and creative motivations of one of the greatest modern dramatists. The conversations range richly across topics such as the notorious McCarthy trials, the intent behind Miller's own work, and his family dynamics and relationships – including his short-lived marriage to Marilyn Monroe. Containing new insights into Miller's celebrated plays, including extensive meditations on *Death of a Salesman* and *The Crucible*, these illuminating interviews also give readers unrivalled access to the playwright himself.

Christopher Bigsby is Emeritus Professor of American Studies at the University of East Anglia, a Fellow of the Royal Society of Literature, a Fellow of the Royal Society of Arts, and an award-winning novelist and theatre historian. Among his many books are his two-volume biography of Miller, along with critical works on twentieth- and twenty-first-century American theatre and drama.

'This is a transfixing, fantastic record of a playwright's vision. As an actor and director, I found it an invaluable piece of work.'

Brian Cox, Emmy- and Golden Globe-winning actor and director

'*The Arthur Miller Tapes* is consistently illuminating, enjoyable and full of unexpected insights. I'd thoroughly recommend it to anyone interested in twentieth-century theatre, culture or politics.'

Richard Eyre, theatre director, writer and former Artistic Director of the National Theatre

'Only Christopher Bigsby would have the deep and comprehensive knowledge of Arthur Miller's life and work to enable him to ask such insightful questions. And because Arthur trusted and respected Chris, he always answers incisively and without evasion. Bigsby enables him to speak uninterrupted, allowing us to hear Arthur Miller's voice as if we were in the room with him.'

David Thacker, theatre, film and television director, former Director of the Young Vic; Professor of Theatre and Film, University of Greater Manchester

Arthur Miller and Chris Bigsby in rehearsals for a gala show at the Theatre Royal, Norwich, to mark the opening, in 1989, of the Arthur Miller Centre for American Studies at the University of East Anglia.

A LIFE IN HIS OWN WORDS

THE ARTHUR MILLER TAPES

BY *Christopher Bigsby*

CAMBRIDGE
UNIVERSITY PRESS

Shaftesbury Road, Cambridge CB2 8EA, United Kingdom

One Liberty Plaza, 20th Floor, New York, NY 10006, USA

477 Williamstown Road, Port Melbourne, VIC 3207, Australia

314–321, 3rd Floor, Plot 3, Splendor Forum, Jasola District Centre,
New Delhi – 110025, India

103 Penang Road, #05–06/07, Visioncrest Commercial, Singapore 238467

Cambridge University Press is part of Cambridge University Press & Assessment,
a department of the University of Cambridge.

We share the University's mission to contribute to society through the pursuit of
education, learning and research at the highest international levels of excellence.

www.cambridge.org
Information on this title: www.cambridge.org/9781009636926

DOI: 10.1017/9781009636940

© Cambridge University Press & Assessment 2026

This publication is in copyright. Subject to statutory exception and to the provisions
of relevant collective licensing agreements, no reproduction of any part may take
place without the written permission of Cambridge University Press & Assessment.

When citing this work, please include a reference to the DOI 10.1017/9781009636940

First published 2026

A catalogue record for this publication is available from the British Library

*A Cataloging-in-Publication data record for this book is available from the Library
of Congress*

ISBN 978-1-009-63692-6 Hardback

Cambridge University Press & Assessment has no responsibility for the persistence
or accuracy of URLs for external or third-party internet websites referred to in this
publication and does not guarantee that any content on such websites is, or will
remain, accurate or appropriate.

For EU product safety concerns, contact us at Calle de José Abascal, 56, 1°, 28003
Madrid, Spain, or email eugpsr@cambridge.org

CONTENTS

Acknowledgements page [ix]
Timeline [x]

Introduction		[1]
1	Beginnings	[8]
2	Michigan	[32]
3	Mary Slattery	[47]
4	Brooklyn	[54]
5	The Federal Theatre, Library of Congress and Radio Plays	[66]
6	*The Man Who Had All the Luck* and *All My Sons*	[100]
7	*Death of a Salesman*	[120]
8	The Waldorf Conference	[149]
9	*The Crucible*	[162]
10	*A View from the Bridge*	[179]
11	House Un-American Activities Committee	[185]
12	Mary and Marilyn	[195]

Contents

13 Inge [219]

14 *After the Fall* and Daniel [229]

15 *The Price* and Vietnam [235]

16 The Eighties [245]

17 The Nineties [254]

18 *Resurrection Blues* [289]

19 Theatre [293]

20 Looking Back [310]

21 Arthur Miller at Eighty [316]

22 Arthur Miller at Eighty-Five [321]

ACKNOWLEDGEMENTS

The interviews which follow took place over many years in many places. Most were private but some took place in theatres, hotels, in cars, universities, or Miller's own home in Connecticut, while I have occasionally drawn on work I did for the BBC, to which I am grateful.

TIMELINE

1915. Arthur Miller is born in Harlem to Isadore and Augusta Miller (whose maiden name was Barnett). Their families both came from the same small town in what is now Poland, though Augusta was born in America. Theirs was an arranged marriage. Arthur's brother, Kermit, is older by three years, his sister, Joan, younger by six years. The family begins their American life in a tenement on the Lower East Side of New York, but subsequently moves north, to the top of Central Park. Miller is born in the family's multi-room 111th Street apartment, but they then move to 110th Street, between Lenox and Fifth Avenues. His father is a successful manufacturer of women's coats. The family has a summer cottage on Far Rockaway, a maid and a chauffeur-driven car. As a child he attends the same local school as his mother had years earlier, PS24. The Millers are wealthy.

1928. Miller takes his bar mitzvah in the Avenue M temple.

1929. The stock market crashes. Isadore's business fails, and the family move to the Midwood section of Brooklyn, first to a two-family home on Ocean Parkway, then to a small frame house on East Third Street, the house in which Miller would later imagine Willy Loman living. The young Miller shares a bedroom with his grandfather. At fourteen, he is already 6 feet tall. Miller goes first to the James Madison High School, later, in 1930, transferring to the Abraham Lincoln High School. It is here he plays football, injuring his leg, the reason he would

Timeline

later not serve in the war. For a while, in 1939, he earns money delivering bread in the early hours. For a brief time, he performs as a crooner on a local radio station.

1931. Miller decides he wants to go to sea as a cabin boy, but this comes to nothing when he discovers that the ship is already fully crewed. His father is reduced to borrowing money from him for a subway ride.

1932. Following a conversation with a student, Miller regards himself as a Marxist. He writes a short story about a salesman, 'In Memoriam'. (The work remains unpublished to this day.) He graduates from Abraham Lincoln High School but abandons City College after two weeks. For two years he then works at Chadick-Delmater, a large auto parts warehouse, the only Jew on the staff.

1934. Learning that the University of Michigan offers cash prizes for those writing plays, the Hopwood Awards, and that tuition, at $65, is relatively cheap, he enters the university as a journalism major, subsequently changing to English. While there, he takes a playwriting course with Kenneth Rowe and wins his first Hopwood Award for *No Villain* (subsequently *They Too Arise*). It would have its first production at the Old Red Lion Theatre, London, in December 2015.

1935. In winter, Mary Grace Slattery arrives as a student at Michigan, one year behind Miller. She will, however, as he did, leave in 1938, but without graduating, instead, it seems, transferring credit when she moves to New York.

1936. Miller is shocked by news of the bombing of the Basque town of Guernica. In an October edition of the student newspaper, the *Michigan Daily*, he writes of fascism in Spain.

1937. While at Michigan, besides winning another Hopwood, for *Honors at Dawn* (which has a strike at its centre), Miller works on the *Michigan Daily*, and meets Mary Slattery, whom he will marry in 1940. She is as radical as him. To make ends meet, he works at various jobs for up to five hours a day, as does she as a stenographer. In his role as a student reporter, he travels to Flint, Michigan, where he witnesses the sit-down strike at the General Motors Fisher body plant. He drives a close friend, Ralph Neaphus, to New York, from where he will travel to Spain and fight in the Spanish Civil War, an issue which engaged Miller then and would later. Neaphus dies there.

1938. In Miller's final year his play *The Great Disobedience*, set in a prison and researched at the nearby Jackson State Penitentiary, comes second in the Hopwood Awards. Following graduation from Michigan, he returns to Brooklyn, with little money and many debts, where he writes short stories (unpublished), one of which, 'Schleifer, Albert', clearly foreshadows *Death of a Salesman*. He works briefly for the Federal Theatre, at $22.77 a week, writing *The Golden Years*, which features the conflict between Cortez and Montezuma. The woman who will become his sister-in-law (Frances, married to Kermit) earns 50¢ an hour working for the National Youth Administration – like the Federal Theatre, this was a New Deal project. Miller makes his money, however, writing plays for radio, his first script being *Joe, the Motorman*, a play about a rebellious subway driver which earns him $100. *The Pussycat and the Expert Plumber Who Was a Man* is transmitted by CBS in 1940. *The Golden Years* is finally staged in 1987.

1939. With Norman Rosten, a friend from Michigan, Miller writes a comedy, *Listen My Children*.

1940. Miller marries Mary Slattery in Cleveland. Her family is Catholic, though she has abandoned her religion. Neither family approves. Directly after the marriage, he goes on a trip onboard the SS *Copa*, hoping to find a story, writing from

Mobile, Alabama, to his wife, whom he addresses as Migg, calling her both 'darling' and 'sister', to say that he has already incorporated one of the sailors into a play. The unpublished novel, *The Bangkok Star*, results from his trip. Written between 1940 and 1942, it is a direct attack on American racism.

1941. Miller is classified '4 F' (or unfit for military service) by his Selective Service Board, a fact noted in his FBI file. He works in the Brooklyn Navy Yard as a ship fitter. Commissioned by the Library of Congress to travel to the South to record local accents, he witnesses a strike by Black garment workers in North Carolina and records their singing. As a result of the Japanese attack on Pearl Harbor, Kermit enlists in the infantry and gains a distinguished war record, even as he is hospitalised as a result of the conditions he has experienced. In later years, this would have an impact on his mental well-being. Miller begins writing for *Cavalcade of America*, a weekly radio series with patriotic themes, sponsored by DuPont (an American multinational chemical company). His first script is about Joel Chandler Harris, a journalist and folklorist. A later play, *Thunder from the Hills*, stars Orson Wells as Juarez, President of Mexico. He writes many plays, including one about the aviation pioneer Amelia Earhart. Playwriting becomes his main source of income, while he also writes radio scripts for the Theatre Guild.

1942. An unpublished and unproduced play, *Boro Hall Nocturne*, highlights anti-Semitism in America.

1943. Miller is hired to work on a film to be called *The Story of GI Joe*, based on the columns of the war correspondent Ernie Pyles. In this connection, the following year Miller tours military bases. None of his script survives into the finished film. He writes *The Half Bridge* and, for Stage for Action, *That They May Win*.

1944. Miller's account of his time researching the film is published as *Situation Normal*. His first play, *The Man Who Had All the Luck*, adapted from an unpublished novel, opens on Broadway on 23 January and closes within days. Other than a brief production in England, sixteen years later, it would be forty years before it was produced again, this time at the Bristol Old Vic in England. His daughter, Jane, is born in September.

1945. Miller publishes a novel, *Focus*, about anti-Semitism in New York. It sells an estimated 90,000 copies. In an article for *New Masses*, he denounces Ezra Pound for his anti-Semitism. He welcomes the use of nuclear bombs on Japan, years later denouncing nuclear weapons. He adapts Ferenc Molnár's *The Guardsman* for radio.

1947. He attends Communist Party meetings of writers. *All My Sons*, based on a story he had been told by his mother-in-law, is directed by Elia Kazan. His first commercial and critical success, it opens on 29 January and receives the New York Drama Critics' Circle Award, beating Eugene O'Neill's *The Iceman Cometh*. *All My Sons* is banned by the Civil Affairs Division of the American Military Government from being produced in occupied areas of Europe. A report to the FBI on the shooting of the film version attacks it as a work of propaganda.

In February, he sails to Europe for the first time, with Vincent Longhi, whom he had met when exploring the Red Hook area of Brooklyn. This would later result in a screenplay, *The Hook*, and later still, in 1955, *A View from the Bridge*. His son, Robert, is born on 31 May.

President Truman signs Executive Order 9835 authorising loyalty investigations into those employed in any department or agency of the executive branch of the federal government, and the suppression of the names of informants. Miller writes a play, *You're Next*, attacking the House Un-American Activities Committee (HUAC). It is performed 400 times in a single year. He attends a dinner of the American Russia Institute, which the FBI classifies as a communist front. In December, he gives a speech at the Zionist Organisation of America, though Miller is not a Zionist.

1948. This year Miller and his wife buy a house in Roxbury, Connecticut, selling it in 1956 for another close by where he would live for the rest of his life, though with time spent at the Chelsea Hotel in New York.

In May, Miller celebrates the creation of the state of Israel, publishing an article in *Jewish Life*, a magazine influenced by the Communist Party, explaining his position as a Jew who writes, rather than being a Jewish writer. He is a supporter of Henry Wallace, a third-party candidate, in the presidential election and begins writing *Death of a Salesman* in a cabin he builds himself.

1949. *Death of a Salesman*, with Lee J. Cobb playing Willy Loman, opens at the Morosco Theatre, on 10 February, and wins a Pulitzer Prize, a Tony Award and a New York Drama Circle Critics' Award. He attends the Waldorf Conference, organised by a communist front organisation, chairing one of the sessions, introducing Aaron Copland, Clifford Odets and Dmitri Shostakovich. He is attacked in the press as a communist. Among those denouncing the occasion is the novelist Mary McCarthy, who would write critical responses to Miller's plays. He later argues that his attendance at the conference shaped the views of some critics even as, for him, it marks the end of his flirtation with communism. He publishes an article entitled 'Tragedy and the Common Man' in the *New York Times*.

1950. *An Enemy of the People* (an adaptation of Ibsen's play) opens on 28 December, starring Fredric March and his wife,

Timeline

Florence Eldridge, both of whom are being threatened with investigation.

1951. He travels to Hollywood with Elia Kazan in an attempt to secure production of his screenplay *The Hook*, set on the Brooklyn waterfront. It is rejected. While there, he meets Marilyn Monroe and attends a party where he stands in for Kazan, who had been having an affair with her. The film version of *Death of a Salesman*, with Frederic March, is released, though only after Miller threatens legal action when Columbia Pictures plans to release a short film celebrating the life of salesmen.

1952. Miller meets with Kazan when on his way to Salem to research what will become *The Crucible*. It is at this meeting that it becomes clear that Kazan, summoned before HUAC, will, under pressure from Hollywood, name names. Miller will not thereafter speak to him until he directs *After the Fall* in 1964.

1953. *The Crucible* opens in January. It wins the Antoinette Perry Award but becomes the centre of controversy.

1954. Kazan's *On the Waterfront*, written by Budd Schulberg, is released, close in spirit to *The Hook* except that it justifies the role of the informer. Miller is refused renewal of his passport to travel to the French-language premiere of *The Crucible* in Belgium.

1955. *A Memory of Two Mondays* and the one-act version of *A View from the Bridge* open in September, followed, a year later, by the two-act version, directed by Peter Brook in England. Miller's involvement in a planned film concerned with juvenile delinquency is ended following complaints based on what are presumed to be his political beliefs.

Timeline

1956. Miller spends time in Nevada, required before he can complete his divorce from Mary. Called before HUAC, he refuses to name those who had attended Communist Party meetings and is sentenced to a fine and a one-month suspended sentence for Contempt of Congress. His sister, the actress Joan Copeland, realises that she has been blacklisted because of her connection to Miller. Miller marries Monroe and, with her, travels to England, where there is a production of *A View from the Bridge* and where Monroe is to appear with Lawrence Olivier, in *The Prince and the Showgirl*. The first signs of tension between them appear within weeks of the marriage.

1957. Monroe suffers an ectopic pregnancy. Miller publishes a short story that would become the basis of his film *The Misfits*. A French-language film of *The Crucible*, with a screenplay by Jean-Paul Sartre, is released.

1958. The Court of Appeals reverses Miller's earlier contempt conviction.

1959. Marilyn has an affair with Yves Montand while shooting *Let's Make Love*. Miller is awarded the Gold Medal for Drama by the National Institute of Arts and Letters.

1960. Miller writes *The Misfits* for Monroe, but during the shooting of the film, which stars Clark Gable, Montgomery Clift and Eli Wallach, their marriage finally falls apart.

1961. Miller and Monroe divorce. In March, Miller's mother, Augusta, dies. *The Misfits* is released.

1962. Marilyn Monroe dies of an overdose. Miller marries Inge Morath, a Magnum photographer he had first met on the set of *The Misfits*. It is his third marriage and her second. Before the ceremony, the couple – a German-speaking woman about to marry an American Jew – go to Mauthausen concentration camp in Austria. Their daughter Rebecca is born.

1963. Miller publishes a children's book, *Jane's Blanket*.

1964. *After the Fall*, Miller's first play since *A View from the Bridge*, and directed by Elia Kazan, opens at the ANTA Theatre in Washington Square Park in January. It is a deeply personal play in which he and Marilyn Monroe are clearly characters, as is Inge Morath. Popular with audiences, it is dismissed by some critics as in poor taste, given Monoe's recent death. In December, he follows it with *Incident at Vichy*, set in Vichy France, and in part prompted by his attendance at the trial, in Frankfurt, of guards from Auschwitz. The play runs for thirty-two performances.

1965. Miller is elected president of International PEN and attends a teach-in on the Vietnam War at the University of Michigan. He turns down an invitation to attend the signing of the Arts and Humanities Bill in the White House.

1966. Miller organises the PEN conference in New York City. His father, Isadore, dies.

1967. Inge gives birth to their son, Daniel, a child with Down syndrome, agreeing that he will be best cared for by professionals. Miller joins leading poets at New York's Town Hall in an event called 'Poets for Peace'. He reads his poem 'What Blood-Red Law' and publishes a short-story collection, *I Don't Need You Anymore*.

1968. *The Price* opens in February. It features two brothers, close in spirit to his relationship with his own brother, Kermit, though Miller himself is inclined to deny this.

He campaigns for the presidential candidate Eugene McCarthy and attends the Democratic National Convention in Chicago as a delegate representing Connecticut, witnessing the violence of the Chicago police. He attends peace talks with the North Vietnamese in Paris.

1969. Arthur and Inge publish *In Russia*, drawing on their visits there in 1965 and 1967. *The Price* opens in Russia. An anti-war allegory, *The Reason Why*, is filmed at his Roxbury home. He and Inge visit Czechoslovakia, where they meet Václav Havel.

1970. Arthur is present, with Inge and Rebecca, in Cambodia when bombing begins. Two one-act plays, *Fame* and *The Reason Why*, are staged.

1971. *The Portable Arthur Miller* is published, with an introduction by the theatre director and critic Harold Clurman.

1972. *The Creation of the World and Other Business* opens in February, a musical version, *Up From Paradise*, being performed in April 1974 at the University of Michigan with music by Stanley Silverman. Miller attends, and writes about, the Democratic Convention in Miami. He grants permission for an all-Black production of *Death of a Salesman* in Baltimore.

1974. Miller becomes involved in the case of Peter Reilly, a local teenager accused of murdering his own mother, the following year persuading a reporter at the *New York Times* to write about it. Originally found guilty, Reilly is eventually released as a result of the efforts of Miller and others. Miller spends some five years on the case.

1975. *Death of a Salesman* returns to Broadway, with George C. Scott as Willy Loman.

1977. *The Archbishop's Ceiling*, set in Eastern Europe, not identified as such but in fact in Prague, opens in April at the Kennedy Centre in Washington for a run of thirty performances. Arthur and Inge publish *In the Country*, which celebrates their immediate environment.

1978. A collection of Miller's essays appears, edited by Robert A. Martin. With Kurt Vonnegut and Edward Albee, Miller protests against the trials of Natan Sharansky and Alexander Ginsburg in the Soviet Union. He meets Aleksandr Solzhenitsyn in America. Inge and Arthur travel to China, resulting in a book: *Chinese Encounters*. Belatedly, Miller is able to attend a Belgian production of *The Crucible*.

1979. Miller protests against the detention of Václav Havel.

1980. *The American Clock* opens at the Spoleto Festival. *Playing for Time*, a film based on Fania Fénelon's experiences as part of the camp orchestra in Auschwitz, is transmitted by CBS, despite protests that the lead role is played by the non-Jewish Vanessa Redgrave, who has a record of support for Palestinians.

1982. Miller directs *Two by A.M.* (subsequently, at the suggestion of Christopher Bigsby, *Two-Way Mirror*), consisting of *Elegy for a Lady* and *Some Kind of Love Story*, at the Long Wharf Theatre in New Haven. He writes *The Havel Deal* to be performed at an evening in support of Havel as part of the International Theatre Festival in Avignon.

1983. Miller directs *Death of a Salesman* in Beijing. While there, a fire destroys part of his Connecticut home. *A View from the Bridge* is revived on Broadway. *Up From Paradise* is staged by the Jewish Repertory Theatre.

1984. Miller publishes *'Death of a Salesman' in Beijing*. *Death of a Salesman*, with Dustin Hoffman, John Malkovich and Kate Reid, opens on Broadway. A televised version is transmitted by CBS the following year, Hoffman winning a Golden Globe Award. Miller is honored at the Kennedy Centre for his lifetime achievement.

1985. The play version of *Playing for Time* opens in September. Miller and Harold Pinter fly to Turkey under the auspices of

PEN. In England, the Royal Shakespeare Company stages *Two-Way Mirror*.

1986. Miller meets Mikhail Gorbachev in Moscow. *The Archbishop's Ceiling* opens in London, at the Royal Shakespeare Company's London base in the Barbican, as does *The American Clock*, directed by Peter Wood, at the National Theatre.

1987. Miller's autobiography, *Timebends*, is published, chosen as a Book of the Month selection. The advance is $750,000. In America, it prompts a number of venomous reviews, in contrast to the reception in the UK. *Danger: Memory (I Can't Remember Anything* and *Clara)* opens in February at the Lincoln Center. *A View from the Bridge*, with Michael Gambon, opens at the National Theatre.

1988. *Danger: Memory*, with Betsy Blair and Paul Rogers, opens in London. Miller visits Grenada and Chile, writing a report on the latter, then under Augusto Pinochet, for PEN.

1989. A fatwa is declared on Salman Rushdie. The Berlin Wall falls. Miller writes an article for the *New York Times*, published in 1990, sceptical of what a united Germany, which he supports, would be like, given its past. David Thacker's production of Miller's version of *An Enemy of the People*, with Tom Wilkinson, transfers from the Young Vic to the West End. The Arthur Miller Centre for American Studies is launched at the University of East Anglia, with a gala performance at the Theatre Royal in Norwich with leading figures from the British stage. In America, filming starts in Norwich, Connecticut, of *Everybody Wins*, based on *Some Kind of Love Story*.

1990. The Young Vic stages *The Price*, directed by David Thacker. Miller attends the Bristol Old Vic production of *The Man Who Had All the Luck*, which then transfers to the Young

Vic. *The Crucible* and *After the Fall* open at the National Theatre. Miller interviews Nelson Mandela in South Africa for the BBC. He voices characters in Ken Burns' documentary *The Civil War*. His film *Everybody Wins* is released.

1991. *The Last Yankee* opens in January as a one-act version at Off Broadway's 52nd Street Ensemble Theatre. Two years later, an expanded version is staged in America and then at the Young Vic, the latter with Zoë Wanamaker and Peter Davidson. *The Ride Down Mount Morgan* opens in London, with Tom Conti. Alex North, who had written music for *Death of a Salesman* and *The Misfits*, dies. 'Miller Meets Mandela' is broadcast on BBC Arena.

1992. Miller publishes the novella *Homely Girl* and is presented with the National Arts Club Medal of Honor for literature. Joseph L. Rauh, who had defended Miller before HUAC, dies.

1993. There is a television production of *The American Clock* on TNT.

1994. *Broken Glass* opens in New York in March and in England in August. Poorly received in America, in England it wins the Olivier Award as best new play. In America, a television version of *The American Clock* is transmitted.

1995. Miller receives the William Inge Festival Award for distinguished achievement in American theatre. He records a series of interviews on his back porch for BBC radio, broadcast on Radio 4. In England his eightieth birthday is celebrated at the Royal National Theatre with a cast that includes Rosemary Harris, Juliet Stevenson, Josette Simon, Joseph Fiennes and Henry Goodman. It is directed by David Thacker and produced by Christopher Bigsby. This is followed at the Arthur Miller Centre at the University of East Anglia by a gala dinner in the company of actors, directors, reviewers and academics. Speakers include David Thacker and Salman Rushdie, himself still subject to a fatwa. Miller spends time in Oxford as the Cameron Mackintosh Visiting Professor of Drama, while, back in America, his birthday is celebrated at New York's Town Hall, with speeches and readings by Edward Albee, John Guare, Carlos Fuentes and David Mamet. The Arthur Miller Society is founded, publishing first a newsletter and subsequently, in 2006, a journal.

1996. A film of *The Crucible* is released, starring Daniel Day-Lewis, who marries Rebecca Miller in November. Miller receives the Edward Albee Last Frontier Playwright Award. *The Ride Down Mount Morgan* opens in Williamstown for a scheduled short run, with F. Murray Abraham.

1997. *A View from the Bridge* opens at the Roundabout Theatre, with Anthony LaPaglia as Eddie Carbone. Both LaPaglia and the play win Tony Awards.

1998. A double bill of *The Last Yankee* and *I Can't Remember Anything* opens, as does *Mr. Peters' Connections*, with Peter Falk, part of a series of Miller's plays produced at the Signature Theatre, where he reads *Jane's Blanket* to an audience of children. A revised version of *The Ride Down Mount Morgan* opens at the Public Theatre with Patrick Stewart, where it runs, initially, for forty performances before returning in 2000, when it runs for a further 121 performances. *Death of a Salesman*, with Brian Dennehy, opens at the Goodman Theatre, directed by Robert Falls. The following year it transfers to New York, where it receives four Tony Awards. Miller attends the Lotos Club in New York, for a state dinner, the history of which stretches back to 1870, previous honoured guests including Oliver Wendell Holmes and Mark Twain. His speech is published in 2011 in *The Arthur Miller Journal*, together with an interview with David Thacker, who has directed many of Miller's plays. *Mr. Peter's Connections* opens as the final play in the Signature Theatre's season of his work.

1999. In June, Inge has an exhibition of her work in Vienna. Controversially, Elia Kazan receives a lifetime achievement award from the Academy of Motion Picture Arts and Sciences. He is supported by Miller. An opera version of *A View from the Bridge*, with music by William Bolcom, opens in Chicago. *The Price* opens at Williamstown and transfers to Broadway. *Death of a Salesman* is revived on Broadway with Brian Dennehy.

2000. Miller travels to Cuba and meets Fidel Castro. Inge has a diagnosis of non-Hodgkin's lymphoma, a cancer of the lymphatic system. They return to England, where he is given the freedom of the city of Norwich and his eighty-fifth birthday is celebrated at the University of East Anglia (UEA), Warren Michell (who played Willy Loman at the National Theatre) giving a speech. During the morning Miller falls and breaks a number of ribs but refuses an ambulance, continuing with the rest of the day's programme, including an interview at the Theatre Royal and a gala dinner at UEA's Sainsbury Centre. There is also a celebration at the University of Michigan, but, because of his accident, Miller has to appear through a satellite link. *Echoes Down the Corridors*, a collection of his essays, edited by Steve A. Centola, is published. He flies to Toronto for the shooting of *Focus*, produced by his son Robert and starring William H. Macy. He is in England for the National Theatre production of *All My Sons* and *Mr. Peter's Connections*, directed by Michael Blakemore, at the Almeida Theatre.

2001. Scenes from a film of *Homely Girl* (to be called *Eden*) are shot at his Roxbury home. The opera version of *A View from the Bridge*, with music by William Balcom, is staged at the Lyric Theatre, Chicago. Miller delivers the Jefferson Lecture for the

National Endowment for the Arts in Washington, subsequently published under the title *Politics and the Art of Acting*. Arthur and Inge are in Paris for television recordings in connection with Inge's project, *Border Spaces*, based on her visit to Slovenia, when news of 9/11 reaches them. *The Man Who Had All the Luck* is revived at the Williamstown Theatre Festival.

2002. In mid January, Inge's condition worsens rapidly, and she dies of lymphatic cancer. The funeral is held in the barn of their Roxbury home, presided over by William Coffin. Later, a memorial service is held at the Mitzi Newhouse Theater at Lincoln Center, Rebecca Miller delivering the elegy. Liam Neeson appears in *The Crucible*, directed by Richard Eyre, at the Virginia Theatre, New York. In October, Miller flies to Oviedo to receive the Principe de Asturias Prize for Literature. *Resurrection Blues* opens at the Guthrie Theatre in Minneapolis. Late in 2002, he meets Agnes Barley, a thirty-two-year-old artist who becomes his companion.

2003. He receives the Jerusalem Prize. His brother, Kermit, dies, as does Elia Kazan. Martin Gottfried publishes *Arthur Miller: A Life*. The Miller family having refused to cooperate.

2004. *After the Fall* is revived with Peter Berg. *Finishing the Picture*, set during the filming of *The Misfits*, opens at the Goodman Theatre, Chicago, in September. In December, Miller falls ill with pneumonia.

2005. On 10 February, the fifty-sixth anniversary of the opening of *Death of a Salesman*, Arthur Miller dies at his Roxbury home, of cancer and heart failure. He is buried in Roxbury. His headstone reads: ARTHUR MILLER WRITER. A memorial service is held in Roxbury and at the Majestic Theatre in New York. Daniel Day-Lewis reads from one of his essays, while Joan Copeland delivers a speech from *The American Clock*, in which she had played the part of her own mother. Robert Miller reads from his father's letter to HUAC explaining why he would not name names. Other speakers include Estelle Parsons, who reads Linda Loman's lines from the Epilogue to *Death of a Salesman*, Edward Albee and Tony Kushner. Members of the public queue around the block to attend.

His estate gifts fifty-five acres to the Roxbury Land Trust, this becoming the Arthur Miller and Inge Morath Preserve.

2006. The Arthur Miller Freedom to Write Lecture is established with PEN, the first lecturer being Orhan Pamuk. In subsequent years, writers include David Grossman, Umberto Eco, Nawal el Sadawi, Christopher Hitchens, Wole Soyinka, Salman Rushdie, Sonia Sotomayor, Colm Tóibín, Chimamanda Ngozi Adiche, Roxane Gay, Masha Gennen, Hillary Rodham Clinton, Arundhati Roy, Richard Flanagan and Andrey Kurkov. The following year, the Arthur Miller Theatre is opened at the University of Michigan with a production of *Playing for Time*. The Arthur Miller Society begins publication of the *Arthur Miller Journal*.

2008. A posthumous collection of stories is published under the title *Presence: Stories*. On 12 December, Mary Miller dies at Laguna Beach, having moved there in 2003.

2009. Methuen publishes Miller's dramatic works in six volumes.

2010. *A View from the Bridge* opens on Broadway, directed by Gregory Mosher and starring Liev Schreiber, Scarlett Johansson and Jessica Hecht. *All My Sons* opens at the Apollo Theatre in London with David Suchet and Zoë Wanamaker.

2012. *Death of a Salesman* is revived, starring Philip Seymour Hoffman. It wins two Tony Awards.

Timeline

2014. Ivo van Hove directs a startling production of *A View from the Bridge* at the Young Vic, while Richard Armitage appears in *The Crucible* directed by Yaël Farber at the Old Vic.

2015. Miller's first play, *No Villain*, is produced at a pub theatre in London. A stage version of *The Hook* is staged at the Everyman Theatre in Liverpool. An interview with its director, James Dacre, is published in the spring 2016 edition of *The Arthur Miller Journal*. *Death of a Salesman* is revived, by the Royal Shakespeare Company, with Anthony Sher playing the part of Willy Loman. *Incident at Vichy* is revived Off Broadway by the Signature Theatre. Miller's centennial is celebrated. *The Complete Collected Essays*, edited by Matthew Roudané, is published. It contains over seventy essays. The complete three-volume collection of Miller's plays, edited by Tony Kushner, is published by the Library of America. *Incident at Vichy* is revived Off Broadway. BBC radio broadcasts *Attention Must Be Paid* in its Radio 4 *Archive* series.

2016. Ivo van Hove's production of *The Crucible* opens in New York with Sophie Okonedo and Ben Whishaw, winning two Tony Awards. The Miller Foundation stages a celebration of Miller's centennial. Penguin publishes *Presence: Collected Stories*. Susan C. W. Abbotson edits his *Collected Essays*.

2017. *The Price* is revived, with Tony Shalhoub, John Turturro and Danny DeVito winning a Drama Desk Award. Rebecca Miller releases *Arthur Miller: Writer*, a film about her father which she has been making over many years, beginning when she was in her twenties.

2018. *Finishing the Picture* opens at the Finborough Theatre in England, while a stage version of *The Hook* opens in Ireland.

2019. Revivals include *All My Sons* at the Roundabout Theatre, with Tracy Letts and Annette Bening, and, at the Young Vic, an all-Black version of *Death of a Salesman*, starring Wendell Pierce. It opens on Broadway in 2022. Other revivals are *The Price*, at London's Wyndham Theatre, and *The American Clock*, at the Old Vic. Rebecca Miller donates her father's studio to Roxbury as a museum. The Harry Ransom Centre, in Austin Texas, opens its Miller archive.

2020. *No Villain* opens at the Studio Theatre of Long Island. *The Hook* is staged by Brave New World Repertory Theatre in Brooklyn. Covid strikes, closing theatres.

2022. Joan Copeland, Miller's actress sister, dies in January, and his first son, Robert, in March. *The Crucible*, with a mixed-race cast, is staged by the National Theatre and broadcast in cinemas the following year. The Arthur Miller Trust celebrates his life by establishing programmes that provide access and equity for theatre education in public schools, promoting theatre education as part of their academic curriculum.

INTRODUCTION

My first contact with Arthur Miller came when, as a graduate student, I wrote to him. He replied from Paris. I wrote again a couple of years later after I had seen the European premiere of *After the Fall*, at the Belgrade Theatre, Coventry (whose ruined cathedral still stands as a reminder of the World War II bombing of the city). I sent him a newspaper clipping about the guilt of the survivor, as this seemed to me, as it turned out to him, to be a central theme of a play concerned with private, public and metaphysical betrayals, the set of which was dominated by a concentration camp tower. As it happens, we had both visited concentration camps a short while previously – I had been to Auschwitz-Birkenau, he to Mauthausen. The play was seen rather differently in America, where the central figure, based on the recently dead Marilyn Monroe, was the cause of controversy. Once again, he replied, beginning what would, some years later, become a regular correspondence, by letter and (fast-fading) fax, along with a series of recorded interviews that would stretch over nearly thirty years.

On an early visit to him in Connecticut, I failed to find a hotel room, arriving in what was known as the leaf season, when tourists flooded in to see trees suddenly flaming yellow, ochre and red. The man on reception in one hotel told me that I would not get a room on the eastern seaboard, while offering to provide me with a cot (or a camp-bed, in the UK) in a room otherwise used for conferences. So it was that I slept, or not, surrounded by tables equipped with paper, ball-point pens and bottles of water. When I arrived at Arthur's, he asked me where I had stayed. As I explained, he told me that in future I should always stay with him, which I duly did. Arthur would be patiently waiting for me at Southbury bus depot, in his red Mercedes, to drive me along the winding rural roads to his house in Roxbury.

In return I once gave Inge and him a gift which might well have killed them – Scottish haggis (consisting of minced sheep's heart, lungs and liver encased in the animal's stomach). It was allowed through customs because, unsurprisingly, the officer could not find it listed on the many pages of banned products. I had, however, carried it for many hours in three airports and on a heated plane. It duly went into the Miller freezer and, given that they survived, never came out again, or was dumped once I had disappeared.

In the summers, I would join Arthur and Inge in their spring-fed pond, its snapping turtles, he assured me, no longer a problem, if not entirely absent. In the winter, the pond cataracted over with ice, and he inducted me into the best way to drive on snow-impacted roads, just as he mended my tape recorder and, in England, my car. No home should be without an Arthur Miller. Over the years he and Inge, a Magnum photographer he had first encountered on the set of *The Misfits* in Nevada, were generous in their hospitality and tolerant of an Englishman with a tape recorder ever at the ready.

Arthur would be a regular visitor to my university, the University of East Anglia, where I launched the Arthur

Introduction

Miller Centre for American Studies in 1989 with a gala performance at the Theatre Royal in which he talked about his plays while actors performed scenes. He subsequently returned to mark both his eightieth and eighty-fifth birthdays. In the case of the former, I produced, and David Thacker directed, a show at the National Theatre in which leading actors performed scenes from his plays in front of the author as he talked about his life and work.

On another occasion, on the morning he was given the freedom of the city of Norwich in the medieval Guildhall, he fell and broke a number of ribs, refusing an ambulance and carrying on with the ceremony, an interview at the local theatre and a Sainsbury Centre dinner, before, the next day, requiring a wheelchair to travel from Heathrow to JFK, where he was not recognised by the driver assigned to meet him and was driven off in the wrong direction.

Quite how the question of my writing his biography came about I am not sure, unless it was the appearance of one by Martin Gottfried that he especially despised, having refused all cooperation with a man who had written hostile reviews of his work. He simply one day introduced me to someone as his biographer, and we were off to the races.

Some interviews I conducted with him, on both sides of the Atlantic, were public, in what Inge called 'the Chris and Art Show'. More usually they were informal, mostly recorded at Roxbury but also wherever we happened to be – whether at home or in rehearsals.

In a collaboration between the Arthur Miller Centre and Methuen, I published a number of the interviews in a book to mark his seventy-fifth birthday in 1990 – *Arthur Miller and Company* – which included pieces by actors, directors and writers, and which I presented to him at a public celebration in New York. To mark his death, in 2005, I followed this with *Remembering Arthur Miller*, which again along with contributions from his fellow writers and those in the theatre world included an extensive interview for the BBC recorded on his back porch, birdsong accompanying him as he looked back over his life.

I still, however, had many tapes, not revisited at the time, and not published, though a couple came from public occasions. In 2022, I listened back to them, and this book is an edited version. The only interview previously published appeared in the journal of the Arthur Miller Society in 2006, recorded just under ten months before his death. Beyond that, a few fragments appear in my Miller biographies and the critical book I published in 2005.

Because these interviews, recorded over several decades, sometimes cover the same ground, I have edited them in such a way as mostly, though inevitably not entirely, to avoid repetition and to make for a largely chronological conversation, even as they were recorded at different times, some, indeed, having no notes on the cassette tapes explaining the circumstances of the recordings. For the most part, it therefore becomes impossible to assign dates to any particular conversation. At first I did try to do so (and very occasionally do), but this proved misleading, as a conversation recorded at one time quickly segues into one recorded at another. As Harold Pinter remarked, in another context, 'The desire for verification is understandable but cannot always be satisfied.' Thus, it will be apparent that Miller's views often changed over time. For a considerable while he despaired of the American theatre, much later noting its revival. I hope that the passage of time is clear, even if not precisely identified. In a sense that reflects Miller's own state of mind. As he

Introduction

explained, in the gala performance at the National Theatre to mark his eightieth birthday, 'I've never been able to make time real for myself. I can't remember when something happened two weeks ago, three years ago or when I was in England last time. The calendar doesn't seem to exist in my head. It all melts together. It always has. It's probably a form of insanity.' Describing writing *Death of a Salesman*, he explained:

> I thought I would try to write that way and simply melt the days, the months and the years because I really do believe that we move through the world carrying the past, and that it is always alive at the back of the head. We are making constant references between what we see now and what we saw then, from what we hear now and heard then ... One of the impulses behind that form was to carry the whole freight of a man's life simultaneously.

Though all the conversations are between myself and Miller, there was a conference where I was simply chairing proceedings at which a question from a member of the audience prompted an interesting response. The question was to do with how far there were real-life models for his characters. His reply is worth quoting. It centres on *The Misfits*, the film he wrote for his then wife, Marilyn Monroe:

> I spent some time in Nevada, and I got to know some guys who were running horses. They would go up into the mountains and capture wild mustangs and sell them. One of these men interested me a lot and it was on him that the character that Clark Gable played in *The Misfits*, Gay Langland, was based. We were shooting a scene out in the country. This was about three or four years after I had known this man. I hadn't seen him in all those years but

there he was, standing in a little crowd of local people watching the shooting of the scene. I thought I had him down pretty well, in Gable's character. He was standing there watching this and listening to his own dialogue. He didn't recognise any of it. So, something happened between the time I heard him speak, and heard his story, which is actually very close to the story that's in the film. So, it's not a case of reportage. It's a poetics.

In fact, there was frequently a real model for his characters, as is evident in his first college play, *No Villain*, as it is in *Death of a Salesman*, his screenplay *The Hook*, *After the Fall*, *The Price* (he was inclined to deny this, though his brother confirmed it), *The Archbishop's Ceiling*, *The American Clock*, *The Last Yankee*, and *Finishing the Picture*. He knew the man on whom he based *The Last Yankee*. As we were driving through Roxbury, he pointed to a nearby hill and said, 'The Last Yankee lives over there', but, as he remarked, this was only the starting point and, besides, 'he never goes to the theatre'. It was, in effect, the spark on which he had to blow to enable it to flame into life. He once, rightly, chastised me for noting the autobiographical elements in his story 'The Turpentine Still', published in 2004, and his last play of that same year, *Finishing the Picture*. The elements are clearly there, but it can indeed be reductive to read works through the prism of his personal experiences. The same could be said of Eugene O'Neill and Tennessee Williams. What matters is the process of transmutation, how fact becomes metaphor. Indeed, he once remarked that he did not write plays, he wrote metaphors, the private world opening the door to public issues and concerns, even as his characters struggle with the business of daily living.

Introduction

On my last visit to Roxbury, Connecticut Limo delivered me two hours late, but Arthur was waiting for me in his baseball cap ready to drive me to his Tophet Road home, where I was to continue working my way through the boxes of papers he had set aside for the biography I was writing. I did not know then that it would be the last time I would see him in the place where, for four decades, he would go to his study every morning to write entries in the diary he kept for many years, along with essays, stories and plays. Written in this small cabin in rural New England, the plays would be performed everywhere – in schools, universities, regional theatres, Off Broadway, Broadway, on the great stages of the world, in multiple languages.

For me, listening again to tapes recorded in so many different places, over so many years, his voice brings back memories. I once accused him of sounding like a Brooklyn taxi driver, to which he replied, 'Who are you to talk about having an accent?' I trust that in reading his words that voice can still be heard as he talks frankly about his work, his relationships, the public world with which he engaged and the private world on which he drew for much of his work. The title of one of the volumes of his essays, *Echoes Down the Corridor*, could apply equally to what follows, a conversation stretching over many years, long stored away in a cardboard box against an unimagined future, a future now arrived.

1

Beginnings

BIGSBY: You are the son and the grandson of immigrants. The family came from Poland. Is there any way in which you think that has influenced you as a person, or as a writer?

MILLER: I am sure it did. In America, the mark of the immigrants was that they had to work harder than other people in order to stay in one place, let alone progress. My parents both spoke English. My mother was born in New York and my father came to America from a little town in Poland when he was only six years old, so they spoke no other language. But the American language, which is always changing, became a fascinating thing for me. They emigrated for two reasons, one was the economic opportunity there was in the United States for them, but the other was fear of hatred in Europe. And that forms a resistance in one's soul, a sensitivity to injustice, and I think that, for some of us, was a product of being the children of immigrants. They were Jews, but they were trying to become, and in some ways did become, indistinguishable from anybody else. You lose roots and you gain something else perhaps. It is a trade-off. It is a question of what you do lose.

Beginnings

BIGSBY: How did your father get to America, because he didn't go with the rest of his family?

MILLER: That is a good question. There is a bit of a mystery which I have never been able to resolve, and neither has my brother, though we have our theories. You see they moved that whole troupe of kids, six or seven of them, from Poland in, I think, two groups. First the father went over with the eldest of the boys, then they made enough money to buy a passage for the rest of them. Everyone excepting my father. We think that they thought he was mentally defective. That is what our theory is. The only internal evidence I have ever had was that my father laughingly told us more than once that he hated Europe. He could not understand why anybody would want to go there. It was a place of oppression, and simply a rotten society. He said at one point that, when they left, he had to sleep with idiots, and he would wake up in the middle of the night and they would be howling and yelling. That was mysterious. Was that a dream or what? Only last year [1995], I think it was, my brother suddenly said, well of course he was in an institution. He was left with an uncle who promptly died and suddenly it all made sense. At some point somebody had said he was not mentally defective, so they sent for him, and he was six by then. He travelled across Europe from Poland alone. They hung a sign around his neck asking a stranger to put him on a certain boat at Hamburg. His ticket was pinned to his underwear, and he ended up on a boat with that ticket. It was a civilised continent in those days, and he was passed from one person to another.

BIGSBY: What sort of education did your mother have?

MILLER: I believe she was the head of her class at school. She probably would have been a great student because she could read a novel in an evening. She was the fastest reader I have ever met and would remember details of minor characters forever. Five years later somebody would mention a character and she would remember. She was a very good example of the way society regarded women, especially in that immigrant group. They really held them down.

BIGSBY: And hers was an arranged marriage.

MILLER: Oh yes, sure. She was lucky because the arrangement was with a very presentable guy who was very interesting for her at that time, although it quickly turned out that he was totally uneducated.

BIGSBY: He was functionally illiterate, but he could read headlines in newspapers.

MILLER: He could read headlines. He could piece out a story, but not a story of any complication. His main need to read was a piece in the *New York Times*, a little column at the back of the paper somewhere, which announced the arrival of buyers. I have not noticed that for many years now – not that I have looked for it. It meant that buyers from all over the United States, buyers of shoes, clothing, you name it, had come into the city to look at goods they were now going to buy for their stores in Minneapolis, Chicago, St Louis, and the rest of it. He wanted to know that, so he could read that.

BIGSBY: Did your mother help him learn to read?

MILLER: She taught him how to read as much as he knew.

BIGSBY: The family was well off when you were a child, and you would be taken down to the family business.

MILLER: I was rather proud to be the boss's son. I was a kid then, of course. I remember I only went there on a weekend, on a Saturday, once or twice. My mother took me because I was at school throughout the week. I remember pushing all the trucks around. They had a lot of hand trucks there that big bulks of cloth were moved around with, and great big scales they had to weigh stuff on that they were going to ship out. He was so excited and proud to have his family in there. They only had partial staff working on Saturday.

BIGSBY: That is the Sabbath. Did that make any difference?

MILLER: Some of them wouldn't work, but others did because they wanted the money.

BIGSBY: Did it mean anything to your father?

MILLER: No.

BIGSBY: But your [maternal] grandfather wouldn't have liked that, would he?

MILLER: My grandfather was a curious beast. He spent his entire working life doing what he had to do, which was working probably seven days a week. When he got to be in his early sixties, and was no longer active, he became religious. It was rather a common thing. The older he got, the more religious he got so he could bother other people with it. He would go around being terrifically godly, but in his working life he hadn't been that way at all.

BIGSBY: Was there a tension between your father and grandfather, because you had to put him up in the house?

MILLER: My father was not in love with him. It was a tiny house, mind you.

BIGSBY: This was when you moved from Harlem to Brooklyn following the 1929 Crash.

MILLER: The first thing to realise is that the Crash of '29 occurred in pulses. It didn't occur in one day for a lot of people. We went downhill in bumps. You were not convinced the end had come for three or four years. So, the move to Brooklyn from Central Park North was not such a catastrophic thing as a recognition that you had to tighten your belt a little bit, and we lived in a perfectly lovely house on a nice street on Ocean Parkway, and I loved it there. It was terrific. And then gradually we had to move to a smaller house because things got tighter, and pretty soon you couldn't pay the mortgage on the small house and the possibility was there that you might be evicted like a lot of other people and then end up, God's knows where, on the street. But this took from, I'd say, 1929 to 1932. Ocean Parkway had about seven or eight rooms. Then we moved to East Third Street. There were three tiny bedrooms. My brother, myself, my sister, my mother, father, and the old man were in those three tiny bedrooms.

BIGSBY: And did you have the furniture there from the Harlem apartments?

MILLER: Some of it they had to get rid of because it was too big. The dining-room stuff remained, and the table ended on the stage for *The Price*.

BIGSBY: In one of your student plays, *No Villain*, the grandfather is always flourishing another piece of furniture he has discovered from the past. Is there any reality in that?

MILLER: Yes, there must have been because I was basically working on what had really happened. He had that Germanic dictatorial nature. Everything had to be exactly so, and he was very clean. Everything around him had to be spotless. He had been driven out of business. I guess he must have lost his way maybe in the late twenties before the Depression.

BIGSBY: And your father's father?

MILLER: My father's father, for some reason which I have never understood, still kept his money. My father's father was not in bad straits. He managed to escape. He must have, because they lived pretty well.

BIGSBY: I get the sense that, as a teenager, Brooklyn was a kind of liberation for you.

MILLER: Oh, I loved it. It was like going to the country. We were out in Midwood. There were empty lots where we could play football, and wonderful weeds and trees. Just a couple of years earlier I had an aunt who could watch her children go to school, six, seven, eight, ten blocks, with no houses. It was all open. That's Willy Loman country, and it gradually got built up, of course, very crowded. Flatbush was never beautiful. It was flat and kind of ugly. But I thought it was great.

BIGSBY: When you went to school, you were not exactly a serious scholar, were you?

MILLER: I went through school invisibly. I was the invisible man. On my last week or so, I ran into somebody who had a camera. I was interested in cameras, and he was in school and had a camera. And I said, 'What do you do with that?' And he said, 'I'm in the camera club.' Well, I had been in that school for four years, and I didn't know there was a camera club.

Years later, a man named Mason, who was the principal of the school who everybody loved, retired. This was already, probably, in 1955, or something like that. They invited me to attend the dinner in his honour, which I did. I sat next to a teacher who said they had all been looking through their records because these teachers were of an age that many of them would have been my teachers. Some of them were seventy. They were all retired. Nobody could find a trace. I left no footsteps behind, and it was a little embarrassing.

BIGSBY: Does that mean there was never a teacher who ignited your interest in literature?

MILLER: They ignited my interest in leaving the school. It was a total loss. I didn't mind it either because they left me alone. The only thing I got out of it was that at some point, in that four-year period at Abraham Lincoln High School – it was a perfectly good school, and a lot of people loved it – I had to write a book report. I knew nothing about anything, so I went to the library and my eye came upon a book called *The Brothers Karamazov*. Well, I was a brother. My older brother and I were at sore points a lot of times, and I thought maybe I could read it. That's where my life began with Dostoevsky. He could have been Joe Smith. I read all his works because something in them meant something to me. Then I began to read a lot of Russian literature – Tolstoy, Turgenev, Chekhov. They were the great teachers.

BIGSBY: When did you work for your father's company?

MILLER: Let's see. I graduated from high school in June '32, and for about a month I worked for him until he couldn't stand it any more. He asked me a wonderful question, and I will never forget it. I swept out the place, arranged stands, just the most primitive kind of donkey work, and we arrived one morning, and he said to me, 'Do you remember where you left off last night?' He could detect, in his peasant way, that my mind was not on this work. I stayed there a very short time because it really was a stupid waste of time. I think that is when I managed to get a job with my friend's father.

BIGSBY: Driving a truck?

MILLER: Driving a truck.

BIGSBY: Some 90 per cent of New York Jews who went to university went either to City College, New York University,

Brooklyn College or Hunter. You were one of the 10 per cent, apart from a brief time at City College, who didn't.

MILLER: Some years ago – it would probably have been in the 1970s – I was invited to City College. I went to City College for about two weeks up on 137th Street, I think. I was working eight to nine hours a day and then going up there to school at night. The required courses were mathematics and chemistry, and I, of course, couldn't add or multiply. They built a new theatre and asked me to come since I had been at that school. One of the teachers looked up my records, and it was the worst record that anybody had ever had. I was half asleep. That was one of the reasons. Even awake, I couldn't do chemistry and mathematics, but asleep certainly not.

BIGSBY: You were fourteen when the stock market crashed. How aware were you of the implications of the crash?

MILLER: It was said that there were only two significant events in the history of the United States, the Civil War and the Great Depression. Everything else affected some part of the country. Those two events affected everyone. I knew the collapse had occurred because suddenly I realised I could not go on to college and that I would have to get a job, immediately. There was a lot of hysteria all over the house and up and down the block. The naivety of the people at that time was remarkable. People really believed that a bank was like the Rocky Mountains. It would always be there. Then, suddenly, one day they came to a bank and all the gates were shut across the door and there was a policeman standing there saying, 'This bank is closed, permanently.' People would stand on the street and ask, 'Where's my money?' And the cop would shrug and say, 'I don't know.' This went on all over the United States. So, there was no question in anybody's mind that a catastrophe had occurred. For me, and for people of my generation, it meant that nothing man made existed which could not be sharply changed, overthrown and turned into rubble at a moment's notice. Out of that mess my generation had to find its way.

BIGSBY: Your father had invested in the market and lost his business as a result. Did he use your mother's money as well?

MILLER: Oh yes, he did.

BIGSBY: And she didn't know at the time.

MILLER: No. Well, she wouldn't pay attention to the whole damn thing.

BIGSBY: And the rows that are in that early play, and in *After the Fall*, did go on.

MILLER: As I heard them.

BIGSBY: And were you just sitting on the stairs listening to this, or what?

MILLER: No, it was just sort of flowing around my head. I didn't take it too seriously. I was too busy doing whatever the hell I was doing, playing ball and roller skating.

BIGSBY: Well, you do at that age. The world just happens. But he tried, did he not, to refloat the company.

MILLER: Oh yes, he started two or three other businesses, none of which worked until World War II, and then he had one which was the best of them, but that was partly due to the war. There was a shortage of clothing, so he could sell this stuff. The basic fact is that the Depression period was a deflation. The price of everything collapsed, so either you couldn't sell anything or, if you did sell it, it was practically at cost or below. Suddenly, in wartime, the prices climbed, because of shortages, so you could now navigate a little better. But once the war ended, he was back where he started. He could not compete.

BIGSBY: Presumably your father was a true believer in the American dream.

MILLER: Yes. He was like all of them. He believed that if you were hard-working and got to know what you were doing, you would succeed. The idea, not just for immigrants but for Americans in general, of course, was that each generation would be richer than the generation before. In fact, this is the first generation in American history which is poorer than the previous generation. That goes not just for immigrants but for everybody. So, he was a standard product of the system.

BIGSBY: On the other hand, he worked his way up until he owned a very large manufacturing outfit employing something like a thousand people, and then suddenly the Depression took it all away from him. Did he stop being a believer, or did he go on believing?

MILLER: He stopped for about a day, not too much longer. Like most people in his class what happened was that they balanced a belief in the future of the system with a deep scepticism about any single measure that would get them out of the woods. Scepticism is very deep from the Depression on, I think. However, it did not really disturb his belief that you could make it if you were hard-working enough, and you were clever enough, and lucky enough. Luck was important. Luck was part of the system. If you were a little cleverer than other people, you still had to have luck.

BIGSBY: At the age of sixteen you wanted to go to sea.

MILLER: Oh yes, I was crazy about that idea. In those times, along the West Side of Manhattan, there were twenty-five ships in berths, big passenger ships. Of course, there were no transoceanic aircraft at that time. The beauty of those ships, some of them, just went to my heart. I remember reading Conrad and the idea of simply disappearing from this troubled time we all lived in appealed. It was so miserably competitive all the time, dog eat dog. You could not take a deep breath; it was very constrictive. There is a myth that grew out of it which was directly opposite to my experience. It is partly the result of literature in those days which suggested that people helped one another. It may have come out of the organisation of the first unions in various big industries, like the auto union and the rubber workers union, and that did take place. But outside of those movements, where the majority of the people lived, including me, the competition was ruthless.

BIGSBY: Because everyone wanted the same job, if there was one.

MILLER: I remember when I worked for my father, one of my jobs at the end of the day would be to ship cartons of clothes to various places in the United States. I had to take them to the post office. I had a little hand truck which I pushed along Second Avenue to the post office, which was somewhere into the Thirties off Seventh Avenue, and they closed at, whatever it was, 7 o'clock in the evening. So, there was a line of guys with their own trucks, and they were climbing all over each other to get to that desk before the office closed. And you had to really fight your way through there to get that done. It was murderous. Later on, when I read John Steinbeck, he had a scene which utterly astonished me. One of the Joads [in *The Grapes of Wrath*] entered a little grocery store along the road and asked for bread. He only had a nickel, or something, but the bread was 8¢, or 10¢, and the owner of the grocery store said, 'That's all right, take it.' I read that book. It's terrific. I never saw anything like that. They would watch you starve to death slowly in New York.

BIGSBY: Is it right that you had a lodger in the basement?

MILLER: Yes. He appeared out of nowhere. Almost every week somebody would come walking down the street looking for work, and a lot of them were literally on the edge of starvation. My mother would give them some soup or something. They knew our house. Word must have got out that you could get a little soup there, or something, because they would come walking down the street. They would avoid all the other houses and come to our house, right down the alley. This guy showed up and he was eager to paint the house, do anything. I think he was Lithuanian. He had an accent, and, for some reason, I think he was homosexual because my mother and the women immediately felt no fear of him; they were alone all day in the house.

So, he charmed his way down into the basement, where one day he lugged a bed he had found in some junkyard and put curtains up. He was a marvellous cleaner. The house was sparkling. He would clean the windows; he would do everything. I am not sure he ever got paid. He got his food. Then he would vanish and get drunk for days. Years went by and he finally made one dreadful error that finished him. My grandfather had made some wine out of grapes. He bought grapes and made wine. It was sweet wine, really grape juice, but it was allowed to stand. He was left alone in the house for one afternoon and drank a couple of gallons of that garbage and got himself good and sick, and my grandfather got outraged because of all the work he had put into this. So, they threw him out, and he never showed up again. He had been a purser on the SS *Manhattan*, which was a big passenger ship, and I went down with him one day to the company, on the West Side of Manhattan, and he introduced me to whoever was there in the office. I thought I could be a cabin boy, do whatever a boy did on the ship. But they didn't need anybody, so I never got a job.

BIGSBY: The central fact of your youth, then, was the Crash, but it seems to have had an amazingly lasting effect on your work.

MILLEER: It had a tremendous impact because I was so convinced of the authority of the system that I lived in, in which my father, at that time, was a great success. Success flowed over onto him, so that what happened was, as it happened to many others, when the physical crash came what it took with it was the authority of anybody who claimed to have [benefited] from it. The fraudulence of the whole thing was simply devastating. So, to a young kid of fourteen you either had to become entirely cynical about the whole world, which I wasn't set up to do, or you had to get busy creating a new one. So that that creation of a new world, and the rejection of cynicism, has been the theme of so much of my work. I am not a fatalist, in the sense that I believe there is no hope, but I do believe that we stand on a very thin edge and that we are liable to go down at any moment.

BIGSBY: There came a moment when your brother took you to a brothel.

MILLER: Yes, that was funny.

BIGSBY: How old were you?

MILLER: I must have been about sixteen.

BIGSBY: It seems such an odd thing to do, but maybe it wasn't in those days.

MILLER: I don't think it was so strange then. It is very distant, very dim. I remember it was an apartment house somewhere in Manhattan, but I don't remember where.

Beginnings

There was another guy, in fact a student at the University of Michigan. He was not much of an intellectual, this guy, a very nice fellow but kind of dumb I thought. Anyway, it was through him that I learned about the University of Michigan. Forty years goes by, more maybe, walking down Park Avenue with Inge [Morath], and there he is.
I recognised him immediately because he never had much hair. It turns out he owns a very elegant chain of grocery stores on Park Avenue and other such places. The stores had a very British name, and here he was, a wealthy guy, on the verge of retiring. Everything connects.

BIGSBY: But what happened on that day? Did Kermit tell you where you were going?

MILLER: Oh yes, sure. I don't remember the conversation, though, if there was very much. I think Oscar put him up to it. It sounds to me like Oscar's doing. Oscar was one of my relatives.

BIGSBY: And was this your initiation?

MILLER: Yes. That was the first time.

BIGSBY: And what was it like?

MILLER: It was very perfunctory, if I remember correctly. Like going to the dentist.

BIGSBY: But what did you feel afterwards, guilty, awkward?

MILLER: It was disappointing. Something was definitely missing.

BIGSBY: And presumably Kermit put up the cash.

MILLER: No, I think I did. That means that I must have been working somewhere.

BIGSBY: Were you able to go off to Michigan because you were the second son, in other words there wasn't an expectation that you had to stay around?

MILLER: I was blessed with having no expectations. My poor brother was supposed to carry the load. It was he who was the responsible party. Early on I was regarded as a hopeless case as far as any kind of responsibility was concerned and, consequently, I always felt free to do whatever I wanted to do.

BIGSBY: Did you ever, then or later, feel guilty?

MILLER: Yes, I did. At the time I felt terrible about it because Kermit had gone to NYU for about a year, and he was a pretty good student, I think. I was a dreadful student early on, and it is he who should have been going to school, not me, because I was too stupid. So, it was unjust, but I didn't resign my position. Kermit dropped out of NYU to help my father. He never went back.

BIGSBY: As you say, your brother did go to NYU for a while. So why didn't you?

MILLER: I wanted to get away from everything, from the city, from my family, and start a new life. That was one thing. The other thing was that my brother had a friend who had gone to Michigan for one year, and he told me there was a Hopwood Award contest. Avery Hopwood was a playwright in the 1920s. He made a lot of money with two or three big, popular successes like *Up in Mabel's Room*, *Getting Gertie's Garter*, plays like that. They made him a fortune. He left it all to the university to start a programme of literary contests, and then walked into the Mediterranean and drowned himself. Each year they were giving out cash money for a play, novel, poetry, written by students, which was unheard of. The fact that they were giving out money for writing was in itself an attraction, but it was also that I realised they were serious about writing. A lot of good writers came out of that. Practically the whole staff of the

New Yorker magazine one year were people who had come out of it. It was very rare in the 1930s. Finally, the tuition at Michigan was $65 a year and that was a great recommendation. Columbia, at that point, was $400. So that was an attraction. I didn't have $65 either, but at least you could imagine having $65, and you couldn't imagine having $400. So, those are the reasons I went to Michigan.

BIGSBY: There is that feeling in *The Price* of the one who stayed and the one who went, the one who went becoming very successful.

MILLER: Oh yes. When I first went to Michigan, I got on a bus somewhere in Manhattan. I remember the fare was $11 to go from New York, and, at the last moment, Kermit went with me to say goodbye because I was going into the Wild West. People didn't travel around the way they do now. Most people didn't have automobiles. Anyway, at the last moment he gave me his hat, which was a very good hat. He loved hats and had a wonderful head for them. I never wore hats, but I took his. I went to school, and kept that hat for about three years, I guess. Then, when I was hitchhiking back home – I was up somewhere in New York State, because I had come across Canada to Buffalo from Detroit and then you went down Route 17 – I got dropped off somewhere next to a beautiful field of grain. Some car stopped and I ran down the road and my hat blew off. I didn't go back to get it. It blew into the field. That is about when I was feeling that I could become a playwright.

BIGSBY: Your sister said to me that when you were both growing up, they thought Kermit would be the writer and you would do something mechanical.

MILLER: Yes. Kermit was very romantic about writing. He loved Keats. I never heard him refer to an American poet.

It was all British Romantic poets, and he had this kind of flowery writing, nineteenth-century stuff. I could make nothing of it. In those days I didn't know about anything, so I didn't try to make anything out of it, but I think that is true. I thought he would be a writer.

BIGSBY: Did the fact that you were a second son have any effect on the psychology between you and your father?

MILLER: I always felt I was to one side of the family, that I had my own career by the time I was six years old. They were all fighting about this and that, or they are happy about this and that, and I was, to a degree, but I had my own space psychologically. Kermit was totally occupied by them. I knew it then. He was the man they relied on to carry on whatever there was to be carried on.

BIGSBY: So, he would have run the business.

MILLER: Yes, not me, and I probably took on the character of somebody who couldn't in order to avoid having to do all that. I think I formed my nature to reinforce what I really wanted to do, which was to have my own career.

BIGSBY: So, you didn't feel any resentment? You were pleased someone was above you.

MILLER: Oh, not at all. I had nothing but the greatest regard for Kermit. His character was much better than mine. He was responsible; I wasn't. And that was a great thing to be.

BIGSBY: Given how important radio was going to be to you later, did you listen to it all the time?

MILLER: That was the major source of entertainment. We kept track of all the new comedians, the singers, Bing Crosby, Russ Columbo, Rudi Vallee. All the entertainment came through the radio.

BIGSBY: And was it a special event? Did the family gather for it?

MILLER: Yes, sometimes. For a singer, everybody sat around. It was very strange. Now I think of it, they sat there judging whether this singer was the best or whether the other one was, and they all sang jazz, of course. It was very important to know who was better and who would be more likely to be the number one person. It is still going on, of course, but now it is far noisier, and more chaotic, because there are more of them. Then you only had a couple of guys, usually men, but there were a few women. Kate Smith was a national heroine. She weighed a good 280 pounds in her stockinged feet, and she belted out these numbers. She had a marvellous voice. She was a little over-enthusiastic, but terrific. I couldn't stand her because she was sort of threatening. Billie Holliday, of course, never got to be a national figure. She was Black, and we couldn't stand for that, but when one did hear her occasionally it was a whole new sound.

BIGSBY: You nearly got into radio yourself, as a singer.

MILLER: They gave me a programme of my own. I had a pretty good voice at one point, and for probably six months I wanted to be a singer, and I did sing on the radio. I was given a programme every week in Brooklyn. I had an accompanist who had a lot of dandruff all over his shoulders. He was blind and was a terrific player. He said they had high prospects for me. I don't know exactly why I quit. I just couldn't carry on with it.

BIGSBY: How did this go down with your family?

MILLER: Oh, they loved it. You know it was very hard to make a dollar, and anybody who could make a whole dollar, especially without working, was okay.

BIGSBY: Because you are talking about the Depression.

MILLER: The Depression, sure. It is unimaginable now, of course, excepting we have an enormous class of people in the

United States who feel the same way, but we don't know about them. They don't show up in the papers, and there are only probably 20 million of them, so it doesn't count.

BIGSBY: To get to university you had to earn money.

MILLER: Until we got into the war, any ads for jobs specified that they wanted White Christians. So as a young kid, looking for a job, I answered the one ad in the paper that didn't specify.

BIGSBY: How far has being Jewish meant something central to you, or is it a peripheral part of your identity?

MILLER: It is peripheral only in the sense that I am a non-believer. Something I have in common with certain priests in this country. I believe in God, but I don't think he is out there. But of course, my background is Jewish, and I think that would probably sensitise me to the whole question of the survival of smaller groups, and to the individual in the face of monstrous power complexes. In that sense, in an ethical sense, it has always meant a great deal to me. I haven't myself felt the menace of fascism, but if both grandfathers had not decided to move from Poland in the last century, I would have been dead by about 1942, I guess. So, the thing is hardly theoretical to me, and I don't think it is theoretical to anybody else, but they probably don't know it. I have always known it, and in that sense the Jewish sensibility is very important to me.

BIGSBY: You did get a job.

MILLER: I worked in a warehouse which was the supplier of a company that I had previously worked for, which was a Jewish company. I had been let go because times were so bad. They did not need a truck driver any more, so I was out of work for a while. Then I saw this ad in the newspaper, and I recognised the firm immediately because, for about a year,

I had been picking up auto parts from that firm to deliver to my firm in Long Island City, which is an industrial area outside New York City. I knew all the guys there, so I hurried down because that was a hell of a good place to work. They interviewed me, and I told the boss who I had worked for before that I was applying and said that if they asked him about me, he should tell a lot of lies and say that I was just great. But nothing happened. So he waited about three or four days, and he called me up and said, 'Did anything come of that interview?' I said, 'No, it didn't.' I was just a kid then, and this was a clerk's job, unskilled work really. He said, 'Well, that is because you are Jewish.' I was shocked. I said, 'Really?' He said, 'Yes, there is no other reason. They wouldn't find a kid your age who knows what you know about auto parts', and I did know about the business. By this time, I had spent a year in it with him. So he picked up the phone, called them and said, 'If you don't give the kid the job he applied for I'll know why.' The next day, I got the job, and I worked there for almost three years. But while I was there I was the only Jew they had ever hired, and probably the only one they ever would hire.

There was broken glass all over the place. You just had to duck. Brake lining came in large rolls which you just had to cut. This was asbestos, compressed with some binders because brakes get very hot, so it had to be something that would never burn. Truck brake liners were very thick. We had to cut them to specifications, to a certain length, when they were ordered. If you twisted the material as it was going through the cutter, the cutter would break because it was made of carborundum. It was inflexible, because any pressure on this, to left or right, it would shatter. We had no eye protection or masks. You could replace a worker for 10¢.

We were unskilled people. It was the largest auto parts warehouse east of the Mississippi. They had six floors of parts, and it was situated where Lincoln Center stands today. The guy who ran that whole business, which was a considerable business, made $35 a week. I made $15, and when you went above $35 you were really in the stratosphere.

BIGSBY: How far do you see the questions raised in the 1930s recurring?

MILLER: I see the same things all over again, but the societies now, I think, certainly the British and American, have learned how to contain these effects far better than they did before. The Depression of the 1930s came out of the freewheeling money hunger of the twenties. There was no social safety net. In the thirties, when a man lost his job he went out on the street. There were no unemployment payments. There was no dole. There was nothing. If people could not pay their rent, they were just thrown out, and the consequence was that a middle class developed on the street. The Roosevelt administration – which came in as a conservative administration, incidentally – was forced to create a law which made it possible for people to own their own home. Mortgages were extended to forty years, instead of the usual seven or eight years. That meant that the payments each month were minuscule. In effect, the government was taking over the financing of homes in the United States. Had they not done that, I don't know what would have happened.

I think there would have been some social upheaval, because this was not the poor. This was employed businesspeople who now literally had no roofs over their heads. Well, when you saw that happening, you knew society was a very fragile piece of work, and that what you had assumed to be the most stable elements in it were really not. After all, the head of the New York Stock Exchange went to prison because he was a crook. This is the chief officer of the New York Stock Exchange.

Now we have got hardened to suffering. I recall in the Depression, in the thirties, if you saw people lying on the street you would call the police to put them in a shelter. You don't do that any more. I was walking in London and there were innumerable people living on the street as though they were in Calcutta. In the worst of the Depression, I don't recall people living on the street. What they did do was erect what were called Hoovervilles. President Hoover was the last Republican president before Roosevelt. People got cartons, and all kinds of junk, and built little houses along the Hudson River which were kind of permanent shelters, but what we have come to is a kind of hardening of feeling towards deprivation.

I see it now and I wonder when does the bottom drop out? And maybe these economies, political economies, just keep it pulsing so that the bottom does not drop out completely. It just leaks, slowly leaks, and I cannot tell you what the end of all this is. We seem to have created a permanent class not only of unemployed, but unemployable people, excess people who are not going to get any retraining for further work. I am speaking of people who were in the auto industry in the United States. British companies are laying off thousands of people who probably won't get back in again. And isn't that the major issue for a society, more important than whether you have Trident submarines or what?

BIGSBY: The Depression keeps cropping up in your plays, sometimes quite centrally, as in *The Price* or *The*

American Clock, but often there as a presence. Why has that event proved so resonant for you?

MILLER: If the democratic system failed, which it seemed that it could do in the thirties, and not only in America, if the economy couldn't be made to work, you had to ask what was next? It would be an authoritarian system of some kind, and that usually brings with it the persecution of minority people. The Depression was the test of the American system, and I have to tell you that we never solved it. When World War II started, it took a year and a half before the unemployed were absorbed into war manufacturing. From our point of view that war was fought by Depression boys. Those guys, many of them, had never had a proper job. The army was the first real pay cheque they had ever had, and you didn't have to be very radical to believe that, when the war was over, we would go back right into the situation as it had been when the war began. In fact, President Truman said as much. He therefore pleaded with Congress to start doing something about providing jobs for those who were coming back, as well as for the rest of the population once we had stopped building planes and tanks and the rest of it.

BIGSBY: There is a play you wrote during the war, which was never performed, in which a central event is German agents removing the buoys which mark the safe channel through the sea. In that play it is as though this was a fundamental breach of the human contract. In a way, isn't that what connects the Depression in America with those events in Europe, that some fundamental contract was torn up?

MILLER: That's right. What the Depression meant in real terms was that when a father of a family couldn't provide for his children he was, so to speak, humiliated. It lasted for a long, long time. I was quite convinced it was never going to end. It was a breach in the social contract. One did feel a betrayal. Political leaders landed in jail, fraudulent businessmen who had been stealing from their own banks. A lot of the great names of the country turned out to be phonies. I think there was a generation that did feel that nothing was real if you didn't re-examine and secure the fact that it was real. And that goes into playwriting. Playwriting presents you with an apparent situation in the first act, and then begins to tear it apart in the succeeding acts. It is really a classic formula.

2

Michigan

BIGSBY: To what extent did you become radicalised when you were at the University of Michigan?
MILLER: Everyone I knew was a radical, excepting for most of the people. They were not radicals. But to me the non-radicals just didn't count. They weren't interesting. They just weren't there. Later on, they ran the whole country.
BIGSBY: Did you join any political groups?
MILLER: I don't really think I became a member of any. There was one possible exception. There was a newly born peace organisation.
BIGSBY: The Oxford peace pledge?
MILLER: Oh yes, that was a big deal then. It was trying to abort World War II. These were all left-wing people, and a world war was to be a war of capitalists. But I don't have any memory of a meeting of any kind, or being in a meeting, excepting as a reporter. You see I was working as a reporter for the paper [the *Michigan Daily*], but, first of all, I was up to my neck in work. I had two jobs. I was washing dishes at a restaurant, the Co-op restaurant.
BIGSBY: And you were looking after mice in a laboratory.

MILLER: Yes, so I didn't have a hell of a lot of time to do anything, especially in the first two years. I was still under the impression that I had got to keep my nose to the books, or they would throw me out of there. I had practically memorised the whole textbook in my freshman-year European history, but when we had an examination I sat there, and my brain froze. The teacher, who was a nice man, obviously must have noticed something, because he came over to me. I said, 'I know all the answers to these questions. In fact, I can tell you the pictures on the pages of the textbook where all these questions appear, but for some reason I am unable to write them.' He said, 'Look, why don't you go home and have a nap.' It was terrific. And he made me promise not to confer with the other students, which I would never have done anyway, because they didn't know any more than I did. He said, 'Come back tomorrow and I will give you an exam', which I did, and the next day I was perfectly fine. This is weird, but I guess it is a form of hysteria.

BIGSBY: How important in shaping your views was your visit, in 1937, to Flint in Michigan for the student newspaper when you covered the strike there? Did that have an impact on you?

MILLER: It certainly did. The prevailing view among a lot of teachers, and certainly a lot of students, was that we were approaching some kind of apocalypse because the Depression never ended. It was periodically supposed to end, but instead it got worse. What is forgotten now is that there was a fantastic amount of racism in this country, not just against Blacks, but Jews, anybody who was a hateful foreigner, especially in Detroit, where I spent some time. There were a lot of Southern workers in Detroit. Ford

especially recruited whole towns in Alabama and
Mississippi, and they were very primitive people.
I remember we had a temporary job doing a census. We got
paid 25¢ an hour, or something, from the sociology
department which had been hired by some corporation or
other to do a census of the workers. Somehow, we got
addresses and went to ask them if they had hot and cold
water, how much education they had, etc., those sorts of
questions. I was really shocked at the way these people were.
When I was talking to them, I heard this rustling under the
porch. It turned out they were raising pigs under the porch
of the house, and it smelt funny. In the middle of Detroit,
where there was running water, there were sewers, they were
living like animals. They were working in the oil plants,
because they were preferred by Ford, who liked them
because they never gave any problems, but these guys got
organised too, and, when they were organised, they were
really murderers.

BIGSBY: How did you reconcile their racism with
a romantic vision of them as workers?

MILLER: This took a lot of doing. You had to cancel out
a lot of what you knew, as you did with a lot of other things
too. My favourite president was Roosevelt, but the truth of
the matter is that Roosevelt really helped destroy the Spanish
Republic, and from time to time we were enraged at him
because he wasn't really acting for the workers. He was really
betraying everybody, so it seemed.

BIGSBY: What was the lesson you learned from the Flint
strike, because that was about unionisation?

MILLER: That was the clear struggle par excellence. It
could not have been more classical. The manufacturing
plant was on one side of the street, a gigantic Chevrolet

plant; the other side was the executive offices of General Motors. Between the two there was an enclosed overpass. At the height of the strike, in order to prevent anybody coming into the plant, they had welded a Chevrolet body on the pass to close the door. It was so pure as a symbol. It was melodramatic. When I arrived, there were National Guardsmen in the street behind machine guns. They were sprawled out ready to fire, while on the roof of the factory were workers walking around getting the air. Somebody told me that they had fired the day before. In fact, I read it in the paper. They had wounded, or killed, two or three people up there. The head of the state was Governor Jackson. He was liberal.

BIGSBY: He lost the next election.

MILLER: He lost the next election. That was typical of the time.

BIGSBY: And it consolidated your views, your interpretation of the world.

MILLER: Oh yes, definitely. There were the workers on one side and the bosses on the other side.

BIGSBY: And the unfortunate thing was that you came from the bosses.

MILLER: But that would help alienate me from the bosses, the fact that I came from them. Meanwhile, though, I was engaged with the idea of how to become a writer, how to succeed as a writer, how to get published. Once, hearing a reading by one of the playwrights – I can't remember who – who said he had gone five or ten years writing without any recognition (I was then, let's say twenty), I thought, 'My God, five or ten years without recognition.' And don't forget that there was no Off Broadway theatre. So, you had to arrive fully formed on Broadway. It was the only theatre we had, with the exception of a few regional theatres, which usually did last year's Broadway hits.

BIGSBY: And the Federal Theatre.

MILLER: Yes, but I was in college then. I had no hope that I would ever be accepted there because the people that staffed the Federal Theatre were fully formed writers. They were ten years older than I was. I would never dream of being accepted there.

BIGSBY: Why was Spain such a critical event for your generation, particularly in America when you were thousands of miles away?

MILLER: One reason, as I read the news, was the feeling that if Spain fell, the next world war was imminent. This was the mathematics of it all. Why? Because Hitler would now have a fascist state.

BIGSBY: But as far as America was concerned, it could keep out of it.

MILLER: A lot of the kids felt we could keep out of it but wouldn't and shouldn't.

BIGSBY: Was that because of Russia's involvement?

MILLER: Yes, probably. That is another good point. You see the Russians would seem to be the only ones who were hell-bent on the Spanish Republic. That was one reason it was good. But the other reason was that the Republicans had been elected, which everybody forgets. We knew nothing of the fighting going on among the loyalists, the fight between the various factions of the left. It was all gloriously unified, as far as we knew. As to why we felt so passionately about it, first of all it was a small minority that was passionate about it. Ninety-nine per cent of the American people, including the students, didn't know where Spain was, and certainly didn't know what the hot issues were in that place. But enough of the conscious people were aware that a contest was going on for the future. Then, of course, quickly, in 1938, two years after Franco had taken over, you had Kristallnacht in Germany. This was such a shock. There were two shocks that I remember. The other was the bombardment of Guernica from the air. I will never forget that because the idea that in broad daylight, with the sun shining, an aeroplane would fly over an occupied town, where people were going about their business, and drop bombs on it was something indigestible, incredible. It is easy enough to say it is barbarism or something, but it unhinged the mind. It just couldn't happen, so you reached for anything that would combat those fascists, whatever it was.

BIGSBY: How real was your temptation to go to Spain?
MILLER: I never really had a feeling that I would go.
BIGSBY: It was just friends that did.
MILLER: Yes. This guy I knew [Ralph Neaphus] found out that I was driving to New York from Michigan, and I took him along. He was going to the Spanish Civil War, where he would get killed, as I thought he was going to. I bought a car for $20, a Model T Ford which was ten years old. [On the way] the car began to sound funny, and I pulled over to a country garage in Ohio and I said to the man there, 'Don't do anything because I've got $2 and my friend has $3, and we need that for gas.' That's all we had. 'So, if it is going to cost anything more than that, stop right here because I will have to hitchhike home.' He said, 'Well, let me look at it.' He looked at it, and the next thing I knew he took the head of the engine off. He found a valve in a garbage pail that would fit the car. He got very interested in that engine. He hadn't seen one of them in ten years. He repaired the thing, put it all back, and started it up. He was so happy to hear it

running, and I said to him, 'Okay, what do I owe you?' And he said, 'I think 25¢ will be all right.' Now, first of all, he was sure we didn't have anything. If he had had the slightest suspicion I was having him on, it wouldn't have worked that way, but he knew we were in the same bucket as he was, and these guys, mechanics, were living on the edge of the world. Nobody paid them. They were getting stuck all the time from unpaid bills.

We stopped over at our house. Another student, named Bob Cummings, went with him. Later Cummings returned, and I met him in New York. He told me that Ralph had been captured and shot. Cummings had been through the war as a soldier. I remember asking him, 'How come you didn't get shot?' and he said, 'I'm too fast. I was running messages from one place to another. I was never standing in the front line near anybody with guns. I spent the whole war in sneakers.'

BIGSBY: This was a period when you were writing letters to your mother describing your commitment to communism.

MILLER: I was probably trying to shock her. You see, they were utterly bewildered by what had happened to them. I was bound not to repeat that. It was very adolescent.

BIGSBY: It was, but some of the pieces you wrote for the *Daily Michigan* had that tinge of a Marxist view.

MILLER: For people on the right side of the liberal position there was hardly a day when some kind of an argument with Marx didn't take place. The situation in the country seemed to be carrying through the prophecy of Karl Marx, that this thing was going to collapse, and that there was no solution to this within the embrace of capitalism. The argument was how to bring it down so that we could start a cooperative society. It was taken for granted that this was a given, that the system had died, or was dying. You see, people on the left were called communists, but communists were people who supported Republican Spain, who were aware of it, who were opposed to the Second World War coming on. I didn't know any party people. I didn't know there was a party there, if there was. You called people communists, but they were usually the militant people of the peace movement and union movements on the campus. It was a generic name for people who were militant and clear about all this, because the majority of the students weren't, as usual. They didn't know what was happening. They were studying dentistry, or whatever.

I suppose the difference would have been between those who were conscious of what was happening vis-à-vis Europe and those who were not. Fascism, then, was the oncoming movement. Lindberg's wife said it was the world of the future. And, in America, there didn't seem to be resistance to it, as such. They were completely unconscious of it. If I used the word 'communist' I wasn't referring to the Communist Party. I didn't know anybody in the Communist Party. Those I knew were those I used to pal around with, the people on the *Michigan Daily*, who were agitated about one or another issue and expressed themselves as such. They were Marxists, or wanted to be Marxists, or were studying Marxism.

BIGSBY: Would you have thought of yourself as a Marxist?

MILLER: I would have wanted to have been one, but I couldn't read very much of it. I had a course in economics. At one point the professor said, 'Who has read volume two of *Das Kapital*?' Somebody stuck his hand up, and the professor said, 'There isn't one.' It was just taken as an article of faith that people understood what this was all about. I was

reading a book called *Constantine's Sword* [by James Carroll]. I read three pages a night and fell asleep.
BIGSBY: About the treatment of the Jews.
MILLER: Yes, the war against the Jews by the Catholic church. I was reading this last night and I really should have known it, but never did. Marx came from a line of rabbis, going back three generations. He was baptised, and was very anti-Semitic, as was the whole society around him. I thought, isn't that wonderful. The Jews were looking to Marxism as the release, while he saw the Jew as representing capitalism.
BIGSBY: So, the Jews were capitalists, and the Jews were radicals. They were both sides of the issue.
MILLER: Wherever you looked, there were Jews. The Jew was on the right; he was on the left. Of course, he was life.
BIGSBY: How much reading of Karl Marx did you do in those years?
MILLER: I remember reading pamphlets of Lenin, including *What Is to Be Done?* I remember that marvellous title. I read some histories of the Russian Revolution by Americans, and John Reed's book [*Ten Days That Shook the World*]. I read a lot about that stuff, basically the period between 1900 and the 1920s. On the Stalin time, there wasn't much to read.
BIGSBY: Were you reading this in Michigan?
MILLER: I started reading in Michigan.
BIGSBY: What was your attitude towards Trotsky?
MILLER: I thought he was a nuisance, basically, that he was getting in the way of this great experiment. I would have been with John Reed, who saw the romance of the whole thing. I was totally misled by the whole business. I don't think there has been such a snow job done in history as was done then. They were self-intoxicated people who were

writing these things. It was not done for the most part cynically. It was done cynically, very cynically, high up, but down below people were passionate. I remember being in Union Square in New York. In those days, on any day of the week during unemployment, you could find a couple of hundred people there, mostly men, talking, usually about Trotsky, the various sects that were breaking off from the Stalinists. There were marvellous speeches being made, a whole group of fifteen men yelling at each other. There were all kinds of strange arguments going on, but they were also about vegetarianism, anything. It was like Speaker's Corner. There was a kind of excitement about all this. Things had got to change. What we were in could not last; it was impossible. One knew one was in a disintegrating situation, socially. The whole thing was coming apart. When, was a difficult question, but it was certainly not going to be there very long.

BIGSBY: You once wrote that Marxism was a kind of religion.

MILLER: That was much later. I would never have called it that in those days. I gave up on religion because, first of all, it was in the zeitgeist. At almost every university it was dying out.

BIGSBY: But there was a moment when you had gone to a synagogue looking for answers.

MILLER: That was when I was thirteen. I tried to carry on for about a year after my bar mitzvah, for which I learned by rote. It was simply drilled into you. The atmosphere was that this was a dying culture. There was nothing there for anybody.

BIGSBY: Looking back over your life, fascism seems to have been crucial to you.

MILLER: Oh yes. That was true because I associated it then with anti-Semitism. That was why I could get so excited about it, but it was also against trade unions, and it reminded me that near where I was going to school was the centre of the labour-organising drive in the United States, Detroit. That's where it all happened.

To me at the time, and even now, there is an element of symbolism in Jewishness. In other words, when the Jews go down, democracy usually goes down with them. It almost never fails. I don't know of a regime that is hostile to Jews that is democratic, including back in 1492.

I was at this Jewish historical society, and I met a neurosurgeon. He was talking about the rise of anti-Semitism in Europe, and he asked me whether this reminded me of the 1930s. It is a different kind of anti-Semitism than Hitlerian anti-Semitism, for which the Jew was almost a carrier of disease. This is, I think, a reaction to Israel and its persecution of the Palestinians, and the occupation of Palestinian territory. It is a political thing. I have been going to Europe since 1947. I didn't run into any anti-Semitism in Europe. No doubt there was some, but it was not significant. But suddenly it got significant, and it corresponded with this dreadful policy, by Sharon and his party, of being aggressive towards these other people. It's not that I blame the Israelis only. I think the Palestinians are just as stupid. This is idiocy from both sides. It's futile to take sides in this, and that's why the blatant anti-Semitism may have risen, but it wouldn't have swept so many other people with it but for some kind of disgust with this.

I think the Jews were understandably justified in trying to find a place where they could be safe after being nearly totally destroyed in Europe, this fine old civilisation. So, I am very supportive. Where I get off the train is when they begin to assert superiority in every direction. It's a simplified nationalism such as we have gotten, and the British have had and the French, and so on. This I find retrograde and stupid. Somebody has got to say that.

I was reading James Joyce's letters again, and it reminded me of my attitude towards the Jews and Israel. He adores Irishness. On the other hand, he hates Ireland. His ambivalence towards it made me laugh. There's a similarity too, because he acknowledges people who are struggling to assert some identity in the face of a world that could squeeze and wipe them out. It's a very parallel thing.

BIGSBY: What about the theatre? Did you try your hand at acting in Michigan?

MILLER: I had the part of a silent bishop in *Henry VIII*. On cue I had to nod. The other job was I appeared in a play called *Excursion*, by Victor Wolfson, put on by the Ann Arbor drama department, in which I played the part of a coastguard officer who boards a New York ferry boat because the captain has taken it out to sea. He is bored going from Staten Island to Manhattan and so takes off, with the consent of the passengers, because they were all trying to escape the Depression. It was a Broadway success. So, I had to board the ship and bang on the door of the captain's lounge, yelling out, 'United States Coastguard, open up!' Through rehearsals I was banging the gun on the floor, because you couldn't hit the set or it would shake, and it made a lot of noise. On the opening night I banged on a board, and it didn't make any noise. I looked down at the revolver head and it had simply fallen apart. So here I am on my hands and knees, in the dark offstage, yelling, 'Open up, the United States Coastguards!'

The captain was played by an Irish actor who would come every year and direct a play in Ann Arbor. He was a great grave digger in many great productions. He, of course, was a professional. The rest of them were students. He opened up the door, and I stood up and had the barrel of the gun in my hand concealing the fact that there was no handle. By this time, I was in total confusion. He put up his hands. My next line was, 'I want everybody up against the wall', but I couldn't think of it. So, he said, 'You want everybody up against that wall?' I said, 'Uh huh.' So, on cue, they all moved up against that wall, and I entered the set. I was just standing there, completely out of it. He said, 'You going to tow us back to New York?' because my next line was, 'I'm going to tow you back to New York.' I said, 'Uh huh', and I think I had one other question or statement, with which he led me off the stage. That was my last acting.

BIGSBY: Did you take any writing courses at Michigan?

MILLER: What happened, was this. I had a lovely professor in the English department. We were all supposed to write something, essays, stories, whatever, and I wrote this play. He loved it. He thought the play was just wonderful. So he read it to the class. His pronunciation was so stiff that instead of 'Oh, yeh' he said, 'Oh yea.' I will never forget that. He said you ought to go and get into Professor Rowe's class, he teaches playwriting.

BIGSBY: Was the play he read out *No Villain*?

MILLER: Yes.

BIGSBY: Do you think you would have become a writer without Professor Rowe? How important was he to you?

MILLER: He was an audience, but quite soon I grew a little bit disillusioned with him, because he kept praising these talentless people who really had no grasp of anything to do with art. Indeed, I don't know of anybody else, besides myself and Norman [Rosten], who had some talent as a playwright, who came out of that whole thing. But he was invaluable as a warm, encouraging presence, and he knew a lot about the history of the theatre. He would talk about style and rhythm. One on one, he was wonderful. It was a great thing to be with him. But when he got into the class, he was hopeless. But he was the closest I had gotten yet to any professional, serious view of what I was doing.

BIGSBY: What did you learn from him?

MILLER: It is hard to say. He was very enthusiastic in general. He loved people writing plays, good, bad or indifferent. I would listen to some of these plays, and I thought they were dreadful. He would always find something good to say about them, so I gradually lost the feeling that he was a proper judge of anything, to tell the truth. But I still prized his affection, and his love for the theatre. Also, I think it was important that he saw the theatre as having a voice which was its own. There was nothing like it. You were in a unique area while you were a playwright. He made playwriting seem terribly important as a social and moral force. That was important. Apart from that it is hard to say that I learned anything.

BIGSBY: What made you decide to be a writer at all?

MILLER: That occurred when I was at Michigan. I wrote [*No Villain*, later *They Too Arise*] during our spring break and got very excited by the whole procedure. It was all very thrilling for me, and it won a lot of prizes, and that gave me the illusion I could go on. I won some more prizes with some other plays, and then I didn't win some prizes, but I had got addicted to the damn thing. It just seemed the most important thing you could do. I should add that in those times, in the thirties, forties and early fifties anyway, writing a play seemed to be socially important, as well as personally. People took the theatre extremely seriously as a way of stating something. It was not merely pure entertainment. It was always entertainment, which it should be, but it was also a kind of tribunal. *All My Sons* is in that spirit and *Death of a Salesman* is too, but that whole attitude, I think, for us, has departed. What they are interested in now is diversion, being purely and simply diverted and entertained.

BIGSBY: Why did you take a course on abnormal psychology?

MILLER: I thought I would find out something I didn't know. God knows. The time arrived, I think it was probably about my third year, when I felt I had had it. I could get everything I needed to know out of the books, because that was what the education consisted of, what I was reading. I only hung out there because I had nowhere to go.

It was a very pleasant environment. But as for pursuing some academic aim, I don't think that was happening, not at all. It was when I got out that I began to circulate. I became part of the Federal Theatre for six months and banged around with the rest of them.

3

Mary Slattery

BIGSBY: Is it right that when you met Mary, your first wife, you actually wrote a term paper for her?

MILLER: Yes. I was able to write on any subject if I knew three things about it, two-and-a-half things. I could write entertaining things and get away with it.

BIGSBY: So, you wrote her term paper on Roosevelt. She had a fraudulent grade.

MILLER Well, she knew all of that stuff. I was only writing what she knew.

BIGSBY: In those days did people live together before getting married? Did you?

MILLER: At the school I had never heard of anybody doing that. We lived together for two years after Michigan.

BIGSBY: Actually living in the same apartment, not having two different addresses?

MILLER: Oh yes.

BIGSBY: What made you decide to get married, because in *Timebends* you say you almost got married because of the opposition. It was the resistance of both sets of parents that made marriage seem a thing to do.

MILLER: I think it was partly the result of my own maturation. I wanted to have a regular relationship, and she certainly did. She was tired of always commuting.

BIGSBY: But you might have thought that with the radicalism of the thirties you would have tended to see marriage as a bourgeois institution.

MILLER: No, not at all. You know the most conformist people were radicals.

BIGSBY: Certainly very puritanical.

MILLER: Puritanical, conformist; it is very strange.

BIGSBY: What was Mary like at Michigan?

MILLER: She was a terrific student, very sharp intellectually, and passionate about things. She had been brought up in Ohio. She came from a Catholic family. They were devout people. The father was Irish, the mother Alsatian. They were one generation away from farm people. They were very devout, and she revolted against that as a young intellectual. She ceased going to church in her early teens. Intellectually, she couldn't accept it any more. She had an older brother who had intellectual interests, and he also left the church. Lakewood, a suburb of Cleveland, was a very heavily Catholic area. There was a lot of anti-Roosevelt feeling once the question came up of being anti-fascist because Franco was a Catholic and the church had long since favoured the fascist side. That is what I think led her away from the church in the first place. By the time I met her in Michigan she was a rebel already. [She went to Michigan for the winter semester 1935, leaving in 1938 apparently without gaining a degree.]

BIGSBY: What did she major in?

MILLER: Probably English. [Michigan has no record of her major.]

Mary Slattery

BIGSBY: Which year did you meet her?

MILLER: I met her about 1937, as a junior.

BIGSBY: You say she was passionate about things. Was she a member of any of the campus political groups?

MILLER: I don't recall her being active that way. She would support them, emotionally, but like most of us had to work. She had jobs, clerical jobs, stenographic jobs, working in the university for her money. There wasn't much time for anything else. I guess I worked two, four, maybe five hours a day on jobs, sometimes two, to stay there. It was the rich kids who did all the organising. The rest of us were trying to get the schoolwork done. Some of the less affluent were on scholarships of one kind or another, and they had to maintain a certain level of grades in order to stay there. So, they were out of it.

BIGSBY: Her family were not well off.

MILLER: Her father was a retired boiler inspector for the city of Cleveland, so I am sure the pension was very modest, and I don't think he had saved any great amount of money.

BIGSBY: Was part of the attraction that you were both by then politicised, thought the same things, or did it have absolutely nothing to do with it?

MILLER: Oh no, part of it was that we shared the same passions about Franco and the Spanish Civil War. That was a passionate issue, and that drew us together. That was very important in the whole thing.

BIGSBY: What form did that take? Did you organise anything, write pieces?

MILLER: I was of no note of any kind. Nobody asked me to make a speech. I wouldn't know how to do it anyway. What I did do was work at the newspaper. I was a sophomore when I was on the *Michigan Daily*, which was then the town newspaper. They had Associated Press and the United Press, and we were very often called by Associated Press in Detroit for what was happening. One of us would write up a story and send it to them. The local paper had no political sense whatsoever, and we were very hip. We were anti-war. Everybody was going to stay out of the Second World War.

BIGSBY: Which of the two of you was more passionate, politically?

MILLER: That is hard to say because both of us were pretty hot about these things, and Mary had a very pure attitude to politics. To her, people were right or wrong. I was more interested in whether right was wrong and wrong was right, but she saw things pretty black and white, even from the beginning.

BIGSBY: How quickly after you met her did you consider settling down and getting married?

MILLER: Oh, I would never have thought of getting married.

BIGSBY: You wouldn't?

MILLER: Oh no. First of all, nobody could easily get a job. It wasn't unheard of that a guy with a law degree was doing manual labour. There was a lot of doubling up of families, twelve, fourteen people in a six-room house to save rent. So, the idea of getting married was out of the question, and I had no desire to get married anyway. I was already thinking, after I had won a couple of playwriting prizes, that maybe I could become a professional playwright.

BIGSBY: Did she have any idea of getting married?

MILLER: Women are always getting married.

BIGSBY: So, would she suggest it?

MILLER: No, we would never discuss that because she knew it wasn't possible. It couldn't happen. I expected we would probably separate by the time we graduated because I lived in New York, she lived in Lakewood, or wherever she was going to settle down. It was only after we graduated that she dreaded going back to that boring place, and so we both went to New York, but we still didn't live together immediately. I had a room on 74th street, on Madison Avenue, in some old decrepit brownstone, because you could rent a room very cheaply. She was living with two other women on Brooklyn Heights, and soon got a job because she was very efficient. It was at a medical publishing house, an offshoot of Harper's publishing. I didn't know where I could get a job. I went home first, but I didn't want to stay there. In the meantime, I was trying to write radio scripts for a living, and I finally did. Norman Rosten was my closest friend then and, somehow, he got some assignment from BBD and O, a big advertising agency. They handled a lot of radio. BBD and O was probably the reigning advertising agency of the era. One of its owners, Bruce Barton, said the greatest salesman in the world was Jesus Christ.

BIGSBY: But how was the relationship with Mary going on then, if you were in two different places, doing two different things?

MILLER: Once I got a room she would stay over once in a while but, basically, she was in Brooklyn with a young woman named Trueblood, and there was one other whose name I have forgotten. Anyway, by 1939 it began to look as though war was coming, and we were all against it. I think most of the country was probably against it, even though we were presented with a quandary because we knew by then that the Nazis were destroying all the trade unions, which we were against. The fascists were eating up Europe, or threatening to. And Kristallnacht had happened. So, everything was now in conflict. Finally, by 1940, probably left to myself I would not have gotten married, but I really admired Mary a lot, and I loved her. I had a great feeling of companionship with her, and we got along great. She was really anxious to get settled down. So, I thought it was probably a good idea to marry.

BIGSBY: That sounds a bit casual.

MILLER: It wasn't casual.

BIGSBY: But you didn't terribly want to get married.

MILLER: No, marriage was not for me. It didn't mean all that much, anyway.

BIGSBY: But by then you were living together.

MILLER: Yes, sure.

BIGSBY: And you were, as you say, drawn to one another partly because you were politically compatible, you believed in the same thing.

MILLER: Oh yes, I think so. Politics in those days was a different quality. It was an aspect of life; it wasn't politics. I suppose it was like being of the same religion, something like that. We were not of the same religion, of course. We were both atheists. I really wouldn't have wanted to lose her. She had become part of my very existence.

She could be very funny. She was very pretty, and a wonderful cook, and there was only one element in her that rankled a little, and that was that her opinions were immovable, simply immovable. They were mostly right, but you couldn't budge her. She had a stubborn streak that was awesome. Everybody knew it who was around her. We used to joke about it. She was granite, and that was her undoing with me, finally. But at the time I admired it a lot because I was not that way. She was rock and I was water. It takes a lot of water to wear down rock, but we had good times for a long time. We were married for sixteen or seventeen years.

BIGSBY: When you first got married how hard up were you?

MILLER: Mary worked. She had a regular job. She made about $25. She was a secretary. I was periodically able to do a radio play, for which I got paid $250, which could keep us for a few weeks or months, or whatever it was. We lived very frugally, never had any money.

4

Brooklyn

BIGSBY: You lived in Brooklyn, and though you moved several times it was always there.

MILLER: Brooklyn Heights, in the 1940s, was the cheapest place you could live in New York City. My first apartment, after I got married, was on Schermerhorn Street. It was a newly remodelled brownstone building. Nobody had ever lived in this apartment before. It had a living room, a kitchen and a bedroom – beautiful. It went right through the building. It cost $35 a month. Even then, elsewhere you would have had to pay double that, and a lot of writers and artists moved to Brooklyn Heights because of that, because it was cheap. But it was also beautiful.

Before the esplanade was built, the promenade there, you looked down on the docks where ships were still being loaded and unloaded, and there were longshoremen bars down there. It was a whole life going on at the edge of the river. Later, it dried up because of the container ships that didn't require longshoremen, but it was an interesting place to live. Out of that came *A View from the Bridge*, because I got to know some of the people down there.

I knew two guys who were trying to organise a movement in the longshoremen's union, which was notoriously corrupt and completely under the domination of the Mafia. They were trying to organise a counter-movement at grave danger to themselves. In fact, a preceding organiser ended up murdered by the union. As I say, I lived in Brooklyn, by now on Willow Street, and saw signs all over the place, chalk signs, saying 'Dove Pete Panto – Where is Pete Panto?' Pete Panto was the original organiser who was murdered. I didn't know what that meant until finally one of these two men came to see me, because they knew I lived in the neighbourhood and they needed support of some sort. That's how I got interested in this whole thing. The story of *A View from the Bridge* came to me through one of them.

Then we had the babies and that took over completely. I lived in Brooklyn Heights for over twenty years, and to me it is now [2004] totally changed. It looks like Philadelphia. I would get lost here, and I used to walk these streets all the time. It got much richer, it seems to me. When I lived here there were a lot of boarded-up houses, especially along Columbia Heights. I can't imagine anything is boarded up now. But it's still beautiful. I love it.

BIGSBY: How did Mary get on with your family?
MILLER: Very well. My mother was probably difficult for her now I look back, maybe because my mother didn't get on too well with most women. She got on with them all right, but I think there was a certain competitive streak in her. After all, I was her son, and she knew what I liked to eat better than any wife possibly could.
BIGSBY: She was being a Jewish mother.
MILLER: She was a Jewish mother. There was a certain strain, but she respected her a lot. Mary was intelligent. She was a good mother.

BIGSBY: When you returned from Michigan, you came back to Brooklyn and initially tried to place plays, the plays you had written while you were in Michigan. But you were also trying your hand at novels and short stories. Was it clear to you that drama was really where you wanted to put your energy, or did you just want to be a writer?

MILLER: I would have settled for anything. I just wanted to be a writer. But I soon learned at Michigan that I had no experience in the theatre. I think I had seen one or two plays as a kid. My mother loved the theatre, and in Harlem, where we had previously lived, up on Lenox Avenue, there were, I think, two legitimate theatres which staged plays. Of an afternoon, the audience was filled with ladies who were wandering around on 7th Avenue or Lenox Avenue. These were mostly melodramas, I think. I saw one melodrama with my mother which really knocked me over. But I was then about eleven or twelve, maybe younger. Anyhow, what got me at Michigan, when I wrote my first play, was that I found I could write dialogue. I've always felt that playwriting was an oral art, as opposed to the novel and short story, which has more to do with the visual. If I can hear it, I can write it. If I can't hear it, I can't write it. And early on I discovered I could hear it, and that began my work in the theatre.

BIGSBY: When you were just married you went on a sea journey. There was a man on the ship who you used as a model both for a play and a novel, a man called Mark Donegal.

MILLER: He hated the captain, as did everybody on that ship. It was the Waterman Steamship Company. They were coastal ships which would go down from New York, to Boston, to the Gulf and back. He had been in the air force in the thirties and got drummed out, I think because he was drinking. He told me he had once flown an air force plane under the Brooklyn Bridge. He was very handsome, a typical Irish ne'er-do-well, but a very funny and a charming guy. His family were quite rich. One day he spilled a whole bowl of soup over the captain, so he lost his job. I am sure it didn't happen purposely.

We got to New Orleans, and he loved New Orleans. It was a hell of a place then, and so I went with him because he knew the city and we ended up in this gigantic brothel which went the whole block long. First of all, you had to sign your name when you came in. He went through the ledger and said so-and-so was here; he knew a lot of the guys. Then he went off to find somebody who he knew was there because of the ledger, because it had the date as well as the name. I walked around in this place. There was a broken wall of brick which was partly destroyed, and I looked in. It was a room and there was a man sitting in there with a bottle of whisky. He was totally stoned in the middle of this ghastly-looking room, amidst a pile of dust and broken bricks. It was really out of some surreal movie. So, I walked in and said, 'Hello.' He just looked up. He was insensible, and so I left him. A woman came in as I was leaving, and she was washing his face.

BIGSBY: What was it all about?
MILLER: I have no idea. I never did figure it out.
BIGSBY: And what were you doing in a brothel?
MILLER: Well, I went in there with Mark. We both left. He didn't go with any women, and we went around the town and listened to some jazz, terrific jazz there in those days. We had to be back at the ship anyway in a few hours.
BIGSBY: Why did you take the ship?

MILLER: I wanted to see what the sea was like. I lived right by the harbour.

BIGSBY: But you had just got married.

MILLER: Yes, well, we had lived together for some time, so it was no great surprise. I had arranged this months earlier. I wanted to write about it. I didn't know what to write, and I never did excepting ...

BIGSBY: ... a sort of O'Neill sea play.

MILLER: I was not conscious of O'Neill in those days. I think O'Neill was out of fashion. People like me regarded O'Neill as being overly fascinated with religion, God, Catholicism. All that was of absolutely no interest to me. I liked O'Neill plays because they were very romantic, whereas the ships I knew about were not at all romantic. They were really hell-holes that people worked on.

BIGSBY: Did you have a story that you were working on, or did you go looking for a story?

MILLER: I didn't have a story. I was trying to find one. I loved the idea of going to sea. I met a number of interesting types on board.

BIGSBY: Were you working?

MILLER: No, I was a passenger. You couldn't get a job on one of them because the union was very strong.

BIGSBY: How could you afford it, because you didn't have any money?

MILLER: It was about $50. There was one guy who would go ashore every time we stopped, at five different cities on our way down. There was an organisation of very upper-class ladies, society ladies, and they ran little places in these ports to help the seamen. He went there and he would bring back the *National Geographic*, or a magazine on travel, whatever, mechanics, leather-working. If it was in print, he would bring it back. He would lie down on his bunk. To him, everything was reading matter. He said, 'I love reading matter.' They were just words, and he spent the whole trip reading it.

BIGSBY: There is part of a novel that emerged from that trip. It is called *Bangkok Star.*

MILLER: I invented a story which I really could not have developed. It was the beginnings of a story.

BIGSBY: Why were you writing it as a novel?

MILLER: When I started, it was a play, and it became a novel. I did that a couple of times. It could have been one way or the other. I can't recall.

BIGSBY: It struck me, reading some of your unpublished stories and novels, particularly one set on the *Bangkok Star*, that you were very interested in race in the 1940s. Can you recall that being an issue to you?

MILLER: When you say that it comes as a slight surprise, but on the other hand it isn't. I was brought up on the southern edge of Harlem, the first twelve or thirteen years of my life, and my school had a lot of Black kids in it, probably half Black and Puerto Rican, although most of them didn't stay. They left, and nobody bothered with them. They just disappeared after a period of time. Only a few remained. I can't say that I was ever a friend of any of them, because they hung together, but they were always figures, to me, of great anguish. I always felt badly about them. Most of the residents of that area were White, up to 116th Street, but school was something around half non-White. So, I was playing ball with them and living right next to them. The idea of these people being treated that way was absolutely outrageous. My parents regarded them, as most Americans did, as being the other side of the river. I probably didn't have the confidence to write about race. I would have deferred to Richard Wright, Countee Cullen, a lot of Black writers who certainly knew it better than I did. It always made me feel uncomfortable. The Black women were always very sweet to me on the street. I always felt they were welcoming.

BIGSBY: There were almost no White writers, outside of Faulkner, who were writing about this.

MILLER: I had a very instantaneous feeling of identification with them for some reason. I felt close to them. We lived on 110th street and, as I say, by the time you got to about 116th street, five or six blocks north, there were a certain number of Black families there. I used to ride my bike through there a lot. They were always very nice to me. The ones who were not were the Italians. They were the enemy. The Italian kids were always looking for a fight, always looking for trouble. The Blacks were absolutely the opposite. I was working out of my own experience. I really had no interest or awareness of what was going on in the literary world. I didn't know there was such a thing.

BIGSBY: You jotted down notes for a play about a salesman and his family in 1935–6. Do you remember anything about that?

MILLER: Yes, sure, I don't know that I ever preserved it. It was about the same people as Willy Loman, but I couldn't engage that broader vision. It all got very petty, little.

BIGSBY: But, back in Brooklyn, you also wrote another story that was a precursor to *Death of a Salesman*. It is written in a stream-of-consciousness style. You are in and out of the sensibility of the central character. Words are strung together, sentences all loop around one another. Can you remember being drawn to experiment in the early 1940s?

MILLER: I read Gertrude Stein in about 1930–1: 'A rose is a rose is a rose.' I didn't understand any single page of it, but I just loved the way it was written, totally incomprehensible as it was. I didn't know what she was going on about. It was like listening to a sort of music. That is the only clue I have as to where I could have connected with that kind of writing, because nothing else I knew of was like that.

BIGSBY: When you first came back from Michigan, however, you tried your hand at a number of stories, which never made it into print.

MILLER: There was one [a little later] based on a man I knew at the Brooklyn Navy Yard [where Miller worked]. His name was Ipana Mike. He was a ship fitter, an Italian, from Calabria. He told it to me in 1942 [a story that Miller tells in his short story 'Fitter's Night' and, somewhat differently, in his autobiography, *Timebends*]. He was in his fifties, so he was talking about the 1920s. He was a working-class guy in Brooklyn. He fell in love with what he called his baloney, an Irish girl, of doubtful reputation. He went crazy about her. First of all, marrying an Irish woman was out of the question. She wasn't Italian. He wasn't sure that he wanted to get married anyway but was spending half his life there. Finally, the day arrived when his grandpa was coming from Calabria, and his family said, when he gets here, he is going to straighten you out, because he was this powerful figure. He is very rich and, if you don't straighten out, he is not going to give you any of his money, and he is coming here to die among his grandchildren. [The guy] had been hanging out with criminals, and the family didn't like that either. The alternative was for him to go to work, which was something he didn't believe in. For money he had been running bootlegged whisky over the Canadian border and was afraid he was going to be arrested. He had also borrowed money so he could pay all the bills. But the family were illiterate, and when a letter arrived saying his grandfather would be coming on Thursday, he told them he was arriving on Friday. So, he figured he would meet grandpa on the dock and prepare him for the criticism he was going to hear from his mother and father.

So he goes down to the pier and grandpa turns up with a big trunk. Immediately he takes him to a saloon and gets him really good and drunk. They become blood brothers. Grandpa's trunk, meanwhile, is full of money. So he finally gets him home, and the family clusters around, all speaking Italian, and everything is going great until the mother reveals that he wants to marry this Irish baloney. Grandpa is outraged. He feels he has been deceived. Meantime, there is an Italian girl in the next house that they had picked out for him. He can't stand her. They insist that that is the girl he should marry. So, grandpa says, either you marry that girl, or there is no money. And he likes that girl because she is very obedient, wears black all the time. Grandpa is a powerful, physical creature. And in an argument, he suddenly slugs him. When he wakes up, he says, 'Okay, I'll marry her. But if I marry her, then will I get the money?' He says, 'Yes, then you will get the money on your wedding night.' So, he marries the Italian woman. This is supposed to be a true story. He comes to grandpa, who says, 'Did you go to bed with her?' He says, 'No, but I'm going to.' So grandpa goes back to the house with him, sits down and says, 'Go in the bedroom.' She has been whining and complaining to grandpa all the time now she is a wife and he never sleeps with her. So he sits looking out of the window. Finally, he comes out and says, 'Okay. It's all been done.' And grandpa says, 'We'll wait until the signs there is a baby.'

Meanwhile, he pays no attention to her and goes back to the baloney. But his wife gets pregnant. So, he is waiting with bated breath for the trunkful of money. Then grandpa begins to act very strangely. By now he knows his way around New York and the situation in America. He looks defensive. He is no longer being so obstreperous and belligerent. He is losing weight and looks morose. Finally, he opens the trunk, and the man starts counting all the money. He runs to the bank and asks them if they will change the money. And they say they will. He says there is 450,000 lire. And they say, 'That will be $222.' I forget how it ended. He is still married to that woman. Of course, he still had a lot of girlfriends all over the place. It would make a good movie.

BIGSBY: Looking at the letters you wrote to your professor, Kenneth Rowe, at that time, you seem to have gone to New York from the University of Michigan with enormous confidence. It was as though Broadway was waiting for you to say, 'Here I am. I am ready now.' Then there was a slow disillusionment as you failed to place stories and plays. *They Too Arise*, a revision of your first college play, was rejected on the grounds that it was too Jewish, even though the producers who were rejecting it as too Jewish were Jewish. Those must have been difficult years.

MILLER: It was tough. It was very hopeless. There was no Off Broadway theatre. There were a certain number of Broadway producers, like Herman Shumlin, who were open to social plays, plays that were not pure entertainment, but the dominant playwrights were all simply entertainers. The only exception was Clifford Odets. The rest of them were what the French would call 'boulevard theatre'. Any idea of a philosophical theatre was simply absurd. So, I felt completely out of it, totally. I didn't know what way you could go with anything that I was interested in. There was no experimentation possible. So, I quickly learned that my confidence was misplaced, I realised this was going to take longer than I had thought.

BIGSBY: But the frustration was that you were picked up by some quite famous names who showed an interest.

MILLER: They were interested in my talent, I suppose, but not in what I was writing. That was the problem. The first one that really showed a real interest was, oddly enough, Joe Fields, who directed [Miller's first Broadway play] *The Man Who Had All the Luck*. Joe Fields, and this is symbolic, wrote plays like *The Dough Girls*, really blatant farces, absolutely pure joke-filled entertainment. But, in his pocket, he always had Baudelaire. He loved French poetry, and he read and spoke French. His sister was Dorothy Fields, who wrote one hit musical after another. He loved *The Man Who Had All the Luck* and insisted that it get on. He had an illegitimate brother, his father's son with a woman who he had never married, who was a very wealthy manufacturer of perfume, men's perfume. He made a mint on this stuff, and he put up the money, directed it, and it closed in a week. But when it closed, he said, 'You go right on doing it because you have got it.' And I went from there and said, 'I am never going to write another play.' So, I wrote a novel, *Focus*, instead.

BIGSBY: You were writing verse drama at the time. Even one of your radio plays was in verse.

MILLER: Well, I made the discovery, which of course goes back to year one, that in verse you are forced to be brief and to the point. Verse squeezes out fact and you are left with the real meaning of the language. I did it for purely economic reasons, in the literary sense. I could say things more quickly than I could by stringing out fully articulated grammatical sentences.

BIGSBY: Is the temptation when you are working in verse to use a heightened language?

MILLER: I wanted not to do that. I wanted to use language so that people thought they were listening to regular language, but what I was slipping over was a hidden pattern which permitted me to say much more in fewer words than I could otherwise. That was really the basis of this. I was very restless with the need to complete grammatical sentences, so that by the time the sentence was half finished, we knew what it was. Why do I need all these other words? I don't want actors to think they are speaking verse because they would put one foot in front of the other and strike a pose. So, if they think it's for real, they will have a different attitude to it.

5

The Federal Theatre, Library of Congress and Radio Plays

BIGSBY: You were failing to place your plays, but there was somewhere else to turn.
MILLER: The first thing I needed to do was to find some means of survival, and I managed to get on to the roster of the Federal Theatre, which was on its last gasp as an institution, and that lasted about five or six months when the whole thing simply vanished.
BIGSBY: The Federal Theatre was part of Roosevelt's Works Progress Administration.
MILLER: Yes, it was basically an improvisation that Roosevelt had allowed Hallie Flanagan, a do-gooding lady from Smith College, and, incredibly enough, completely an amateur, with no experience whatsoever, to set up. It was a nationwide theatre which employed hundreds of people and did some very interesting work. In fact, they probably invented the only new form of theatre of the twentieth century. I don't know whether they have ever got any credit for that. It was a theatre which was basically a journalistic theatre. They made no bones about it. They were dealing with the big issues of the time, the question of medical care for people in need, the question of the agriculture of the United States which was falling apart with the Depression.

We were slaughtering little pigs to keep the price of pork up even as people were starving in the cities. It was insanity. They would tackle these big issues with an editor and numerous writers. It was really like the nineteenth-century novelists' approach.

BIGSBY: That was the Living Newspaper [plays devised by journalists and playwrights on major social issues]. But when you joined you did not write that kind of play.

MILLER: No, the division I was attached to was the playwriting division. This was a new idea. People were paid $22.77¢ a week to go home and write plays. There were more than a couple of dozen writers in New York. There may have been more in Chicago and San Francisco and New Orleans, but in New York there were, let's say, as many as thirty or forty such people, and they were all busy writing plays. I never heard of any of them becoming playwrights, but it kept them off the street and it kept them alive.

BIGSBY: And you did write a play for the Federal Theatre. It was called *The Golden Years* and featured Montezuma and Cortes.

MILLER: I wanted it to be a metaphor for what we were up to. You may remember that the Spaniards invaded Mexico, about 350 of them, and in one of his armies Montezuma, the emperor of Mexico, had about 30,000 men. The story basically was the paralysis of Montezuma in the face of the evidence. The Spaniards were killing thousands of people, burning up villages, stealing everything in sight, but he had convinced himself that they came from God. The Mexicans had a white god, among the gods they believed in, who had vanished across the sea, walked on water. When the Spanish came they were preaching Christianity and told the story of Christ walking on water, and their god was a god of peaceful pursuits. Montezuma thought, having conquered the entire world as he knew it, that they had come there to carry him off to heaven, because that was all that was left for him to do. Of course, they were all the time planning how to decapitate him. He was a metaphorical figure for me, reflecting the paralysis of the West, the disbelief that fascism intended literally to destroy our societies. Nobody could quite believe that until it became evident that there was no way round it.

BIGSBY: It then disappeared without trace, finally surfacing in the late 1980s on BBC radio and then on television. In a way that is a play, written for the theatre, that nonetheless works very well on radio.

MILLER: Because the use of language in it was vital. I was trying to create a language that would translate seventeenth-century Spanish and Indian into recognisable contemporary speech, and at the same time keep a flavour of some antiquity. So, the work on the language was more important than anything else, and therefore it probably has some vitality in its language.

BIGSBY: Can you remember what it was like to suddenly hear a play that you had written decades before, and had never been performed anywhere, suddenly on the radio?

MILLER: I thought it was an interesting experiment to try to do that, and I enjoyed listening to it. Of course, they had some very good English actors in that. They were terrific people. Anyway, my time at the Federal Theatre gave out and, meantime, as it was giving out, the only possible way to make a living was on radio. There was, of course, no television at the time and the radio was purely commercial, excepting for one programme on CBS by Norman Corwin. They had given him, I think, an hour a week, and he did anything he wanted to do. He had this kind of Whitmanesque style of chest-beating lyricism, but they were very effective plays. Some of them were oratorios; some were documentaries. He was always interesting. He had a considerable audience for a year or two, and I wrote one play that he bought for $100. It was the first time I ever made any money writing, and they broadcast it. I was thrilled. That was *The Pussy Cat and the Expert Plumber Who Was a Man*, a political fantasy. Everything was politics in those days. That set me off thinking that I might be able to make a living.

BIGSBY: Did you just submit that out of the blue, or did he know about it?

MILLER: I had no agent. Nobody knew me. I can't remember how I got it to him. I could have dropped it off with CBS for all I know. Hearing it on the radio was thrilling. As a matter of fact, I heard it at sea. As you said, I decided to make a trip down to the Gulf on a freighter, and I was at sea when the thing went on, and I could only get snatches of it on the ship's radio.

BIGSBY: Did that impress the people on board ship?

MILLER: They couldn't care less. They didn't know what I was talking about anyway, but I had some friends who were already working in radio who were a little older than I was. Of course, you have got to remember that in those days hack work was regarded as essential if you were going to be a writer. Faulkner used to write mystery stories and haunted tales, and of course Fitzgerald worked in the movies, which was the same thing. It was cooking up stuff.

BIGSBY: But, at the same time, you wouldn't go to Hollywood.

MILLER: If anybody had offered me a job in Hollywood then I probably would have taken it.

BIGSBY: In fact, you were offered a job in Hollywood when you just graduated.

MILLER: Yes, at a certain point I was. You have got to remember that they were turning out a picture a week in those studios, and they needed stuff to put into these movies. Somebody got the bright idea that maybe they ought to get some young guys in who had never done this. So, they sent a man named Colonel Joy to New York to ride herd on a group of writers who they would corral onto a train and take to Los Angeles. I knew a couple of those guys, and they offered me a job, but I just couldn't think of doing that because you have got to remember that the movies then, despite the legends that have sprung up since, were junk. They were known as junk; they were made to be junk, and they were junk, and they have now become classics. They are classic junk. Anyway, I didn't want to do that. I had higher ambitions. Finally, I got a job writing for the Cavalcade of America, which was a DuPont corporation programme that went on every week and dealt with historical events in American history.

They were dramatisations of Benjamin Franklin or George Washington, or the invention of the cotton gin, or the Wright brothers flying the first aeroplane, harmless stuff, and I got very good at it finally. I could write twenty-eight minutes of text, and that gave them two minutes to do their spiel. It may have been twenty-seven minutes. They had a forty-piece orchestra to do the musical bridges between scenes. Fourteen violins picked up and played four notes. It was really some production, and they had big movie stars playing the parts. They would bring them in from the West Coast. From that point of view, it was a very high-level programme, and was probably the best there was at the time.

BIGSBY: When your radio career was just getting under way, you became involved in a project with the Library of Congress. How did that come about?

MILLER: Desperation. I had no money and a friend of mine, Joe Liss, had this job in Washington in the Folklore Division of the Library of Congress. They were actively going around the United States, and had been for God knows how many years, collecting folklore from various parts of the country before it got devoured by commercialism and the entertainment industry. They would talk to Indians, they would talk to Spanish-speaking people, people from New York State to California, from Canada to Mexico. They were looking for somebody to go down to collect Southern accents in North and South Carolina, because in both places there is a large variety of Southern speech, some of it going back to Elizabethan times, because some of these places were isolated over the years and never got corrupted by modern life. So, they gave me a van with an engineer, because in those days you cut a record. There were no tapes. There was a record-cutting machine. unbelievable as it is. I interviewed people who were willing to talk to me and collected a variety of accents.

I got involved in the town of Wilmington, North Carolina, which had been a receiving port for slaves back in the nineteenth century. I would go up to somebody, maybe a guy standing around in the street, and tell him what I was doing. I made no secret about it. I said, 'Will you just talk? I am trying to find out the way you speak.' I had this van with a sign on the door saying United States Library of Congress. About ten years ago I found out that they had made tapes, because we made acetate records, and if you play an acetate record twice it crackles, wears out that quickly. Someone told me, and I wrote them. There are about a dozen tapes, and some of them are quite lovely, one especially. I made thirty records or so, because each record only held about two minutes.

There was a strike going in Wilmington, in a shirt factory, the Block Shirt Factory, owned by people from New York, as everything was down there. The South was in a colonial position. They were all Black women workers, and they were marching up and down on a street singing. Some of the voices were unbelievable. The people were singing beautifully. There were about thirty women on a picket line, and they were adapting spirituals to their struggle. One of the songs was, 'Oh, Mr Block, Halleluiah, you think you can do as you please.' Their voices were fantastic, and I got involved with one woman who was a contralto and had a fabulous voice. She was about late twenties, early thirties. So, I found an old barn and we all went there, and I recorded her singing. I had a lot of fun doing all that, and meantime I was collecting accents. It moved me, deeply, because those people, if not penniless, were close to penniless. Imagine the morale, the spiritual strength these people had to sing like that. Probably some of them were hungry. It was so stirring. They had pitched their tent. They weren't going to take this humiliating situation any more. They just wanted to be paid for their work. And this was the middle of the South, where they could expect no help from the government, from the town, from the White majority. They were on their own. It was one of the most moving situations I have ever come across.

BIGSBY: How long did that job last?

MILLER: About two or three weeks. There were still people around, one of whom was a woman named Lucy

Cantwell, who claimed to remember slave ships coming in. I don't know how that was possible, but it may have been some memory she had collected in her childhood.

BIGSBY: One thing that struck me is that she refers to an event that took place in 1898, when 'the White gentleman' had put 'troublemakers' on the train. In fact, the events of 1898 were the beginnings of segregation in the South, and nine Black people died in Wilmington. Did you have a sense that you were being offered a gilded version of the past?

MILLER: Of course. You would have taken it all with a grain of salt anyway, no matter what she said. But she was very charming. She wasn't stupid at all. She was just naive. So, as I say, she claimed to remember sailing-ships coming up the bay and landing. If I am not mistaken, her window faced the harbour. She said, 'From this window I would see Black people being taken off those ships.' But the dates don't work out. I don't see how she could have done that. She may have imagined it. She was extraordinarily well spoken. She composed her remarks in sentences, but what was so terrible about the whole thing is that she was a very sympathetic lady but what she was describing was probably the Ku Klux Klan or some similar organisation which were bound to keep the Blacks subservient. I am sure she was not motivated by hatred. It is decorum she was interested in, keeping people in their proper places. She sounded like one of Tennessee's women in *The Glass Menagerie*.

I found the Black people very welcoming to me, and they were perfectly at ease. I will tell you something about the South. The Southern White has far more contact with Blacks than the North. As I said, I was raised in Harlem. It was then a White enclave, but I had Black kids in the school, so I was used to that. It didn't seem very strange to me. I never found them difficult to have contact with, maybe because I didn't think they were all that different from us.

BIGSBY: Was this the first time you had been to the South?

MILLER: I guess I had never been down there before.

BIGSBY: What sort of impact did it have on you?

MILLER: It was very primitive, from my point of view. They were still reacting fairly violently to labour organisations. They were still hunting down labour union organisers. One day I was out in the town square in Wilmington and suddenly discovered about thirty or forty automobiles, broken-down trucks, spread all over the square. There were Black people who seemed to be doing nothing. They were sitting there. I got talking with one of them. They had built a shipyard in Wilmington. They had been brought in from the countryside. They had never been in a city. The building of that shipyard required them to work in water up to their hips, and it was tough going, but when the shipyard was done, and they were getting ready to hire labour to build the ships, they were all fired because their work was the tough work to build the goddamn shipyard. This was just leading up to our participation in World War II. One of them said a line I have never forgotten. There was no provision for these people at all. They were just told to go home. They were uprooted families. Where were they going to go? They had no jobs and one of them, a bright young guy, said to me, 'They've got me just about tripped, captain' – a White man was captain – 'just about tripped.' He was at his wits' end. He didn't know what the hell to do.

I interviewed the head of the shipyard – he was from Connecticut or Massachusetts – and I told him about this.

I said, 'What about that?' He said, 'Well, their work is done.' I said, 'Couldn't they be hired as labour in the making of the ships?', because the available White labour there wouldn't have had any experience either, and they were probably illiterate, the school system being what it was in those days. 'Oh no, the Whites wouldn't work along with them.' And that was the end of that.

I was astonished. I don't know why I was astonished, because it wasn't a hell of a lot better in New York. But this was such an overt act of discrimination, it was kind of breathtaking.

BIGSBY: And this is only a year after Richard Wright's novel *Native Son* had come out, a book that you found powerful and influential.

MILLER: Oh yes. It was fierce. What else could you say about it. It was total.

BIGSBY: I suppose driving round the South with a van with the insignia of the Federal Government on the side would not necessarily guarantee a welcome.

MILLER: We were guaranteed a welcome in some places, but in other places it was hell. We were looking for a quarry, where I was told there were all kinds of strange accents. We were vaguely pointed in a certain direction, and we went through a heavily wooded area where there was just a track. We came to this enormous pit, probably a quarter of a mile in diameter, and way down at the bottom, maybe six storeys down, were these workers mining stone. I was wondering how we could get down there when I turned my head and there was a truck right next to us, and from this truck was protruding a large shotgun. It was an octagon-shaped barrel. I will never forget it. It was about 2 feet away from my face, and at the other end of it was this infuriated man. He began railing against Jews. Johnny Langenegger, who was driving the van, put it in reverse and went backwards at about thirty miles an hour down that track. This idiot was obviously boozed up. His wife was pulling on his arm so that the gun was waving all over the place. We got out of there.

I wondered how he knew I was Jewish. Johnny had the answer. 'We have got this Library of Congress, Washington DC insignia in big gold on the door, and they think anybody in Washington is Jewish.' They called him [Roosevelt] Rosenfeld. This was the going anti-Semitism down there.

One of the places that was supposed to be rich in accents was this mining place. To get there, I hooked up with the head of the public health service in North Carolina, which was a very progressive one. His name was Dr Vestal. He agreed to take me around. He was quite eager on his rounds because he enforced the rules about manufacturing, about health risks [even as] his breakfast consisted of three bottles of Coca-Cola and two bags of salted peanuts. In a corner of his office was this pile of cases of Coca-Cola bottles. Each case, I imagine, must have held a dozen or more, maybe two dozen bottles. These were not refrigerated. It was just warm Coca-Cola, and, once fortified, we went on the road and got to his talc mine. Talcum powder comes from stone. It is just rotted-out limestone, I suppose, but it was down a hole, and we went down in an elevator. He was there to inspect whether these workers were wearing masks, because talc is extremely bad for the lungs. It consists of very fine particles, and you can't get it out of your chest once it is in there. It is like inhaling rock, and they would get all kinds of diseases from it. He was very strict about it, a good scientist, and I was very impressed with him. He was also absolutely outraged that there was a report on the radio that Hitler had supplanted the cross on some church in Germany with the swastika. He was out of his mind. He was ready to go to war that morning against Hitler. This led me into the complications of human life.

One of his other stops was a forging shop where they were making stoves. It was a large floor with thirty or forty workers. At that point I accidentally ran into a friend of mine who was directing an industrial film, also for the Library of Congress, about health issues, I think. His name was Oscar Shaw. We were in this shop, and he had the cameras focused on a row of machines when the cameraman said, 'Hey, could you ask that guy over there to just step away?' I stood there while my friend was moving people around, and there was a Black worker standing in a certain place and my friend wanted him to be moved aside so that he could get a straight shot. So, I walked over to the man and said, 'Excuse me, sir, could you just move a few steps this way', and the guy instantly complied. I came back, and Dr Vestal looked like he had been hit by a rock in the head. He was white with anger. He said, 'Mr Miller, will you step outside.' I walked outside and he said, 'You must never address them as sir.' I said, 'What am I to call them?' He said, 'Boy.' The worker was about in his fifties or older. I was twenty-four or whatever. That's the time that gave me a clue about racism.

BIGSBY: I was struck by all the interviews you did in Wilmington. You quite often asked how fascism differed from American values. What were you after when you were asking that?

MILLER: All the time I was collecting accents I guess I was trying to figure out the mind of this country more than anything else. It was a way of trying to penetrate what they were really about.

BIGSBY: This was two months before Pearl Harbor. You were there in October 1941. It is almost as though you are looking for an idealistic motive on their part.

MILLER: I was very young, and I thought people were moved by these thoughts. They are, of course, but I was asking questions to see if there was any conceptualisation of where we were vis-à-vis this tremendous war going on. Of course, there was practically no idea of what was happening in the world, any more incidentally than there is now. The people is a great beast, and it moves at its own rate of speed. It gradually engorges whatever is important to it, but it takes an awful long time.

BIGSBY: Not long after this you were going to be researching a film, *The Story of GI Joe*, and were asking the same question on American military bases of people who were actually involved in the war. I think you got similar answers.

MILLER: I learned through all this that we don't proceed with ideas. Feelings are what rule the human race. It is only writers and commentators who ascribe ideas to these feelings. Ferdinand Bruckner, a[n Austrian] playwright, came to America because he was an anti-fascist. He was not a lefty guy. He was basically a nationalist but was anti-Hitler. I sat with him in a room when the Russians had started to move west. He was glued to the radio. Why? He was waiting for the German revolt against Hitler. He said, 'All these workers are armed. He has armed all the workers.' I looked at him and I thought, how could he think that these guys are going to revolt? It was what he felt.

It reminds me of my father. Adlai Stevenson was running against Eisenhower, and my father was a Democrat. He would have voted for Stevenson no matter what, but it happened that Stevenson made a speech on television, followed immediately by Eisenhower. They were both running for president. I asked my father, 'Well, what did you make of this show?' 'I thought I liked Eisenhower better.' I said, 'Why?' He said, 'I could understand him.' He had a feeling for Eisenhower. Stevenson was balancing one idea against another idea and trying to come out with some comprehensive concept of where we were. My father got lost in the woods. The Korean War was on. My father heard one line that Eisenhower had said. 'If elected I will go to Korea.' He didn't say what he was going to do in Korea, but he said he would go to Korea. What Stevenson was promising was victory. My father wasn't interested in victory. If he had any interest at all, it was to stop this endless war, and Eisenhower won the election that night with that line which meant nothing. He could go to Korea to encourage the troops to stay there indefinitely, who the hell knew, but it was a feeling he gave off that he cared about these people. Maybe he did. I don't know.

BIGSBY: The job in Wilmington lasted only a few weeks.

MILLER: Yes, but it paid $200 in those few weeks.

BIGSBY: And was that primarily why you did it?

MILLER: I needed the money. I had no money at all. I got a lot out of it, and it interested me. I wouldn't have done it probably if it was not without some interest, but I liked the idea of having the excuse to talk to people. I talked to miners and schoolteachers, and all sorts of people. I got a good idea of what was happening in the country. I have always been interested in knowing what the hell is going on.

BIGSBY: To what extent did that work you did for the Library of Congress, talking to a wide variety of people with a wide variety of accents, different backgrounds, help you when it came to writing plays in which you had to inhabit the lives of people and inhabit their language?

MILLER: It probably did enlarge my awareness of different kinds of speech because in truth, not boasting, my plays involve people speaking a variety of languages. I was always a mimic. I could always mimic the way people spoke. In fact, during World War II I made a speech in Italian, of which I understood nothing, on an international broadcast from Washington. I can't remember now why they picked me out, but they asked me to read this speech, which was in Italian, and I read it with great vigour and passion. Years later I was in Italy and some guy came up to me, who was an interviewer, and started speaking Italian. I said, 'I'm sorry, I don't speak Italian.' He said, 'I heard you on the radio.' I can imitate any language, except Danish. Danish is impossible. But almost all the others I can mimic, and doing this speech stuff in the South I was very good at imitating the way different guys spoke. In North Carolina you can go a quarter of a mile and hear an entirely different speech. I am not sure if that is true any more, because television has evened it all out. In Carolina you could hear the language being sculpted by history. They came from different parts of Africa, or they came from different parts of England, but they were distinctly different within two miles. That is why they sent me down there. That is why they picked that area, because it was so profuse in the number of accents.

Of course, my plays are about people, and it has always interested me to hear what they have got to say about stuff. It is often confusing, terribly discouraging. I had a cleaning woman here for years, a very intelligent woman, and she had a mother and a father who were on social security. She turned to me one day and said, 'Roosevelt put in social security, didn't he?' I said, 'That's right.' She said, 'Was he a Democrat or a Republican?' She was quite intelligent. She had gone through high school, but it had all gone down the drain, these so-called political ideas. I mean, to ask me whether Roosevelt was a Republican. The Republican Party fought social security tooth and nail, and they are still fighting it, and she couldn't figure it out. She had no idea. So, she went with the feeling. She felt she liked Roosevelt. She liked social security. It just simply didn't matter to her that much to enquire as to how that programme came about.

BIGSBY: There was a very surprising moment on the Library of Congress tape after protest songs sung by women strikers. Someone sings 'Ol' Man River.' It is you. Do you have a memory of doing that?

MILLER: The only memory I have is that, when I got back to Washington with all these records, at the Library of Congress they had a recording studio, and there was nobody there, and my friend Joe was there, and an engineer, and I said, 'Hey, I'll do an impromptu performance.' So, I did a monologue on Buffalo Bill and his tragic ending.

I remember doing that, but I don't remember singing. It was taken down from my improvisation. We had finished whatever we had been working on and were in a studio in the Library of Congress and had some tape. I don't know what got into me, but I had just been reading about Buffalo Bill, and I started spitballing about him. There were four or five people there, and they were all laughing. I can't remember how it got written down. What interests me about Buffalo Bill was that he ended up a show-business guy. He was on Broadway. Everything in America ends up in entertainment. If it is there long enough, whoever is doing it ends up being an actor. Funny.

Meanwhile, as I say, they bought a play of mine called *The Pussycat and the Expert Plumber Who Was a Man*. That introduced me to radio, and I survived on it. Radio is a lost art, but it could have been important, as the British have proved. I wrote half-hour plays for the Dupont Corporation. They would give me the research, and I went home and used to be able to do them in a couple of hours.

BIGSBY: One of your first radio plays was about Joel Chandler Harris, who wrote the *Brer Rabbit* stories.

MILLER: Joel Chandler Harris was a Southern writer from Georgia who wrote *Brer Rabbit*. Brer Rabbit was brother rabbit, an incarnation of the Black personality in the shape of a rabbit who was extremely clever and outwitted the White owner of whatever it was he was trying to steal. [I was] assigned this by *Cavalcade [of America]*. Joel Chandler Harris was a darling of the very conservative Southern White culture, but in truth he had a radical streak in him. He used to hang around railroad stations as a young fellow and pick up stories from the Blacks who were looking for work, and he got to love them. For example, the rabbit is caught by the owner of a vegetable garden eating the carrots. He is about to shoot him when [the rabbit] engages him in conversation, and as he is engaging him in conversation he is just sidling over to a hole. At the optimum moment he disappears down the hole. It was typical of Brer Rabbit that he could talk his way out of anything, and it was delightful. He became a national figure, but nobody ever thought of Joel Chandler Harris as a radical, when in fact, quietly, he had a radical streak in him.

For example, he wrote a story about this hunting dog, and the hunting dog has a great nose. He is a beautiful animal. Every morning, he wakes up, goes to the door, his master comes out and throws him a chop or something and they are off. They go hunting in these marvellous woods, and it is a kind of pristine American scene. There isn't a house or human being in sight, and they are out there all morning hunting whatever they are hunting. One morning he wakes up and goes to the door and it doesn't open. After a while it does open, and there is a woman there, he has never seen. She yells at him to get lost, and he doesn't know what to make of it. She slams the door in his face, and a little later in the day he yelps a bit to get attention. She opens the door and throws a pail of water at him, and overnight he waits for his master, but the master doesn't come.

The next morning, he tries again and once again is rejected. So, finally, he hits the road, because he is desperately hungry, and he comes to a town which he has never seen in his life, and he smells meat somewhere. He follows this smell and ends up in front of a butcher's store. The ladies are buying meat, and he sees them put down this metallic stuff on a counter and a man gives them meat. As he is sitting there, watching, one of these coins falls on the floor. He grabs it up in his mouth, springs up the counter with his fore-paws and drops the coin on the counter. He charms the butcher, who gives him a scrap of meat. The customers are delighted, so they start throwing him pennies, and he begins to get food, and he begins to get fatter and fatter. He is just sitting there with the money in his mouth, and pretty soon he can't eat any more, so he keeps the money in his mouth. He can't keep it in his mouth indefinitely. He is getting too much, so he runs around to the back of the store and digs a hole and drops the money in and comes back to the store because he doesn't want to miss any money. He gets more money, and he puts it in the old hole, but then he thinks some other dog is liable to dig this up, so he goes to a different part of the garden and digs another hole. Pretty soon he has got six holes all over town, and they are full of money, but he can't sleep because, when he goes to sleep, he is sure a dog is digging up all his money. Meantime he is losing his fur. He is getting overweight, because he doesn't run around any more. His eyesight is failing, because he is not used to looking at long distances, and that is the end of him. He just runs around digging up his money, half-blind and crippled with arthritis because he has no exercise. And that is the story. That is not the story of a conservative Southern gentleman, but it attracted no attention whatsoever. He was the darling of the Rotary Club because he could tell these wonderful tales.

BIGSBY: Could you breathe something of your own politics, your own radicalism, into the plays you wrote?

MILLER: Up to a point I could, but in this case it was quite obvious that this man was an anti-racist, so I could simply tell his story. There were several such occasions. One of them was very comical. They had the hundredth anniversary of the DuPont Corporation, something like that. It was going to be a big occasion. All the DuPont offices all over the world were going to listen to this programme. It is one of the largest companies on earth, and in Delaware, which was the home of the DuPont corporation, was the DuPont family. They were all congenitally deaf, so they had special things hooked up to the radio so they could listen. They gave me this book about John D. Rockefeller who had some relation to the DuPont company. John D. Rockefeller, the old man, was a notorious bastard. I was a little surprised they had given me this book and thought, well, they must know what they are doing. It was a story of the discovery of the largest iron mine on the face of the planet.

The story was simply that there were a couple of brothers, called the Merrick brothers, who were iron miners and very religious. One of them, one day, went prospecting out in the country for signs of iron they could dig up, and he came upon this Indian. He described what he was looking for, because iron stains the earth and it makes definite signs of its presence. The Indian said, 'Oh yes, you go that way and there is a lot of that out there.' The Indian had no use for it, and nobody owned the land. It was the frontier. He went out there and looked around. He had his pick and shovel and he dug up iron. So, he staked a claim. The claim was awarded. He came back and followed the veins of this iron. It turned out it was endless. Not only that, but it was right on the surface. You didn't have to go digging a mine. He and his brother set up a business, and quickly got a crew of people out there. They were shipping out iron but were running out of capital and so they needed to borrow money.

Meantime, the news had trickled back to New York, and John D. Rockefeller heard about it. And what did he do? He found out very quickly that these were two very religious men, so he sent out his personal minister who talked to these fellows and offered them x millions to set up a real operation, but it was a carefully monitored amount of money. It wasn't forty million; it was like four, so there would be enough to set this thing up, but he knew, goddamn well, of course, that they would be running out of money in a short time. Anyway, the minister said that God had led the brother to the Indian, and the Indian was there in order to provide the people of the earth with all the iron they needed. Anyway, to make a long story short, they continuously ran out of money because a thing like that requires enormous capital. You have got to have big shifts to take the stuff out, crews, etc., and pretty soon Rockefeller owned the mine, and later on, in the 1890s, there was a federal investigation of this whole thing, and one of the senators asked one of the brothers, 'What did you end up with?' He said, 'I didn't have the fare to take a trolley car from one end of Duluth to the other.' This was the book they sent me.

I called [Homer] the producer and said, 'Are you sure you want me to do this thing?' He said, 'Why?' I told him quickly and he said, 'Well, the DuPont family selected this book.' I said, 'Okay, if that's what you want, that's what you are going to get', and I wrote the story and they broadcast it. I said to Homer, 'You explain to me what gratification they got from this rapacious event?' He said, 'Very simple. It showed how a capitalist benefited humanity by exploiting a natural resource which now went into the manufacture of motorcars, stoves, and the benefits of capitalism.' I said, 'You know, that never occurred to me.' They loved it.

BIGSBY: Were there occasions in which DuPont pressured you to cut things?

MILLER: One time they wanted me to do a show about Juarez, who fought against Maximillian, dictator of Mexico, and finally overthrew him and established the Republic of Mexico. Orson Welles did the part. At one point Abraham Lincoln, in order to support Juarez against the French in Mexico, had left quantities of rifles and ammunition on the United States side of the Rio Grande River for the revolutionaries to take and use against the French. The guy who was vetting this script for DuPont said, 'You can't have that.' I said, 'Oh.' By the way, this programme was to be broadcast on Pan American Day, to show the cooperation of the United States with our little brothers in South America. I said, 'Why? It shows the cooperation of the United States in the formation of the biggest government, the best government, in Latin America.' He said, 'No, you can't do it.' I said, 'Why? It is a marvellous scene.' 'No, you can't do it.' 'Can you tell me why we can't do it?' 'Well, the DuPont company owns Remington Rand, Remington guns, and we are constantly being accused of gunrunning in Latin America and stoking up revolutions just to sell the guns. This will reinforce the idea.' I think it remained in because it was so absurd that even they caught on that it was idiotic. I also had a line in there referring to parrots flying, and they looked it up and found there were no parrots in Mexico. So, I had to pull that one out.

BIGSBY: That play came to be made in rather strange circumstances, didn't it?

MILLER: I had the script in my pocket when I came to deliver it to Homer [Fickett], and it turned out he was in rehearsal with another show. So, I went over to the studio of NBC and, as I walked in, there was a shouting match going on between Orson Welles, who was the star of that show, and somebody behind the booth. I couldn't see who it was. It turned out to be a Yale historian who was a real alcoholic, and Orson was furious with the script he was supposed to be performing, saying, 'This is all shit', because Orson's grandfather, or something, was an official in the United States State Department and Orson knew from firsthand what the story was that this was dealing with. The role of the State Department had been dreadful, and they had made it seem as though it was just wonderful. It was a whitewash of American policies vis-à-vis something in Latin America. Some woman had written the script, and he said, 'This is no good. I am not going to do it', although they were in rehearsal. That was about a Tuesday, or a Wednesday, and it would be going on the air the following Monday. I walked into this argument, and they came to a stop. Everything stopped, so I went over to Homer, who was a very sweet, overweight man, but who was simply helpless. He tried to assuage Wells. As I say, it happened that I had a script in my pocket, about the triumph of Juarez in the Mexican Revolution. So I said to the director, 'I have this script. The trouble is that I wrote it by hand.' I didn't type in those days. I said, 'It's got a great part for Orson, because there is a long narration.' He loved that. So Orson read it and said, 'This is terrific. Let's do this one.' They quickly typed it up, and he had this marvellous cast, from the Mercury Theatre, and in an hour and a half they had a production going that was unbelievable. That is how that happened. It was a hell of a show. So everybody was happy. That was a good day.

BIGSBY: It is a play in verse.

MILLER: Orson knew how to talk. He understood the microphone like nobody before or since. He would wrap himself around that microphone and come out through the wires. He was amazing. So, whether it was in verse or not, you never knew. He managed to make that sound marvellous, as did the others. They were all trained in Shakespeare. They did marvellous Shakespeare productions. They understood language. Otherwise, I doubt it would have been done.

BIGSBY: The actors were often Hollywood stars. The play *Captain Paul*, the story of Captain Paul Jones who founded the American navy, starred Claude Rains. Did you get to meet these people, or did you just hand your script over?

MILLER: Oh, sure. They would bring them in from the West Coast. It was a very high-level programme. I had to be there because sometimes changes had to be made in the script. It might be a few seconds too long, or whatever, so I had to be there. That was part of the deal. They took me out once to Chicago, where Alfred Lunt and Lynn Fontanne did *The Guardsman* by Ferenc Molinár, and they were fantastic actors, both of them. I had to sit there and make adjustments to the scripts so that they could do them.

BIGSBY: That was for another radio series.

MILLER: That was US Steel Company. I only worked for the best.

BIGSBY: Some of the productions were by the Theatre Guild of America. Was there much to and fro between theatre and radio?

MILLER: Well, they not infrequently did a play in thirty minutes of radio time. US Steel was an hour, because I remember having to rustle up a terrific plot of *The Guardsman*, which took about two hours and fifteen minutes on the stage, into less than an hour.

BIGSBY: They delivered the script very fast.

MILLER: Yes, they spoke at a rate which, for Americans anyway, was extremely fast, but you heard every syllable. They were marvellous.

BIGSBY: Was there a sense in which you saw some of your radio work as a contribution to the war effort?

MILLER: I thought some of it was. I never had much illusion that it was vital to the war effort, but these things had sizeable audiences. They went into the homes of millions of people, and one was aware that we had a very strong isolationist sentiment in the United States. I would have said that, prior to the attack on Pearl Harbor by the Japanese, an honest poll would have shown that most Americans would have been opposed to us entering World War II. I don't think there is any doubt about that.

BIGSBY: And you would have been one of them.

MILLER: Early on I probably would have been the same way. It became a real local domestic political problem for the administration, and one saw rising in the country a pro-German, pro-Nazi feeling on the part of various churches, various individuals. I am not sure how it would have ended if we hadn't been attacked. So, I felt I had to contribute somehow.

BIGSBY: There is one series of which that is particularly true. It was called *The Doctor Fights*. It was about doctors who were serving in the military, both in the Pacific and in Europe, and you did some research for that by going to a hospital.

MILLER: That sprung from a story of a plastic surgeon. He was quite famous, and I went down to that hospital in Pennsylvania where he worked and watched him restore guys who were badly wounded.

BIGSBY: You wrote a memo at the time which said that this series should not pull punches. It should not be sentimental. It should confront the fact that people are actually being injured.

MILLER: As in all wars, the grisliness of the horror of it all is concealed under patriotic flags and music and garbage. Once I saw what was really involved, I thought that, out of respect for these guys, we shouldn't make it sentimental because, in many cases, it would change their lives forever.

BIGSBY: Did you have any difficulty in getting that idea accepted by the producers of the series?

MILLER: They didn't want it that way. It was dangerous. It would put people off the military, and not only the military but the whole idea of resisting fascism, which is what it all ended up being. But I felt that it would be better to tell them the truth, and then they would understand better what was involved in this struggle.

BIGSBY: There is one of those plays, set on a bomber raid out of England over Germany, where a doctor goes on this raid. How did you research that?

MILLER: By talking to the people involved in it.
I remember one guy who was hit by shrapnel, and he ended with his face on the floor of a bomber, and the floor froze and his face froze to that floor. I will not forget that. They had to cut him away from that floor, and this doctor restored that guy's face. I saw the photographs of the procedure as it went on over a long time, months and months and months, as he gradually restored this guy's face. Another guy's lips were blasted away. The doctor never went to sleep. This man must have worked at least eighteen hours a day, going from one to the other, to the other, seven days a week. They were heroic people. It was very moving to me. I was terribly moved by confronting some of this stuff because they were all very young. These guys were even younger than I was. I was probably twenty-five or something, and they were eighteen, nineteen, twenty years of age, and marked for life. A number of them were blinded, and you couldn't turn your back on them. I just felt I owed it to them, remote as I was from it. I wasn't flying over Europe and being shot at. But some of them were roaring around in wheelchairs with their legs off, playing football. They were rolling down the aisles of a hospital tossing a football to each other. It was just

excruciating watching them, and their spirit was fantastic. They were the best of the best, those guys.

BIGSBY: In the late 1940s, and into the 1950s, those who had written for Hollywood films that celebrated the alliance with Russia suddenly found themselves being questioned and blacklisted. How far did that reach out into radio?

MILLER: Once the anti-communism started, it had a direct impact on radio, but by that time I was half out of it. I was no longer really writing radio any more. I was writing plays and getting produced. There was a publication called *Red Channels* which was a racket run by a guy called J. B. Matthews. He had a long list of people who should be barred from writing radio for the innocent American public. It involved every good radio writer there was, including me, and I can't remember what the charges were, excepting either you were a communist or you were sympathetic to communism, or whatever, and that began a real massacre. Producers would avoid using those people. The way to get off that list was you went and paid him $100 or $200, and he took you off the list. It was a real racket. Or else you pleaded with him that you no longer were on the left, you were cured somehow of that disease, and, with a sufficient contribution, you would manage to get off. The producers for radio, for a couple of years maybe, cleaned out leftism quite early and without much ado. I don't recall any great publicity about this. It just happened. You just knew it was going on.

BIGSBY: One of your plays was very directly and deliberately political. You wrote it for the American Federation of Labour. It was an attack on the Taft–Hartley bill, which was seen as an anti-union bill.

MILLER: The American Federation of Labour of course was a very conservative labour organisation. It was nothing to do with anything except raising wages and keeping that bureaucracy of the American Federation of Labour which was later overturned by John L. Lewis and the CIO [Congress of Industrial Organisations], which was itself an attempt to organise labour on a different principle. On American radio you could just buy time. The American Federation, just like some toothpaste company, buys time, and the object was to defeat this bill in Congress. They asked me to write a script, which I did. I don't even remember whether it was broadcast or not, and I don't remember the script either. It couldn't have been one of my sterling efforts.

BIGSBY: You wrote a play in June 1942 called *The Battle of the Ovens*. It features a baker in the Revolutionary War and starred Jean Hersholt.

MILLER: He was one of those very sentimental, grandfatherly actors who always played the part of the good grandpa who comforted the heroine by patting her on the back and holding her hand and telling her it was all going to be all right. He always played the same part.

BIGSBY: What did you learn from writing radio plays that was going to prove useful to you later?

MILLER: They did have [live] audiences. That was very useful to me, to see that what I had written could hold people, keep them focused, interested, and sometimes moved to laughter or to something else. It was my Off Broadway theatre. Inadvertently, I actually benefited from writing these things. You couldn't possibly write a whole story in twenty-eight minutes, minus probably a minute-and-a-half or so for various announcements, so it was probably more like twenty-six-and-a-half minutes, without learning something, and I learned how to compress stuff in a way that was infinitely helpful, and to tell a story.

My model is the Book of Genesis. You read the creation and, in about a page and a half, you have got the human race. That is pretty hot stuff. That is the way to tell a story, and a story that never dies. It is the imprint of a hot iron on the soul, and when I see a book of 400 pages I wonder, couldn't this be 80 pages and make it better? It taught me a lot about how to tell a story.

BIGSBY: And is that the process, for you, when it comes to writing theatre plays, one of cutting down?

MILLER: Less is better. Why? It is very simple. It is like dreams. Dreams are very brief, and some of them you never forget because they are so discrete. Nothing is wasted. No dream has got excessive material in it. It all counts, and that is the ideal.

BIGSBY: Was it fun being involved in this radio work?

MILLER: What I found positive about it all was that very often they would be in rehearsal with some play – I think they began on a Tuesday – and by Wednesday afternoon they realised it was a dead horse. There was no way they could ever broadcast it, because some of these guys didn't know how to read a script, and they didn't realise until the actors got hold of it, that it was impossible. So, they would call me up and say, 'We've got a subject. We have got to go on tomorrow night', and they would send a messenger over with a book which would arrive at about 2 o'clock in the afternoon and they had to be rehearsing that thing the next day at 3 o'clock in the afternoon. I would sit down, and these were not electric typewriters, they were slow typewriters, and I would write the whole damn thing and get it off. Then you would change one or two lines, if that. I took great pleasure in being a good mechanic, and they got them on. By that time, I was getting $500 a shot.

BIGSBY: Besides working in radio you also worked in the Brooklyn Navy Yard.

MILLER: When the war began, and I was not accepted for the armed forces because I had a broken knee, I went into the Navy Yard. I was in the ship-fitting department. A ship fitter, in normal times, before World War II, took about six years of training. Usually, very young guys did this work. For six years you were a helper and then, after about four more years, you were ship fitter third class, and then second class, and then first class by the time you were in your forties. A ship fitter was supposed to be able to do every job in the Navy Yard. He had to weld, burn, chip, read blueprints. He could build the ship.

I entered the Navy Yard just after the war started, and we were ship fitters in six months. I could barely read a blueprint. How we ever got those ships made is a mystery. Every time a ship floated out of the dry dock, guys would stand there, watch that thing and say, 'How the hell did it ever happen?' But it did. We patched it all together and somehow or another it went to sea. However, I was writing radio plays at the same time. I'll tell you a funny story about that.

I had a friend named Sammy Casalino who was, like me, an ignoramus about what we were doing. Anyway, when the men sat around for lunch – I worked from four in the afternoon to four in the morning, eleven out of twelve days, with a day off on the twelfth – they all talked about their former work in real life before they became ship fitters, or whatever, in the Navy Yard. One guy was a boilermaker, another was a truck driver, while another was whatever. I couldn't tell them I was a writer, first of all because they would never believe me, and secondly, I just felt it would make me look peculiar. So I never talked about it. I'd see Sammy several hours a day because we worked together a lot. They probably thought I had been in prison. Finally, I said, 'Look, I'm a writer.' It turned out that just a few days later I had a programme going out on *Cavalcade of America*, about Amelia Earhart, who had been lost on a trans-Pacific flight. She was one of the first women pilots, that ilk who were very brave people pushing the envelope of aviation. She'd flown her aircraft out to do something, I never understood what, into the Pacific, and that was it. She never showed up again. They wanted me to do a programme about her life, and they gave me research. I did the programme. However, I added an ending which had her calling for help from her plane, but the radio conked out, and she was all alone in the dark and disappeared.

I said to Sammy, 'I have a programme coming on Monday night' – Monday was a day off – 'You can listen to it.' He was very sceptical about this but agreed that he would. He came back to work on Tuesday, and I expected a real welcome from Sammy, but he never said anything. So, I waited another day, and he still didn't say anything. Two or three days later I said, 'Well, Sammy, did you hear the programme about Amelia Earhart?' He said, 'Yes, I heard it.' I said, 'Did you hear them mention my name?' He said, 'Yes, I heard that.' I said, 'Oh well, I just thought you should know.' He said, 'Yes, but it was all true.' I said, 'Yes, but these are actors, Sammy. These are not the real people.' He says, 'Yes, I know. But it was all true except the end. I figured you wrote the end.' He gave me an insight into the audience's mind. In fact, now that I think of it, a year ago [2002] I had this play, *Resurrection Blues*, at the Guthrie Theatre in Minneapolis. Now, I'm sitting in the back of the theatre watching the play, and in the interval a woman came up to me. She recognised me and said, 'Did you write everything they say?' I thought of Sammy Casalino. So that is where we left it, and I have wondered ever since what the audience really makes of movies, radio plays, anything.

I know a fellow whose mother used to go to double features. For 25¢ you went to a movie theatre and you got two movies, and she saw Clark Gable get killed in one movie and in the next movie there he was again. This threw her into a state of mind that was hard to extract her from. She couldn't figure that out. It is an interesting study, what the audience makes of these transformations. I don't know what they make of them.

BIGSBY: An interesting feature of the Amelia Earhart play is that it is about women getting into the workforce.

MILLER: In those days it was a revolutionary idea because women belonged at home, and the only women you think would be working would be ugly women, or women who were spinsterish. Any woman who looked like anything couldn't possibly want to. The convention was that they didn't belong outside the home. She, by the way, was extremely conscious of this feminist problem. It was one of the reasons that motivated her to make that fatal trip. Lindberg had gone to Paris. There had been other transatlantic things, but the Pacific, of course, is much bigger and easier to get lost in, and she succeeded in doing that.

BIGSBY: And, of course, those shows went out live.

MILLER: Oh yes, live. Of course, there was no such thing as recording. They rehearsed two days, all day, and they broadcast, I think, on the third day in the evening. They would call me in the morning and say we are going to send over a book. You read the book fast on Monday morning and Tuesday morning you started writing. I wrote the whole damn thing in a day, and I made $250, which was a lot of money then, and, as I say, I got up to $500.

BIGSBY: You were saying you didn't want to go to Hollywood because that was hack work, but you were prepared to do that on radio.

MILLER: This was a day's work. If you went to Hollywood you had to sign a contract for a number of years, or at least a year. I don't think you could do it for less than a year unless you were a very important writer, and maybe you would write one movie. I am sure Hemingway could have made a deal, and Faulkner no doubt did. That was a common thing.

BIGSBY: You have dismissed radio drama as trivial, and you have also said that it can have real power.

MILLER: I think it can be a terrific, perhaps minor, form but a terrific one. It awaits its Shakespeare, so to speak. The whole art of that kind of radio drama, which almost always consisted of adaptations of a book or something, was that you had to condense an enormous amount of material into twenty-eight minutes. As I said, learning how to condense is invaluable. If you can condense a 400-page book into 28 minutes of dialogue, then you might be able to condense your own elaborate fantasies into a time that people would be willing to sit there and listen to. I learned how to condense and to do it gracefully.

BIGSBY: They paid you well. You had been earning very little at first.

MILLER: About $200 a year. But I soon started to make more. In the 1920s my family had a seven- or eight-room apartment facing Central Park right off Fifth Avenue. It cost about $110 a month. A Cadillac probably cost $900. Sandy

Calder [Alexander Calder] lived near me in Roxbury. In 1936–7 he paid $3,500 for a farm and 15 acres. I paid $28,000 for my place.

BIGSBY: Among your papers are so many aborted beginnings of plays. I suppose that is the nature of a writer's life.

MILLER: You see where it goes, and then it sort of goes into the sand and you don't have the impulse to write any more. If I had had a theatre, easy access to a theatre, I would have had many more plays because what would have happened, I think, is that I would have written the beginning of something and got a couple of actors in to start to play around with it, and then I would have got enthusiastic and cooked up the end of it. It is so painful in this system we have got. When I was coming up, there was simply nothing there. A professor from what they called a speech and rhetoric department ran a little theatre at Ann Arbor. It was a nice little theatre of three or four hundred seats, and they did the previous year's Broadway hit. At one point I said to them, it must have been after I started really writing plays, 'Why don't you do student plays, new plays?' And he said to me, 'But how would we know if they were any good?'

6

The Man Who Had All the Luck and *All My Sons*

BIGSBY: Your first Broadway play, *The Man Who Had All the Luck*, was not a spectacular success. You could have chosen a better title for a play that was going to close in four days. Did you know, before the reviews came out, what a disaster it was going to be, or was it only the reviews that told you that?

MILLER: I can't say that I knew, but I suspected that it wasn't going to work because I couldn't recognise the production. I had no experience in theatre. It just seemed to me completely divorced from anything I had imagined. Indeed, the critics were completely baffled by it, with the exception of one who worked for the *World Telegram*. All the critics had criticised the play, among other things because they couldn't believe the story. There's a baseball player in it, a young fellow in a small town, who is trained to pitch by his father in the basement all winter. And he's a great pitcher, but when anybody gets on base behind him, he goes to pieces. He can't play the bases and, instead of being in the big leagues, he is finally rejected and becomes a tragic wreck. They couldn't believe this was possible. Now this one critic had been a sportswriter, and he wrote a whole-page article about his experience with pitchers who couldn't play the bases. Of course, the play was closed by then. He was a very well-known critic, but he was the only one who had anything good to say about that play. Now, of course, it's been revived.

BIGSBY: It was finally revived in England at the Bristol Old Vic [in 1990]. What was your response to seeing that production?

MILLER: Well, it was a great evening for me because I was amazed at how good it was. I think the director, Paul Unwin, had found a key to that play. It failed originally, in my opinion, because none of the people involved, including me, had a clue as to how to act and produce that play. It is not a realistic play, but it has realistic dialogue. It is a metaphorical play, and yet it makes you laugh and even maybe weep, so it doesn't fit the categories very well. It is very difficult to know how to do it, but he has done a really spectacular job with it, and I was happy seeing that it had been confirmed as a play. I didn't publish the play for a few years because I was convinced by the critics that I was totally incompetent. Only recently had it been published in Britain as a result of you and your encouragement. I think it is pretty good. I think it means something, so it was a great pleasure to see it.

There was a good production up in Williamstown, and then they did it at the Roundabout [2002]. [In 1944] they thought it was a realistic play, and it was directed as such. I couldn't locate myself in that play. Due to the developments in the theatre over the last half century and, I think, civilisation, you don't expect ordinary street realism any more, and the consequence was it became wonderfully moving to people.

As you say, my play was not a success when it was first staged, and I resolved never to write another play, so I wrote [a novel] *Focus*, and that was fairly successful.

BIGSBY: Why, after the success of that novel, and the failure of your first Broadway play, did you go back to theatre?

MILLER: The prospect of writing another novel was [daunting]. There were just too many words. So I decided to write another play. I would either be the best playwright in America or I would go into another line of work. That was *All My Sons*. I suppose one of the reasons it took that form was that I had written about six or seven or more plays before, and none of them had been produced. There was only Broadway or nothing, so I had nothing. Consequently, the form of *All My Sons* was very conservative. It was written in a form I wasn't accustomed to. Before, I had written plays more lyrically, more experimentally, and got nowhere with them. I was approaching the age of thirty and wasn't about to spend my whole life failing if I could help it. So I thought I would write one play that maybe I could get produced. It took about two years to do. It followed a form which in our culture was originated by Henrik Ibsen. It is a conservative form of storytelling. It is very traditional, and very effective. It is the basis for most of the movies that were made at that time. I found it extremely useful because I learned a lot about playwriting by writing that play.

[Beyond that], I think the playwright is an actor, and an actor needs an audience, he needs contact with an audience, he needs the feeling of instantaneous contact that will energise him and the audience and the entire world. With a novel, if somebody buys your book and sits on the train going somewhere and reads it, and you never see him, you do not know what his reaction is. In the theatre you can feel it. I think that is part of it. The other part is that I have always tended to think in terms of scenes, confrontations, and it is much easier for me to write plays than to write books, prose. I have a pretty good ear, and I could use that in a way I could not do in the novel. Playwriting is a largely auditory talent. People with dead ears are at a disadvantage when they are writing plays. O'Neill struggled with this problem all his life. He couldn't hear anything, but he is a great exception. So, I think because of the auditory nature of the theatre I am rather taken with it. I love music, and music meant a lot to me then and does now.

BIGSBY: How was the idea for *All My Sons* born?

MILLER: It came out of a remark by my then mother-in-law about a story she had read in a newspaper in Ohio about a young girl who had reported her father to the authorities because she had discovered he was shipping faulty parts to the army or the air force. That stuck in my head, that this child would be able to do that, that she would have the moral courage to do that. She wanted to stop him from doing that any more. We were at war. Everybody was intensely patriotic, especially in that part of the country. That was the genesis of *All My Sons*. I changed it from a girl to a boy. I didn't understand girls too well at that time.

BIGSBY: But the play doesn't exactly follow that original incident. It doesn't turn out to be a play about someone who informs.

MILLER: No, it turns out quite differently. I didn't know the original people. All I had was a report from [my mother-in-law] who had read this in a newspaper. So, I simply latched on to that and ran with it. The original lost all significance for me, and I forgot all about it.

BIGSBY: This was a play written during the war but produced after it. What do you think the response would have been had it been produced during the war?

MILLER: It would have been very explosive because during the war the idea of somebody in effect betraying the troops in that way [by forwarding faulty aircraft engines] would mean that I would probably have been crucified for even mentioning this. Everybody knew that a lot of hanky-panky was going on, a lot of illicit fortunes were being made, a lot of junk was being sold to the armed forces. We all knew that. The average person was violating gasoline rationing. All the rules were being violated every day, but you wanted not to mention it. The idea of saying that some important businessman was a crook, or unpatriotic, was not going to go down very well. However, it was fortunate that, as I finished the play, the war ended. So I was able to do it in peacetime, and by then people were far calmer about the whole business, and they could confront the facts of what they had just been through.

BIGSBY: You might think that that play was very rooted in its time, but that hasn't proved to be true, has it? It has gone on living.

MILLER: I suppose it is because, by some instinct, at least when I am lucky, I latch on to what is a prominent dilemma. I suppose what people are responding to now, as opposed to the past, is a more social theme, the basic conflict between the father and the son, the idea of the parents and sons being in conflict. I think that those conflicts are probably never going to go away and will never change.

I saw that play in Israel once, and I was sitting next to the prime minister, who was then Yitzhak Rabin. Later he was thrown out of office by the right-wing government [and assassinated in 1995], but I didn't know it yet, and at the end of the production the audience simply got up and left. There was no applause whatever but, clearly, they were deeply moved. So I asked him what was going on. He said, 'Well, this is an Israeli play. This play could have been written in Jerusalem.' I said, 'Why?' He said, 'Here we are sitting watching a play and the kids are out there getting shot at and there are people here making money and having a good life.'

I have had this same thing just recently in Sweden, of all places. They had a production, which was quite a sensational thing for them, and I met the director and he said, 'We have never had a reaction like that to a play in this city. Swedes are not demonstrative like that. In the theatre when they are pleased, they sleep a little more lightly', but he says, 'This one is simply phenomenal.' I said, 'Why is that?' And he said, 'Well, they are guilty.' I said, 'About what?' 'About not being in a war, about selling all that stuff to the Nazis, that the king was openly pro-Nazi.' You see that guilt had really no direct connection with the plot of the play. It was very strange.

BIGSBY: Guilt is something that recurs in your work, as does betrayal.

MILLER: I suppose you cannot be speaking of any kind of an order, whether it be a moral order or a political order or whatever, an order of civilisation, without the idea of violation and betrayal. After all, the first story in the Bible has got to do with betrayal.

BIGSBY: Joe Keller, of course, justifies his actions to himself.

MILLER: I think that the justification Joe Keller makes, that everybody does this, and that you do what you have to do in order to survive, is very understandable. It is always understandable, and it is always unacceptable finally. I think the audience today feels 'Thank God I am not in that position.' But they know pretty well that, given the kind of pressure that Joe Keller was under, they might well have collapsed, too. In other words, people participate in the conflict. They don't entirely stand apart from it, because they know they are vulnerable. The thing about Joe Keller is that he feels justified, but he feels guilty, too. He couldn't help it, because the whole surrounding society would have condemned such actions. It would take a sociopathic person, a person who is really a criminal – which he isn't – to say, 'I don't give a damn whatever anyone else says, I am okay.' Joe Keller does feel guilt about what he has done. At the same time, he feels that there was no other way for him, that he couldn't have done anything else. It is a crazy quilt of motivations and contradictions.

BIGSBY: How far does he justify himself in terms of survival and how far because he wants to hand the business on to his son?

MILLER: That is terribly important. If he went bankrupt, say, or he badly damaged his business, he would have had nothing, or very little, to hand on to his son. For a man like Joe Keller, that would be a fate worse than death, because one of his psychological supports is that he is a provider. He is the father of the house. He is the man from whom all power and energy flows. That he couldn't hand something down to his son is something he couldn't bear to see. It is his great pride in life that he can leave all this to his son.

BIGSBY: Does this suggest that the family is in some ways a source of danger, of conservatism?

MILLER: There is a danger. There is a certain antisocial element in a family. The family is a selfish institution by its nature. It wants to provide for itself at any cost, and sometimes that cost can be the social existence of other people. So there is a real conflict in all family life, the conflict with society, even though it supports society.

BIGSBY: There is, surely, an echo of the 1930s in the title, the conviction, on the part of writers like Clifford Odets and John Steinbeck, that there has to be a solidarity beyond the family.

MILLER: I hadn't thought of that. I suppose at the time, 1947, less than a decade after the Depression and the ethos, habits of thought, of the Depression, it may well have been that I was influenced by that, but I don't recall it.

BIGSBY: Do you find yourself having sympathy for Joe Keller?

MILLER: Oh yes. I can't write a character convincingly with whom I don't sympathise. On some level I have to participate with him in whatever nastiness he is involved in. They are all projections of the writer, after all. Every character is. To some degree, he is me. But I hope not altogether.

BIGSBY: What aspect in particular do you feel some sympathy for?

MILLER: It is probably that we are both fathers. We are both sons. We both want to be of use to our families. Family means a lot to both of us. I recognise his weakness in both trying to satisfy his own needs and to be a socially responsible person, which he is trying to do.

BIGSBY: Joe Keller is not the only guilty person in this play. How much does Joe's wife, Kate, know?

MILLER: They all are, for different reasons. She knows everything from the moment the curtain goes up. She knows all the facts because she was there. Her life has consisted of trying to deny what she knows. The same is true of her son, Chris, but with him it is buried deeper because it is so intolerable, the idea of his father betraying him and his comrades. So, he fiercely defends Joe. He will simply not consider it until he is forced to. Everyone in the play has a share of guilt. It is part of the system of thought that goes through a related group of people if one of them is guilty.

BIGSBY: How far could you accuse Chris of cruelty?

MILLER: You can. Without that streak in him he could not have spoken as he does. He has got to feel a certain almost vengeance upon his father, or he would not have been able to do as he does. If he were completely passive in relation to all this, nothing would happen. He has got to feel the anguish of resentment and hatred for his father, to some degree.

BIGSBY: When the play has ended, has Chris been left with a burden of guilt?

MILLER: Probably to the end of his life, in part because it would have taught him that he really knew better when he was denying all this, that he should not have participated in the business without clearing things up earlier on. I think the recrimination against himself would continue for a long time.

BIGSBY: And then there is the guilt which comes from his having effectively forced his father to commit suicide.

MILLER: It is awesome, terrible. And yet there was no other way for him to have behaved. He could not have accepted that crime. There was no alternative for him, given who he was, given his experience. He had to attack his father. It is part of the structure of the play that that whole story cannot be otherwise. It must go the way it goes. There is no alternative.

BIGSBY: Why do Ann and George choose to believe Joe Keller rather than their own father?

MILLER: First of all, the crime is horrendous, and Joe Keller was not on the scene when it happened. Their father was. The court believed Joe. An objective judge believed that this weak man, who was on the scene, and whose job it was to see that these cylinder heads went through in good condition, was capable of letting them go through under great pressure. It made sense. Keller had a perfect excuse. He wasn't there.

BIGSBY: Was Joe Keller's death inevitable? Did you start the play with the idea that he was going to die?

MILLER: I began the play with that idea. Everything in the play moves like the bow of a ship towards that point.
I believe it had to happen, because his whole ritual was being supported by this fiction that he was innocent. When it was exposed, his whole nature was in a state of collapse. I don't see how he could survive this thing, psychologically. He would have had to destroy himself. I think, too, that there is an element in his suicide of his justifying himself. Most suicides are in part a blow against somebody. The Chinese hang themselves in the doorways of people who have offended them. I think that part of his suicide is
a counterblow to his wife and son.

BIGSBY: In fact, the central character in all four of your first major plays dies. Is there a sense in which you felt that the death of the central character raised the odds, enhanced the significance in some way?

MILLER: They are all quite different in the reasons these deaths occur. Why I would have done this, though, is mysterious to me, but at the same time one element is clear, that is that the tragic structure is based upon a death, and I was deeply involved in trying to create tragedies. It was the cast of my mind that made me feel that I had to write in this way. When I wrote *The Man Who Had All the Luck*, John Anderson, a newspaper critic who I did not know, called me up and we had a drink. He was the first one who said to me, 'You should be writing tragedies.' That play was not a tragedy. He said, 'There was a sense in this play that a death was looming.' That was very perceptive of him, because that play was being written about a man who did in fact kill himself, but I didn't have the tools yet to write a tragic play. I wrote the whole tragedy, but the man lived. His saying that released something. I saw immediately what he was driving at. I saw that that was what I really wanted to express, the sense of a clarifying death. From that play, I proceeded to *All My Sons*.

BIGSBY: The title implies that the individual is responsible for his actions, and to his society.

MILLER: It was John Donne who wrote 'Never send to know for whom the bell tolls; it tolls for thee.' Joe Keller was both responsible for, and part of, a greater web of meaning, of being. He had torn that web. He had ripped his part of the structure that supports life. The society is that web of meaning, and the person who violates it, in the way he did, has done more than kill a few men. He has killed the possibility of a society having any future. He has destroyed the life force in that society. So it does express the social side of that story.

George Deever [son of the man imprisoned for Joe Keller's crime] is about the return of the truth, the return of the repressed, in psychological terms. He is what you wish you could forget and what you wish would disappear from the earth. He is the evidence of the facts, and a frightened figure. He also reminds us of some of the original pre-crime atmosphere of that house, and the happiness that was in that house before that dreadful war, before all the sacrifices that had to be made in war, and the way they were produced by circumstances. George is the broken promises of the past. Everybody in the play is denying something. I would say that you can't live without denial. The truth and denial are cousins, not brothers and sisters. You can try to get away from them, but you have to deny something in order to survive.

BIGSBY: So how do you draw a line between what Ibsen called life lies, necessary denials, and those which are damaging and deadly?

MILLER: Of course, the denial that Joe is engaging in is the denial of a deadly crime, which is quite different from what the others are denying. But these lines are always very difficult to contemplate. It is hard to say what is permissible and what isn't.

BIGSBY: By now, presumably, your financial situation had improved. When was the first time you were able to buy a house?

MILLER: The first time I could buy a place was as a result of *All My Sons*. I bought a two-family, beautiful house on Grace Court. This was at the end of a garden, a fenced-in garden, beautiful. It took up two-thirds of the street. It was a dead-end street. At the other end was the river. It was a bit like a mews in London. It was two duplex apartments. The lower one was rented out already, when I bought the place, to the head of a Brooklyn savings bank and his wife. The upper two floors we lived in, but I got sick and tired of being a landlord. I couldn't stand this guy, anyway, and I sold it to W. E. B. DuBois, though I didn't know that because he was hiding behind a guy named Ross.

BIGSBY: Were there any other Black people living in the area?

MILLER: No, he was the first. I bought another house two blocks away, because that was a single-family house. That house must date from the 1880s. It was built a long time ago.

As a matter of fact, it is one of those houses you cannot tear down. The city made it part of a preservation zone. Mary sold it maybe twelve years later for about a million dollars.
BIGSBY: That was in the sixties.
MILLER: I wouldn't be surprised if that building now was in the two-million range. The other one, the Grace Court one, is probably up to three because it has a duplex apartment for rent in there.
BIGSBY: Immediately after the success of *All My Sons*, you took yourself off to do manual labour.
MILLER: Yes, that's true.
BIGSBY: It's as if you wanted to balance that success with being in touch with ordinary people.
MILLER: Actually, I smelled a story. Here's the thing. I was living on Brooklyn Heights, which is bordering the waterfront. That was when I saw those chalk signs: 'Dove Pete Panto.' I didn't know what the hell this was. Mitch Berenson came to see me, he and Vincent Longhi, with whom I later travelled in Italy. They were a conduit into that life. They were looking for help in reorganising a corrupt union. In 1950, I wrote a screenplay about it, *The Hook*, which was hijacked by Kazan and Budd Schulberg [*On the Waterfront*]. It had to do with social reform, being on the left and all that. I never knew what they were doing as communists, but that was outside my interests. It was a story about colourful people, about heroic people. This guy Panto was killed because he was trying to stand up for those guys who were standing around in the rain at four-thirty in the morning waiting to get hired. The injustice of the whole thing was glaring, and there were shootings. I was not going in there to make some kind of a political statement, and, indeed, I ended up with *A View from the Bridge*.

The Man Who Had All the Luck *and* All My Sons

BIGSBY: When you were in Hollywood pitching the idea for *The Hook*, it was proposed that you should change the gangsters in that script to communists. The proposal came from a man called Roy Brewer [head of the Hollywood unions]. In his autobiography Kazan says you were in the room. In your account you only heard about this when you had gone back to Brooklyn.

MILLER: That's the way it was. I met with Harry Cohn and Cohn's labour relations person, a man who loved the script, incidentally, thought it would be a great movie. That guy worked for Columbia, and when I left for New York I considered that we had a deal. I was in New York, what, a week when Kazan called me and said they wanted to make some changes and the changes consisted of changing the gangsters in the film to communists, and I said, 'Well, you can't make the film. That's the way it has got to be because that would be a laughing stock.'

BIGSBY: I have read an account given by Brewer which implies that he had been told to make these remarks.

MILLER: This is not impossible. You see Cohn didn't care about the movie one way or another. In those days, let's remember, a film like this was impossible to conceive in Hollywood. There was no love story. It was a dark film about corruption. Nobody made pictures like that. There would have been a revolution if they had made a picture like that and, indeed, when Cohn showed the slightest interest in it, Kazan and I were both quite surprised. But he said to Kazan, at one point, and I remember this, 'This picture is not going to make a dime. I want you to direct for me.' That was the only reason he was interested at all. He made no secret of that.

BIGSBY: It was in 1947, the year of *All My Sons*, that you went, by ship, to France, the first time you had been to Europe.

MILLER: Yes. On the ship there was this little jockey, travelling from New York to Paris. He had about four women fluttering around him. He was a tiny little man. It was like a harem of very elegant women. They were all over him, all the time. If he lifted his finger, they put a cigarette in his hand. They gave him a coffee and a brandy. He had a silk dressing gown, and he never got out of it. He would walk around the ship with this beautiful silk dressing gown. I was going to Paris. In those days, when you got out at Cherbourg, the roof of the railroad station was all gone. It was all glass. There wasn't a pane left because they had fought. The war was still there. I went over with [Longhi], an Italian American, purely as a tourist. We toured France and southern Italy, Sicily, which was in ruins at that time. I was aghast at the whole thing. It was beyond me to deal with it. I simply could not grasp it. The enormity of the whole thing was too great.

BIGSBY: Just after *All My Sons* Israel declared its independent existence.

MILLER: It was in 1948 that Israel came into being, and soon after that the Russians recognised it. Nobody else did as yet. I regarded Israel as a curiosity. It was a place where the kind of Jews lived that I had never met, farmers, soldiers, none of whom existed outside of Israel in that way. Well, there were some farmers here, there were a lot of chicken farmers in New Jersey who were Jews, but I had never met them. Anyway, it was a very peculiar place as far as I was concerned. Then, in 1948, some committee of people who

were passionate about Israel invited me to attend a dinner for the inauguration of the state.
BIGSBY: Why did they invite you?
MILLER: *All My Sons* had come out. They just wanted some cultural figure. It was probably an afterthought of some kind, but I was curious, and I went. That was the first time I met that kind of passion on the part of Jews for Israel, and I approved of it. I thought it was pretty terrific that for the first time since ancient times, since the Roman period, there would be a totally Jewish society of Jewish bus drivers, Jewish prostitutes, Jewish heroes, Jewish everything – like normal people. Apart from that, it would be a place where Jews could safely live.

I was never a Zionist, because I had the delusion, like a lot of people, that the Arabs could live happily side by side. It never dawned on me that this was being set up as a clerical kind of a state, because the Orthodox didn't recognise Israel. Everybody has forgotten that. They said, this is not the reinstitution of the ancient state because that could only happen with the return of the Messiah, and no Messiah had returned. And, since no Messiah had returned, this was a quasi-state. Indeed, they did not serve in the army. Everybody has forgotten that, too. They were a special small caste, if not sneered at then only tolerated by the genuine Israelis who were busy building up an army, an agriculture, a scientific establishment, and the usual accoutrements of a modern state which these guys couldn't care less about. They were ghetto Jews, and they created their own ghetto inside of Israel where nobody else ever went.

What attracted me was that this was going to be a modern state, not a racist or racially exclusive place by any means. Indeed, they had a number of Arab people living inside

Israel perfectly happily, and they still live there, though I am not sure how happy they are. I oftentimes feel a certain tug of pride whenever they do something decent, which they have done, along with this dreadful right-wing crap that they have indulged in in the last few years.

BIGSBY: Would you like to see a Palestinian state?

MILLER: Sure. Most of the Israeli people wanted a Palestinian state. Right now, if you took a poll, they would want a Palestinian state, because that would take responsibility. The problem, from their point of view, is that they have nobody to talk to who can say, 'Yes, this is the deal', because Arafat was up against his own problems. But they would have to withdraw those settlements. They should never have been put out there in the first place.

BIGSBY: But no Israeli leader has been willing to do that.

MILLER: No, because he couldn't stay in office. It is a real tragic situation, but one knew it then, I have to tell you, when they first started putting settlements out there. A lot of the Israelis complained about it. They predicted, quite correctly, that this would be the cause of an endless battle.

BIGSBY: The Jews have always had a double commitment. They live in a culture and a society, but they also live outside it by virtue of believing themselves to be chosen. It is that ambiguity on which they have been historically caught, because it is their very self-separation in certain regards that has been reflected in the attitude of people towards them.

MILLER: I agree with that. I used to admire my father, who travelled the United States, on and off, for a good part of his life. He had no political or ideological idea of anything. Everything was behaviour, that's all, and so he found himself in Chicago, or Iowa, or wherever, dealing with gentiles all the time, and he had very good friends. But, of course, he didn't look particularly Jewish. He looked maybe like some Scandinavian or Irishman. Not that he ever hid it; it never came up. People would attribute some virtue to somebody because he was Jewish and he would say, 'No, he's not Jewish. It's got nothing to do with him being Jewish.' You couldn't kid him about how all the Jews were virtuous, because he knew better. He taught me, inadvertently, that life is a matter of a particular people rather than labels that are supposed to count for something when they really didn't. I think that has carried over into my private and political life. I have written more about Jews than practically anybody around, but I haven't come out as a programmatic, born-again Jew or something.

BIGSBY: What has been the attitude of Jewish society to you?

MILLER: They are very positive toward me. I am glad they like what I do, and every little bit helps. I identify a lot of my sensibility as being tempered somehow by that mysterious Jewishness which never really goes away.

BIGSBY: Are you an absolute, dedicated, out-and-out atheist, or is a part of you something else?

MILLER: I am an atheist because I think that it's kind of a miracle that we are on this spinning ball at all. I just can't imagine a transaction between some being and us, and I don't see why it is necessary. However, I find myself, because I am at the end of x number of generations of people who did this, looking skywards now and then, before correcting myself because it is an ultimate absurdity, the whole thing, the idea of God. Suddenly, after the Holocaust, it was pretty tough to justify it. The Book of Job tried to make a stab at it, but let's say Job had been the survivor of six million dead instead of this individual out there in the desert, maybe the conversation would have been a little different.

BIGSBY: I wonder whether your early fascination with tragedy itself was a reaction to the Holocaust. I remember Hemingway saying about the First World War that it had destroyed tragedy, because death was arbitrary and sudden. The Holocaust allowed people no time at all to be heroic or anything else. For the Nazis, Jews were just junk to be disposed of.

MILLER: I wanted to give value to human beings. I wanted to do it in the American context because I felt the American situation was wiping out the individual. You couldn't tell the difference between one person and another any more, and that was one of the functions of the theatre, I thought. I did think that, objectively, if one could be said to have had an obligation of some kind, it was to reassert human value, the value of one person again. The Holocaust, among other things, represents a defeat. It is a defeat of the people. It didn't look that way, but it is as though there was a war and you lost, and there is an ambiguous reaction to a lost war.

Take the American South. There is a feeling of inferiority, that they were beaten, a feeling of resentment that, if there was any justice in the world, they would have won. It was not only a physical defeat, but all the values that civilisation allegedly still held, and which one implicitly relied on for defence and protection, had been destroyed. There was nothing between individuals any more. Therefore, there was a silence, an inability to digest the depth and breadth of this kind of defeat. It was unclear if there was an answer to it.

I think the fact that it took so long to respond to the fact of the Holocaust is partly a product of guilt. The guilt of the survivor was very strong. People had no reason to feel guilty, no objective reason, because they were not even on the same continent, but they did feel it. My grandfather was very pro-German. A lot of Jews from Europe were, and he always said that the Russians were the barbarians, while the Germans were civilised. That is another reason to keep your silence, because there was no explanation for this. One did not want to regard humanity as being evil by nature, or inevitably evil, and yet that event proposes the idea that civilisation is only an excuse, a thin cover for what is basically a totally barbaric centre.

BIGSBY: Is this why you so frequently invoke the figure of Cain?

MILLER: The rabbis, when they put together the Bible, had numerous texts to choose from with respect to which one was going to be the first story. After all, they were the editors. They had the Book of Job lying on the table along with sixteen other events. They chose that because that was the reason why there had to be a Bible. This is the matrix for everything. That a brother could kill a brother means there has to be some kind of disciplinary belief to keep people from doing that. The rest of the Bible is supposed to supply that in eighteen thousand different ways.

When you ask about my relationship to God, I think that in some way I do think that God is Jewish. The idea is profoundly Jewish, the idea of there being one rather than a whole slew of Gods which are much more convenient. I can see where life would be much happier if there were a God of the Hearth and a God of Swimming and a God of Dentistry, and so on.

7

Death of a Salesman

BIGSBY: After *All My Sons* came *Death of a Salesman*.
MILLER: The circumstances were extraordinarily long and complicated. It went back to the era of my youth, because I had always had a long relationship with an uncle of mine, even though it was distant. I never saw him for more than an hour and a half in my whole life. But his was an image that was powerful and, after *All My Sons* was written, I wanted desperately to write, as I had written before *All My Sons*, a more lyrical kind of style. This man, Willy Loman, was a lyrical character. He was totally divorced from the normal processes of thinking. He could contradict himself within the same sentence. He was living on a quite different plane of consciousness from other people. But how to do this? It could not be done in the form that *All My Sons* had been done. It had to be done in a play that was tracing the character's inner life from the first line. It therefore required a wholly new form, a form in which both the past and the present exist together, concurrently, in which you would know, by certain signals in the play, when he had drifted back into the past and when he had moved forward into the present. There are scenes in *Death of a Salesman* in which the past remembers a further past, in crude movie terms as

a flashback within a flashback, and which I think corresponds with the way the mind works.

The whole point of the structure, and the storytelling, of *Death of a Salesman* is to absolutely stick with the way Willy imagines himself, life and the circumstances surrounding him, because one of the main points of that form was that I could account for the social and economic life he was living, which was crucial in his case, as it is in most cases, the way he earned his living, the way he valued himself as a wage-earner, or a commission-earner. All that had to be in the same web of storytelling, with no breaks between them. This required a different technique and a whole new form. Incidentally, it is not a form that has ever been repeated, and I doubt that it can be. It is a very strange play in that respect.

BIGSBY: The past that we see is the past as Willy remembers it. Is there a gap between the reality of his memories and reality itself? How can an audience work out what really happened in the past from what Willy chooses to remember?

MILLER: In a way that is beside the point because it is the way he remembers it that affects him. Willy asks for a New York job instead of having to travel on the road selling and ends up being fired. If you asked the boss what the reality of that situation was you would get what is in the play. You get the feeling from the boss that they no longer trust his judgement. They think he is not a good salesman any more, that he needs a rest, in other words that he needs to get out of there and never come back. It is strange, but I think it is one of the good ways of telling that story, that Willy remembers it that way. It is accurate. What he completely misjudges is the power of the love that surrounds him. Everybody loves Willy, except Willy. At the end of the play, ironically, he realises that he is loved, and that obliges him to do what he does, to kill himself and arrange for his insurance to go to his sons.

BIGSBY: Is Linda responsible for the way Willy is? What if she had decided early on not to support his dreams?

MILLER: She tries not to support his dreams. If you look at the early dialogue in the play, every line she has got is a corrective of his vision. She is the reality principle. She is doing everything she can to make him face reality. She is the one who tells him that they need money. She is the one who presses him to the wall as to how much he has sold in reality. More than that, no psychiatrist could do. He is constantly being pressed by this woman to confront facts. When it doesn't work any more she drives the sons out of the house. I don't agree that she is supporting him. She is trying to keep his nose to reality.

BIGSBY: Could Willy have survived without Linda?

MILLER: It is almost impossible to conceive him without her. He says as much. He says, 'You're my foundation and my support, Linda.' Without her, he would probably have become a totally different person. If she had died before him, I conceive of him as just going silent and, in effect, spiritually vanishing.

BIGSBY: Biff is disillusioned with his father because he discovers him in a Boston hotel room with another woman. Why does that have the effect that it does on the whole of his life?

MILLER: Biff is a creature created by Willy. It is unimaginable, the power of Willy in Biff's early years in creating this illusory young man whose whole confidence derives from his father's admiration. When that father becomes a dubious, or non-existent, moral force, the air simply goes out of him. He feels he is nothing. The support he had in life turns out to be a farce. The streets are full of these people who have lost the one support they had. It could have been that, or a lot of other things, that Willy betrayed.

BIGSBY: Despite that, there seems to be a powerful, surviving, love between them.

MILLER: It is a love story. They are lovers, Biff and his father. They are trying to get together at the same time they are being driven apart. The impulse to come together ends up by being the most powerful one. It was initially, in its first production, directed just like that. It was directed as a pure love story, and when it has been at its best that is the way it is directed. That is the way it was conceived.

BIGSBY: You have seen a lot of actors play the part of Willy Loman. They have brought different approaches. They have had different physiques. How would you compare, say, Dustin Hoffman with Lee J. Cobb or Brian Dennehy?

MILLER: If you had King Lear played by a five-foot actor, it would already be a different Lear than if he had been played by a tall, noble-looking actor. Dustin is a very good actor, and his Willy was very persuasive. But the whole effect of it was somehow circumscribed by his very physical nature. It became very realistic, and his acting was marvellously realistic. For some reason, when you get to the bigger actors, they are less realistic, and they are probably more lyrical as a result. They are relying on a different force in themselves, since they can really bellow out some of those lines. They become part of you. I think that the forces in those big men do power up. You get the feeling of some big thing falling. I remember when we were first casting the play, I had originally thought of a small man with a large wife. We went through all the small actors, but it wasn't working, though some of them were damn good actors. When Cobb came in from California – he was a friend of Kazan's – it was a completely different effect. It suddenly had a grandeur about it that I had connected with when I wrote it. *Death of a Salesman* has speeches in it some of which are right out of the nineteenth century. 'May you rot in hell when you leave this house!' Who says that any more? You have got to have some super-real force behind all that or it doesn't quite happen. I will always be grateful to Dustin because the reality of his performance was marvellous. I do think, though, that probably a different dimension comes in with a Dennehy or Lee Cobb.

BIGSBY: It has always struck me that there is something curious about the timing of *Death of a Salesman*. You wrote it in 1948, in the immediate aftermath of the war, when most Americans' primary concern was to get back to normality. It was time to let the dream live again. Yet here you were, offering a play about the death of a true believer.

MILLER: It was also the beginning of the largest boom in history, and that's when I chose to write this play. I wasn't aware the boom was going on, but it was. The stock market started to take off. The end of the war meant that we had the only money that mattered in the world. America was the centre of production. That's when I wrote about the failure! It was completely without design. I hadn't figured that out. I just did it.

Maybe the best way to explain it is this: in one production, years later, an actor came up to me and asked when the play takes place, what year it takes place. I said that I had never thought about that. It was just suspended in time. And he said, 'A lot of it sounds like it was in the Depression period, but they had been in the war.' And I said, 'That's right, they have been in the war. All I can tell you is that I think it is suspended out of chronological time. I simply melded two periods together. It sounds absolutely insane, but that is really the case.' In other words, in one sense, it is a play in which the war has not happened, and, in another sense, it is a post-war play, because they refer to the war in the play as having happened a little while before. It is a bit like a dream. In a dream you are in two places at the same time, and *Salesman* is in two places at the same time. It is suspended over time. It is not by design; I mean I didn't work this out, or something. It is a very interior play. The play is referring to social events and a social situation, and Willy Loman is in a concrete social position, that is he has got a boss and a salary. The play is full of the most concrete evidences of living in this country for that class of person. But it is also suspended over that. I think that is why it has lasted this way. It transcends all that.

BIGSBY: You said your father was a believer.

MILLER: He was probably closer to Charley than to Willy. Charley is a believer in the sense that he certainly has no idea of socialism, or some other substitute for the system they are living in, but he is not a romantic about it. It is all very real. Willy has connected this to a romance. He is a lover. Interestingly, when I directed the play in China, Ying Ruocheng, who played Willy, one day said, 'You know, I'm finding it very difficult to generate what I conceive to be his romantic feelings about business. First of all, in the Chinese scoring system, which derives from Confucius, there were ten categories of society: at the top was the warrior and the philosopher. At the very bottom was the businessman. So you will never find a Chinese putting his name on a business. It is always the White Flower Tea Shop, or the Green Leaf Laundry, but never his name, because there is something

beneath contempt about a person who is dealing in money all the time, even though they are masters of the art of dealing in money.' And he said, 'So I'm looking for an image that will substitute for it, and the only one I've come up with is this. In the nineteenth century the Chinese were building railroads, like everybody else, and these railroads were going through country which practically only had one little dirt road for vehicles in order to get from city to city. Consequently, the railroads were constantly being robbed by bandits who would stop the cars and rob all the people. So a group of outriders grew up who were hired by the railroads and rode on horseback alongside the railroad car, which couldn't have been running very rapidly, and they would defend the railroad. These guys formed a kind of a rough human comradeship. They all knew each other and, occasionally, they would find themselves together somewhere and go and get drunk. And they were daring men. They were brave men. Finally, they died off because the country got pacified and they were no longer necessary.'
I said, 'Well, that's a good image.' Isn't that interesting, that he caught the romanticism of Willy, and there was no counterpart for that in Chinese culture except for the outrider who was part of the society, of course, who got paid by the railroad, but was also apart from society.

BIGSBY: The Americanness of *Death of a Salesman* seems to come partly from America being an immigrant society in which belief in a better tomorrow is factored into everybody.

MILLER: Oh yes. I think that was there from the beginning. After all, Puritans were going to create that City on the Hill which never existed before in the world. It was the new Jerusalem, and they literally called themselves the Society of Saints. It was to be a completely new civilisation. And, of course, when immigrants come in – and it is still the case today with Latin Americans and people from Asia – they recreate this dream of a society where there is no rank, excepting the rank of money, which they would like to join. I think the answer lies in the fact that we never had feudalism. Europeans, no matter where you go, have the remnants in their heads of feudal relationships, very strict class demarcations. They never existed here, and so consequently, from the beginning, the country was an arena where you could enter and fight the battle. And I think it is as strong today as it ever was among those people. In second-, third-, fourth-generation Americans it withers, and especially now, with globalisation and consolidation of business, I think it is getting weaker and weaker among them, but not necessarily among the mass of people. I think some of the Blacks have it, too. They are going to go out and make it. There is very little excuse for anybody.

BIGSBY: *Death of a Salesman* is thought of as being a quintessentially American play, about a quintessentially American figure – the salesman. On the other hand, that is a play which has become a classic in almost every country.

MILLER: I doubt that there is any such thing any more as a local culture. Those days are over. The American culture is simply international. It is everywhere. I just came from Switzerland, from Frankfurt, Berlin and Paris. There are productions in all those countries of *Salesman* and *The Crucible*. The thing is that I can't any longer detect any great differences. There are adaptations, but the origin is perfectly clear as being American. The attitudes are. After all, we are all trying to do the same thing – get rich.

BIGSBY: I'm intrigued by the fact that this is a play that, in a sense, begins in the West, not in the East. What led you to that?

MILLER: It was part of his nature, to me, that he sprang from people who were wanderers in the mountains.
BIGSBY: Willy's father was a salesman as well.
MILLER: Of course, but he was making those flutes.
BIGSBY: And that is the difference, then, between somebody who works with his hands and then sells the products of his hands, and somebody who now has to sell, well, anything. He is simply a salesman.
MILLER: Exactly. He is selling himself. He has got himself.
BIGSBY: So is that the historical change you are looking at, as America has moved from a time in which people worked with their hands, and sold the products of their labour, to one where people are now detached from the making of things?
MILLER: I think so. I have always felt that about it. Where I live, in Roxbury, there used to be, even in my time, which is only half a century, blacksmiths who actually made stuff, useful implements, frying pans, all kinds of stuff. There were still ploughs being used, and in fact here and there you would find a pair of horses drawing a plough. And those guys sold what they made, or they adjusted stuff that was store-bought, as they called it, and changed it around. It is part of our agricultural legacy. Of course, farmers used to make practically everything they owned. A farmer had to know how to work metals and wood; he was an artisan as well as somebody working the land. Willy's yearning for some relationship to the world is substantial.
BIGSBY: And it is that side of him which is represented by Biff, who at the end of the play seems about to return to that world, to that relationship with the natural world. Does that

mean that there is a kind of romanticism in you, too, for some lost America?

MILLER: I feel it. I've always resisted this departure from any concrete relationship with my environment. This is why I make furniture occasionally. I like to fix things myself or rebuild stuff. Before I wrote *Salesman*, it was early April I think, I built myself a place to write the play in, and it probably had something to do with that. I just wanted to construct a world of my own instead of buying one, or renting one, and I made that building, which was really badly built. I used two by fours under the floor, so it bounced when you walked in. I didn't know any better. But it is still standing there half a mile down the road from where we are sitting. I can see it from the road. In fact, another writer [Tom Cole, 1933–2009] has bought that house and is sitting in that studio hoping to be struck by the same lightning.

BIGSBY: Writing is making too, though, isn't it?

MILLER: Writing, of course, comes out of you and you sell it, but you are selling what you have made. I think that the loss of that has terrific consequences. We have taken it for granted for so long that there is no going back and, of course, nobody is going to abandon machine-made civilisation, nobody is going to sit down and make himself an automobile, if it were possible. But it is not just here. I'll tell you a story.

I had a friend, when I was at school in Michigan, whose father was a Russian immigrant who worked in Detroit as what was called a forging expert. He worked for General Motors Chrysler. What he did was, he went around to these places and tested the sand in which forgings were made. He could tell by picking up that sand whether it was exhausted or not, whether or not they needed to replace it. The

Depression hit and the Russians came to Detroit and bought the Ford plant lock stock and barrel, the whole thing, and shipped it to Russia, to a place nobody had ever heard of called Stalingrad. They hired my friend's father, who spoke Russian, to come back and run this plant, which he did. He was born in that area. He brought with him several hundred Detroit auto workers who were unemployed because of the Depression. They went to work in a Stalingrad tractor plant which was basically a Ford plant transported to Russia.

Anyway, when he got started, he went back to his native village, and there was a metal-working plant with four employees. The boss had a beard down to his belly, and they made all the ironwork that was used in that whole area. They were all excited because they knew about this Stalingrad plant, and they asked him how many tractors he was going to make. He said that, when they were underway, they would expect to make about a hundred a day. Well, they couldn't believe it. They said, 'We'd like to make them too. We'll make some part. What can we make?' He said, 'You guys are working by hand. You can't possibly catch up with that machinery.' But they said, 'Give us the plans and we'll make you some.' In those days they were all building Great Russia, socialism. So, he was touched by the sentiments, and he brought them plans, thinking nothing would come of the whole thing. He figured that nothing much could happen, and, after a couple of weeks, he went by again and they had made about ten chassis over that period of weeks, and they were very proud of those chassis. He said, 'Look, it's wonderful, but we make that in about twenty minutes.' They said, 'Wait and see. We're going to catch up with you.' He was so moved by the whole thing that he kept coming back and they were making five a day, seven a day, but they all looked like they were going to collapse. Nobody went to sleep.

I never forget that story because he, who was a machine man, who worked out of the biggest manufacturing company in the world at that time, was romantically attached to the idea that these five or six guys were banging these hammers producing hand-made objects. It was with great difficulty that he finally got them to come to the plant and see the way the tractors were made in order to make them realise it was an impossible task to keep up with this. I knew the old man, his father, and when he told this story he was so moved that he was near tears himself, that it was all gone. Those rugged old guys hammering away, were hopeless, useless. So, something has gone out of the human animal which is probably irreplaceable.

BIGSBY: And you come back to that, surely, much later, in *The Last Yankee*, in which you have two men, one a businessman who sells things he doesn't make, and the other a carpenter who settles for less in the way of money but has more meaning in his life.

MILLER: You know, there are so many elements in the things that a man or woman makes that you never even think about. The whole question of time is different. A man who is, say, a good carpenter will look at a job and immediately he has got to think of how long this is going to take. The ordinary person looks at a wall and sees a wall, or a bench, or whatever it is, but that is really congealed time, and what the machine has done is, in effect, to destroy that element of the human mind for a lot of people. They no longer respect the time embodied in the object. It is human time. So, they get disembodied. They lose contact with reality, which is also a question of the rolling away of your life, in terms of its minutes and seconds and hours. It is terribly important, and I don't know what the substitute is. I often wonder whether this lust for sheer entertainment isn't the way people try to fill the gap. It is a distraction from death, from the movement of time. We are now living other people's lives. Television, in this country, is on all night and all day, and it seems a pity.

BIGSBY: *Salesman* begins with flute music, because Willy's father makes and sells flutes, but there is a lot of music in *Death of a Salesman*. Was it always there? Did you hear the music as you were writing the play, or did the play exist first?

MILLER: When I wrote the play, I put in the stage direction that we hear a flute. It was woven throughout the script from the beginning to the end. But Alex North was brought in by Elia Kazan, and Alex wrote a score which was not just a flute: it was a flute, a bass and two or three other instruments. It was a quartet. And, of course, that expanded the thing immediately. Incidentally, in the original production we had four guys up in a room playing these cues every night. The recording industry hadn't progressed so far that you could push a tape-recorder button and get the sound; and the loudspeakers weren't what they later became. So you heard the actual quartet. It was piped through a loudspeaker. Anyway, the music I had written in grew somewhat.

BIGSBY: What is the interplay in your mind between the music and the action?

MILLER: Willy's attitude towards the past is always romantic. It is one of his problems as far as getting on in the world is concerned, because his brain embellishes everything. For Charley, what is real is real, and so the sound of music seemed to me to be the way to express that romanticism.

BIGSBY: What contribution did the stage designer Joe Mielziner make?

MILLER: Enormous. It was wonderful. I couldn't imagine a set, so I wrote it for three platforms. One would be the kitchen, one would be Willy's bedroom and the third, elevated higher, would be the boys' bedroom. The other scenes would be taking place on the stage level and various parts around this group of platforms. Well, Mielziner took those three platforms, and he made a house out of them in a most marvellous way, because the house seemed to be floating in space. You could see right through everything. It was basically an outline of a house, of the roofline, and it expressed the romanticism that Willy feels towards that house. As he says, there isn't a crack to be found in it any more. He has reworked the whole building fifteen different ways. So it is part of his romance, and that set was the same.

Also, it was terribly practical, because it was so open. You could move in and out of it wherever you wanted to. We were still rather tied to marking where reality ended and dream began by having the kitchen on a slightly raised platform, maybe six inches off the floor. Normally people would go in and out of a door to get into the kitchen, but as soon as Willy starts to get swept away by his memories he goes right through the wall. He steps off the platform onto the surrounding stage, and the first time it happened you could feel the audience take a deep breath. Here they had been taught, so to speak, that this is a real kitchen. Incidentally, the marvellous thing about the set was that the entrance to that kitchen was just 5 feet 11 inches off the ground. That is the way it had to be because there was a bedroom above it. But Lee Cobb was about 6 feet 2 inches, so to get into his kitchen he had to bend down to get under that lintel. But it didn't bother anybody because by that time they knew they were in dreamland. It was quite wonderful.

Of course, the lighting, which he also supervised, was phenomenal. People got attached to that play in a way I have never seen since. A man who owned the Century Lighting Company, which supplied lights for all the Broadway shows, Eddie Cook, simply fell in love with the script. So, he ceased being the head of his company. He knew more about lighting than anybody, but normally he never did any lighting himself. He just sold and rented the equipment. With *Salesman*, he moved into that theatre personally, and never left. I remember one day I arrived in the theatre about 1 o'clock in the afternoon and they were working, he and Mielziner, on hanging lights to hit the boss' chair in the scene where Willy is talking to his young boss. When the young boss leaves him alone in that office, what you see on the stage is a little reduced-size desk and an armchair, and, at a certain point, Willy starts to talk to that chair as though the boss were in it. So they wanted to hit that chair with light as though the light were coming from the chair. Therefore, they had to eliminate any shafts of light coming from above. The only way you could do that was to have an enormous number of lights, each barely lit. On a count of one to ten they would be one. And this effect lasts through two speeches, a period probably of around a half a minute. They worked from that afternoon right through the night to get that effect. Sane people don't do that. They will find some way to get around it, or just give up on it and hit it with beams of light. It would be okay. But by doing it the way they did it, it was the most marvellous, eerie thing. That chair seemed to be elevating off the stage for that moment, and it drove you right into Willy's head. You entered Willy's head as a result of that light. I've never seen that done again. I mean nobody's going to spend that time.

The distortions in that set were violent. For example, the kitchen table is probably about 20 inches long by 16 inches deep. That is ridiculous. The bed in the bedroom is about 5 feet long, so Willy had to be sitting up in it, practically, and screwing his body around so he looked as if he were in a full-size bed. The entrance to the kitchen, as I said, was 5 feet 11 inches. He had to do that; indeed, the stage was probably not deep enough for him to make those dimensions. They had to take out two rows of seats in the orchestra because we built an apron out so that they could play scenes in front of the house when they are tossing the football around, or when he goes to see his boss and there is a tape recorder, a wire recorder. That scene was played downstage on that apron. The whole set was a distortion of a most wonderful kind. It was very, very, adeptly designed.

BIGSBY: Did you make any changes during rehearsals?

MILLER: There was one scene I had to rewrite. There is a scene in a restaurant, where Biff comes to tell his father about his attempt to raise a loan from a businessman called Bill Oliver. It was written so that sometimes Biff was telling a fact, sometimes it was sort of a half-truth, sometimes it was an outright invention, to suit Willy's demands. We were rehearsing it one day and one of the actors, Arthur Kennedy, stopped, which he had never done before, and said, 'You know, I can't act this . . . I can't jump from telling a real lie to half a lie to three quarters of a lie.' So, I had to go home that afternoon and clean it up so that it was simpler. As far as I recall, I think that was the only change.

BIGSBY: You've seen numerable productions since with different designers.

MILLER: Nothing has ever come up to that.

BIGSBY: But each new designer subtly changes the play.

MILLER: If anything, it disturbs the relation of dream and reality when they fool around with it. There is a new production coming up as we speak which has a more cinematic approach [Robert Fall's production at the Goodman Theatre, Chicago and Eugene O'Neill Theatre, New York, 1999]. The play is cinematic anyway, although I hadn't thought of it in those terms when I wrote it. It is the blending of one scene into another. This new production is like a black-and-white film, and there are four or five turntables, revolves. It creates a very interesting kind of interior life. It is not particularly romantic. It is rather harsh, but it is the nineties, and I find it very interesting. I think it is well done. You don't have to keep doing the same thing over and over again. So, I went for it. I think it is a good treatment.

BIGSBY: To what extent do you see Willy Loman as a tragic hero? After all, you wrote an essay about tragedy and the common man.

MILLER: That depends a lot on whether you can really attribute a tragic circumstance to a person of that class, of that nature. We generally don't. I personally think of him as a tragic hero, but I can see why some people would not be able to. But every one of my plays has to do, somehow, with somebody who has a heroic size, or in my imagination has.

Thomas Mann saw that play. I had never met him before, and he wanted to meet me. He happened to be in New York, and we sat and talked, and he said, 'You know the thing about the play is that it is a lyric play, but you never tell them what to think. It is simply an experience that they cannot escape.' This is part of the reason there is always a debate about the play. I never allowed them to go beyond their intellectual and emotional capacity. There is no line in there that goes beyond what they could possibly have realised. The consequence is that, unlike standard tragedies where you have the right, formally speaking, to make self-aware statements, where the character is aware of the play he is in, I would purposely never let them become aware of the play they were in. All that was driven out ruthlessly because I resolved I was not going to allow the audience to escape. Every scene in that play begins late. There are no transitions. It starts with a man who is tired. He does not get tired. We know that from the first second of the play, from the way he enters that play. He is on and he is moving, and he is on his way. In the first line he says what has happened. He is exhausted. The same is true of every scene in that play. I completely drove out the usual transitional material. That is the form of the play.

BIGSBY: Has *Death of a Salesman* changed over fifty years?

MILLER: It is hard for me to say. I am not quite sure what the audience is making of it. They have been telling me for years now that Willy's situation, if anything, has become more desperate in reality. Today, people are tossed aside ruthlessly by downsizing corporations, or corporations moving out, so that it is not at all infrequent that a man of fifty, at the height of his powers, finds himself without a job. He can't get a new job because they don't want somebody who is liable to be a burden on the health care plan which is costing them money. They would rather have young guys who will start at a reasonable salary, because they are not married yet, and not likely to get sick, not as likely as an older guy or woman. The woods are full of these people, especially in my state, Connecticut.

First of all, it is a highly industrialised state, despite the fact that it all looks like it is woods. It is the richest state in the union, because of the very profitable businesses here. The insurance companies are clustered up in Hartford. Anyway, I am told by people who have never seen the play before that they can't believe it was written fifty years ago, because it seems to be now. This happened just recently in Chicago, where a number of the reviewers – these guys are in their thirties and forties and weren't born when this play was first produced – found it amazing that it was so topical. And it is partly because industry has been so ruthless tossing people aside. But I have a feeling that there are other things involved, interpersonal relations, which don't change very much.

BIGSBY: America is hardly less dedicated to materialism now than it was in 1949.

MILLER: Well, it has got richer. When you get richer you get all kinds of stylistic things that obscure the reality. But, for a lot of people, life is too real, those people who are getting kicked around. However, I'm not sure that that is the essential thing anyway. I think it may be that these relationships – father, mother, son, and so on, the family relationships – though they may change to some degree remain essentially the same. I have a whole younger audience now, and I don't think they are there because of the industrial side of the story. Kazan said something one day. We had a few minutes' break and he had just discovered something on stage. He said, and I mentioned this earlier, 'You know what it is. It is a love story. This is a love story.

Willy and Biff are behaving like two lovers.' And since then, I have realised that everybody in this play loves Willy. They care terribly about him. Even Happy loves him. He thinks he is marvellous, but he is not going to go out of his way to help him. Both things can exist in the same person. He says, look, he is no great selling man, but he is a hell of a nice guy. He is full of affection for him. It is just that he is a selfish person and is not about to put himself out for him all that much. But Charley, Linda, Biff, Bernard, Happy all love him. It is a rare thing in a play, I think. We are faced with the spectacle of all that love being lost on someone who doesn't, who can't, receive it. The secret of playing Willy is that the audience have got to fall in love with him too and, if it is done right, they do. They don't want to see him go down and are terribly moved when he does. He can't help himself. It is unfortunately life. Listening to the play, I still get moved to tears occasionally. I was watching it in the Chicago production that has now come to New York, and I did.

BIGSBY: Which are the parts that move you?

MILLER: It could be anywhere. The first time I heard it and was listening to Lee J. Cobb – and it was not a particularly emotional part of the play – I was suddenly overwhelmed by the struggle of this man simply to stay alive. It is nothing to do with anything, it is just that struggle, that human struggle, to not be wiped out. That's mainly what it is about.

BIGSBY: One part that does move people to tears is the epilogue.

MILLER: Which they wanted to cut.

BIGSBY: Why did they want to cut it?

MILLER: Well, as Kazan said, 'The play is over. Willy has gone. They are going to get up and start picking up their coats.' And I just said, 'That is the best writing in the whole play. Don't tell me it is over.' And, of course, it was a complete miscalculation, because the audience want to know what all these people made of it. Many years ago, a guy came to see me from Norway. He ran a Norwegian state travelling theatre, because in Norway they have settlements up in the fjords and in the Arctic Circle, or they had, and they had a travelling acting company that went by ship and visited all these little settlements. They brought a company playing *Death of a Salesman*, and the only hall they had was a local little church. When this company finished, they went to bed. The next morning there was some fog, so they were delayed a few hours and, about noon, probably 200 people started showing up again at the church. So the director said to the minister, 'What's going on?' He said, 'They came to see the rest of it.' And he had to explain to them that that was all. But what happened to these sons? They thought it was a saga, and a saga goes on forever. You go down generation after generation after generation, and they were very unhappy that they only got the first part. The impulse behind that was that they felt you could not just leave it hanging in the air in that way.

BIGSBY: Would Willy have failed in any system?

MILLER: Let me put it this way. That play was a great success in Western Europe, Eastern Europe, Japan; it hardly mattered where it was done. I suppose you would have to have some kind of commercial civilisation for it to work at all, but not much. Anyway, I talked to people twenty years ago from the Soviet Union where it was playing. They said there are people all over the place who have reveries of how they are going to conquer life.

BIGSBY: But there is an irony, isn't there, because in some ways you are yourself the epitome of the American dream. You have become extremely successful. Yet your work offers a critique of aspects of that dream, right the way through from *Death of a Salesman* to *The Last Yankee*.

MILLER: That is partly because I was impacted by the Depression. As you said, I was about fourteen when it hit, and that is a very delicate age. So, my faith was deeply shaken. Before that, I didn't think we lived under a system. I thought it was something that had existed since Adam and Eve. There was no such thing as an evolution, a historical evolution. We all thought that way, I think, and then suddenly, with the collapse of that system, you began to wonder how long anything would last again, how secure even people were. So the belief in material things was shattered. I no longer believed that money was the main value. It could easily disappear. When you saw great fortunes simply disappear in a matter of weeks or months it made you realise that man was a very fragile thing, and that the system was especially frail, and I think that this idea is very deeply engrained in Americans to this day. People who do not know where that idea came from, to this day do not think that because they have two cars and a beautiful house and a swimming pool, they are safe. I think Americans live in a fear of falling.

In recent years a considerable number of people have gone backwards. They have been fired from their jobs in big corporations. In my state, where I live, there is an organisation put together by former executives of large corporations who were making $150,000 to $200,000 a year and were suddenly fired. Their expenses were enormous, and they were in danger of bankruptcy. Many even went bankrupt, and they formed an organisation to help each other locate new work. This was an organisation of the bosses, you might say, who suddenly found out they were workers. All this spreads the news, which I got in 1929, that the framework is built not on sand but a very unstable base which can shake itself at any time. That spills into my plays, of course.

BIGSBY: In the 1930s there were some writers who thought that the theatre could have the answer, that they could play their role in transforming society, changing the world. The writer who was dominating in American theatre when you started to write was Clifford Odets, and people went out of his *Waiting for Lefty* shouting 'Strike! Strike! Strike!' The early student plays you wrote were rather like that. Did you believe that the theatre could transform the world in a literal way then, and how do you feel now?

MILLER: Well, of course so-called social protest theatre was a small corner of the large theatre which was not involved in those ideas at all. I think you could count in the few thousands the number of people who ever saw a play either by Odets or his contemporaries. I was part of a movement who thought of ourselves as some kind of a vanguard. We thought we were leading the country somewhere and, as it turns out, we were not, as every vanguard in history has discovered. However, it gave great energy and optimism to what we were doing, and you had to believe that literature could change the world, though there was no evidence of it. All the radical playwrights that I had heard of were either German or Middle European, maybe a few French, no English, and those countries were moving rapidly towards fascism, regardless of these protest movements. So you cannot say they led anywhere. However, they carried the spirit of resistance to the awful materialism of the moment, and, like all such narrow movements, they were places where other people could come to drink and return to their merry ways, wasting their time, but at least having had a sip of the spiritual leadership that we were trying to provide. It was all very romantic. It was a romantic kind of Marxism where the working class was basically moral and the other people were not, and you know where that gets you. We did not know then where it got you, and we all felt that there was great danger in the world, as I still believe.

That danger was German fascism, to a lesser degree Italian fascism. We believed that one had to link up with one's contemporaries to resist the chorus of German fascism which, after all, had appealed firstly to intellectuals. Large numbers of the first members of the Nazi Party were poets, philosophers, intellectuals. We had no such movement in the States, but we were conscious of having to resist this, and I think that was the spark really which gave shape and form to – I wouldn't even call it a movement – a tendency in our theatre and literature in general. Sad to say, it is hard now to recall a play written in that period, or a novel, which one would be interested in seeing any more, and that has been true for some years now. Odets wrote a few plays that still have an appeal because of his poetic use of language, but I do not think the content of the plays is really relevant to where we are.

BIGSBY: There is a Faulkner character who, in *Requiem for a Nun*, says the past is never dead, it is not even past. In some way the past is the present in many of your plays, and that distinction is not a real one.

MILLER: I think it comes partly from the surprise I felt when everything collapsed in my early youth. I had thought everything was pretty solid. It turns out that it was an empty shell, so that when the real collapse came and, for example, there was no money for me to go to school any more and I had to take very many menial jobs in a job market that was violent because everybody wanted the same job, the past became profoundly attached to the present. I have never lost that notion of reality, that the present is merely that part of the past that is showing its face at the moment, and my plays probably reflect that.

BIGSBY: They reflect it not just in the subject matter but in the style. *Death of a Salesman*, *After the Fall*, even your autobiography braid past and present.

MILLER: Yes. The technique of *Death of a Salesman* was invented in order not to make flashbacks [while using that term earlier]. Flashback means the action stops and you go backwards for a bit and then the action continues. In *Death of a Salesman* the action never stops, and yet you are in the past and the present concurrently because that is the way I think we think. You can think two things at the same time, and the concurrence of those two lines of mental activity and their collisions are what *Death of a Salesman* is from.

BIGSBY: On the other hand, you live in a culture which has little interest in the past, which leans into the future.

MILLER: I have a lot of trouble with that of course, a lot of trouble, but I keep making the same preachment to the young writers whenever I meet them that every good play is the story of how the birds came home to roost, which is always news to them.

BIGSBY: Does this interest in the past and the pressure of history have anything to do with your Jewish background? Does this sustaining history have a moral quality to it?

MILLER: Moral to most people means good and evil. To me it means order or disorder. It can also mean good and evil, but it means people not going out into the street and tearing each other's throats out. The fascists were interested in the Jews, of course, but really it was the Christian religion they were after in the end. It was paganism, and barbarism in the full sense of that word. Incidentally, the representatives who were practising the Christian religion in their rituals, and in their tenacity being reminiscent of the Early Church, were the Jews, and that is why they had to go.

I think my Jewish background probably supplied me through my epidermis, because we were not an especially religious family, with the idea of order and disorder. From 3,000 miles away, I could feel a tremor in the earth which was going to destroy that democracy. That sense of being personally involved in something distant has always been with me, I think, partly because we are a very few people on the face of the earth. It is miraculous that when a real reactionary regime begins it goes after us very early on. So we must be doing something right. Of course, there are people who know nothing whatsoever about Judaism, its codes, its rituals or anything else, who have precisely the same feelings as I do. They have a sense that the end of the world is out there someplace looking for them. I wouldn't lay it all on Judaism, but I think some part of it is.

BIGSBY: What led to the Chinese production of *Death of a Salesman* in Beijing?

MILLER: They were just coming out of the aftermath of the Cultural Revolution. In the Cultural Revolution the leadership of the so-called Gang of Four, which included the widow of Chairman Mao, declared there were four acceptable plays, and that was it. They had so constricted the repertoire that for a period of, I guess, six or seven years the people had no contact whatsoever with anything but these little communist theological works. Now she was gone. She had been arrested, and a new regime was in which was far more liberal in their terms, although not necessarily in ours. These theatre people wanted to subject their audience to a kind of play which would be at the same time dealing with large themes of society and individuals along with a new technique, because the only techniques they really had permitted themselves were taken from the Soviet models of realism, that is, plays by Gorky and a few other very realistic and conventional writers, conventional in theatrical terms. They thought *Salesman* would be a good introduction for the audience to the non-strictly naturalistic or realistic theatre, and so they asked me to go over and direct it. I should say that *The Crucible* was produced by them at a different theatre in Shanghai before I got there, a year earlier, so they knew about that.

BIGSBY: Why was it so successful in China?

MILLER: There was a terrific actor playing Willy, Ying Ruocheng. The Chinese, in effect, invented the family. The family is at the centre of Chinese culture, and especially the males of the family. Every father wants his son to be what they call a dragon, meaning the boss. He has got to dominate. They understood Biff's relationship with his father instantly. They knew all about that. They understood the thrust towards success, even though they had been through fifty years of communism. It fell away as though it had never existed as they sat watching this play. A few years later, the whole system collapsed. I suppose it represents to them one other thing. The opening night, Columbia Television interviewed young people coming out of the theatre. They asked one what he thought of it. He said, 'Wonderful.' 'Why?' 'Well, Willy Loman is right. Everybody wants to be number-one man.' He said, 'Biff, he's the problem, because Biff is being a pest with all the problems he's got. Willy wants power.' That was very interesting. They had turned the whole play around. This was a Marxist country, which shows you how superficial all that politics really is. What they saw in it was a man trying to convey power to his son, and his son refusing it.

BIGSBY: Charley says Willy had all the wrong dreams. Did he? What is wrong with wanting to succeed, to be well-liked, wanting your son to embrace the same values as you do?

MILLER: There is nothing wrong with wanting to be well-liked, or to be successful, wanting to be number-one man. In one way or another everybody wants to do that. The question is how you get there. Willy had no sense of the stages of preparation for anything. If he thought of something, he had it. It was just a question of being able to grab it. The idea is well expressed in the play. Biff says in effect you cheated me out of everything. Instead of confronting me with reality, you always made me the leader of men. There was no question of preparing myself for any of this. You see it in the scenes with the young Bernard, where Bernard is trying to get him to study, and he is fooling around with a football. There is nothing wrong with the aim, it is how to get there. He turned it into a dream, instead of a reality.

BIGSBY: I can see why Willy needed Linda. Why did Linda need him?

MILLER: She adores him. They are in love with each other. If you can explain that, you are better than I am. She thinks he is funny, tender, full of imagination, is never boring. He has always got a new story. She is simply delighted with him, most of the time. When he gets depressed, that's a problem. But when he is not depressed, he is one hell of a guy. He is certainly more interesting than Charley, who is a real boring person.

BIGSBY: You must go and see productions of your plays around the world and presumably much of the time in languages you do not understand. Can you tell whether a play is working when it is in a language that is not your own?

MILLER: I directed *Death of a Salesman* in Sweden, in Stockholm, and in Beijing, in two languages that I know nothing about, and I found I could tell very accurately whether they were doing it as intended or not. You can certainly tell what the audience's reaction is, because people are people. When they are bored, they begin looking at their watches and leaning back and yawning and falling asleep, but if they are interested there is a certain tension in the audience, whether it is China or Sweden or Britain. Language is remarkable. In China, for example, I could tell, although I know not a syllable of Chinese, when they were slipping off the lines and not really invigorating their language. I would tell them, 'I think you are just coasting here', and they would break and say, 'How did you know?'

8

The Waldorf Conference

BIGSBY: You were perceived by those who were Trotskyites, many of whom wrote for *Partisan Review*, as a Stalinist in the 1940s. How far were you aware that that kind of battle was waging between the Trotskyites and what they characterised as the Stalinists?

MILLER: I knew about it. The parting of the ways was in 1949, at the Waldorf Conference. Up until that point I was aware of two different kinds of left, and I didn't know any of these people personally. The people I knew on the left were all people who were pro-Soviet. I don't think there were anywhere near as many of the anti-Soviet left around. They were a minority within a minority, because the regular communists and left people were the ones that were organising unions, and all the rest of it. I had never heard of any Trotskyites organising unions. They were basically a New York literary phenomenon more than anything else. They were political all right, but I didn't know of them as being active in the creation of unions or electoral politics. But in 1949, when the Waldorf Conference was organised, no doubt by elements of the Communist Party, my sympathies were with keeping our alliance with the Russians, out of pure gratitude I suppose. Anyway, I couldn't see any way of backing out of it. It seemed to me, first of all, to be objectively necessary. It seems impossible now, but there were days when it looked as though they were generating a real war spirit in the United States, and a kind of vindictive hatred was growing which I found alarming. So, they asked me to show up.

Salesman had opened not long before, so I was being very much touted around. Some American scientists were terribly worried about the whole thing. They were genuinely concerned that this thing was going to come to an atomic exchange of some kind, and they were trying to tell everybody that the conventional idea that the Soviets could not add nine and eleven was a mistake, and that they probably had a high level of atomic armaments. That also contributed to my decision to show up at the Waldorf. I do not know whether some of those who turned up were actually Trotskyites, but Mary McCarthy was one of them.

BIGSBY: One of the things Mary McCarthy did was to read out a list of writers who were imprisoned in Russia. Were you aware of just how repressive the Russian regime was then?

MILLER: Not really. Once you accepted that the Russian Revolution had been necessary, in the sense that the decrepit tsarist regime which, incidentally, was so repressive itself and was killing a lot of people, had to go you accepted a lot of other things with it, namely that they were going to repress the counter-revolution. I have often regretted that I was amenable to all that.

BIGSBY: Because you managed to swallow the show trials which turned a lot of people off.

MILLER: They turned me off, too, but on the other hand to take a position against them meant putting myself in the

The Waldorf Conference

lap of the State Department, as I saw it. It was just incredibly crude in its anti-Soviet positioning. After all, they were the ones who were denying people passports.

BIGSBY: But a lot of people on the left became Trotskyites a) because of the show trials and b) because of the Hitler–Stalin pact. You managed to go through both of those crises and still remained loyal to the idea of the Soviet Union.

MILLER: Well, that was a pretty bitter pill. I was on the edge of the abyss, I thought, if I thought about it at all very much, the abyss being as you slid into a position which was also equally intolerable to me at that time. It was to deny, for example, the sacrifices of the Russian people in the Second World War, because I don't think it is too much to say that Russia turned the Hitler machine back compared to what the West was able to do. It was minor compared to what the Russians did. I felt a kind of loyalty to these men because 40 million people got killed over there.

BIGSBY: Can you chart for me the process whereby you did move away from the stance you had adopted at the Waldorf Conference?

MILLER: Ironically, or maybe not ironically, by the end of the Waldorf Conference I really felt alienated from the left. It just seemed to me to be accepting too much from the Russians. It was a kind of osmosis. I began to smell a rat. *Salesman* was still running, and I lived on Brooklyn Heights, and nearby was this minister who ran a big Episcopal church, I think the oldest Episcopal church in Brooklyn. He called me up one day – he had been the president of the Russian war relief effort in the United States during the war, and they were collecting clothing for the Russians and the usual good works – and he said, 'There are a couple of Russians visiting me in my house, why don't you come over?' I was curious about it. I had never really met a Russian, white, red or otherwise.

So I went over. I don't know who they were, but they were probably from the Russian cultural organisation in the United States, which was still going at that time. They may have been from the embassy, or the consulate, for all I knew. I am not sure if they had any importance, but one of them said to me, 'We saw your play and we would like to do it over in Russia.' I said, 'That would be nice.' 'But, of course, the reason you only had one set', he said, 'was because of the commercial theatre. When we do it, we will have a different set for each scene.' I said, 'That's wrong. You don't want that.' I then experienced a tone that I had never experienced before. He said, 'No, no, you don't know what you are talking about. This needs six different sets.' I said, 'No, the virtue of this play is that it is moved through his mind, not through his body.' They said, 'We are going to do it right', and I smelt a certain kind of arbitrary power there. It stuck in my head because I had never run into such a thing and, if I were a Russian writer, they would be telling me what I was supposed to be doing, and here they were not even in Russia. They were in New York, and that kind of rattled me.

That meeting ended on a very tense note, although there was nothing to be done about it. If they were going to steal the play they would steal the play, which is what they did anyway. When they did *Salesman* I was told they made Charley a kind of a clown, because he was a capitalist. They didn't know what to do with him because he was a generous capitalist, a sentimental capitalist, and they distorted that whole part of the play, and that alienated me from them. It was a gradual thing, I think. It got more and more strange and foreign and less like the sentimental kind of leftism that I attributed to it.

BIGSBY: The reviews written by a lot of those people on the Trotskyite left identified you as a fellow traveller.

MILLER: I was signing petitions which were set up really by some front of the Communist Party. But they were for good causes. Sometimes I would suspect that it was a front but, what the hell, it was a good cause. I would sign the damn thing, and when I got before the Un-American Committee, they had about two hundred of them, and I think I said, 'Well, yes, I have signed all of them.'

BIGSBY: But the Waldorf Conference itself must have given you pause for thought because there was Shostakovich obviously saying what he had been told to say.

MILLER: That is a vivid image. That was the first time in my life that I had really met a Soviet, if you could call him that, and I didn't know what his situation was in Russia. I had no idea. I don't think anybody did. He was a practising composer. He was famous in Russia, so he had to have some favour in the Soviet Union, or he couldn't have gone on, or so I had assumed. But he was totally incommunicado. There were some Russian-speaking people who were not with the Russians, but they were American exiles who wanted to talk to him. I remember that. He just stood there.

BIGSBY: What did you do at the conference? Were you chairing a session?

MILLER: All I did was recognise speakers.

BIGSBY: Did you hear any of the speeches by those on the other side?

MILLER: Yes.

BIGSBY: What did you make of them, people like Mary McCarthy? Incidentally, their suite was paid for by the CIA.

MILLER: So, I wasn't wrong.

BIGSBY: No, you weren't wrong. Not all of them knew this, but it was.

MILLER: The keel of the ship, as far as I was concerned, was another war. I remember before the Waldorf Conference meeting a flier in the American air force who had been delivering fighter planes to some port there on the Pacific coast of Russia. He said to me, 'Get ready. The next war is with the Russians.' This was within a few months of the end of the war, and I said, 'How can you say that?' And he said, 'They are getting ready, and it is going to be a big one.' I thought it would be the end of the world. I was right about one thing: the Americans simply had no conception of the nationalist dedication of the Russians to their own soil. When the war started, all our military experts said it would be over in six weeks because of the superiority of the German technology, better tanks, better this, better that. When it didn't happen, they were completely unable to explain why. So, they extended the time another four weeks, another eight weeks, and then finally that petered out. They stopped talking like that because they recognised that something else had entered into it.

People were now completely wiping out of their minds the solidarity, despite whatever else was going on in Russia which we would confront. It is a bit like now. I am quite sure that, misled as they are, if we walked into an Arab situation we would be in bad trouble. People don't need high-tech weapons. That is quite obvious. Six guys with explosives can do a lot of damage. The point is that at that time I believed that whatever the differences inside the Soviet Union, nobody was going to win that war easily, but the general idea was that we had 'won the war'. One out of a hundred

Americans would realise the contribution of the Russians to the winning of that war. As far as they were concerned, Eisenhower had won the war. Maybe Montgomery had a little to do with it, but I am sure none of them could name a Russian general, nor identify a Russian battle, or the largest tank battle in the history of the world.

BIGSBY: But given that that was your position, and that was why you were at the Waldorf Conference, how come, within a few months, that was counterbalanced, in your mind, by the repressive nature of the Soviet state?

MILLER: It was exactly counterbalanced. I was suspicious by now. I will tell you something else. *Focus*, which I wrote in 1945, was about anti-Semitism in New York City. I went on a radio programme to flog the book, and there was another writer who preceded me. This was a book programme, and they interviewed writers. We chatted for a minute, and he asked me what my book was about, so I told him, and he said, 'Well, it is a widespread problem, especially bad in Russia.' Of course, in those days, 1945, the war was on, and the Soviet Union had the only constitution that forbade anti-Semitism. Anti-Semitism was the socialism of fools, according to Marxist ideas. You couldn't have anti-Semitism in Russia. So, I said, 'Why do you say that?' He had some connections with people in Russia, and he started to tell me about this, and that really shook me. But all I knew was the anti-Semitism in New York. That I knew about, and this hung over my head for some time. It was an entry point. But, of course, even then, excepting that in the Trotskyite press, which I never saw, one didn't see anything about it until later, and then it began to really shake me up. Little by little, one blow after another, I changed, but I guess I was clinging to the old idea that this was to be a new society. It turned out to be older than any society.

BIGSBY: How far do you think that conflict between the two sides of the left accounts for some of the responses to your work?

MILLER: A lot. I didn't think so at the time. I didn't know anything about it, but, looking back, I think it was very important, because a lot of them were important critics, and they influenced other critics and academia especially. It was important. If I have persevered at all it is because my plays exist for the audience. I don't really think, excepting for a *New York Times* critic, Brooks Atkinson, I ever had a critic on my side.

BIGSBY: But that persisted, didn't it? It wasn't just in the 1940s.

MILLER: It went on and on and on. I am sure it had to do with Robert Brustein's hatred, though recently he has turned completely around. He has completely changed.

He has written a play, not bad, about the head of the Actors Studio [*Nobody Dies on Friday*]. It is not great, but it is okay, and I think he basically wanted to be an artist, desperately, and, since he couldn't be, the next best thing was to destroy everybody around and to lift up those who he regarded as inferior to him. This is my interpretation of it.

BIGSBY: There is another strand to this, though, and that is that the Trotskyites, through magazines like *Partisan Review*, were enthusiasts for European modernism, and so anything that seemed to them popular, realistic, would be attacked.

MILLER: If *Death of a Salesman* had been rejected, they might have accepted it. The reason they hated Tennessee, too, I am sure, is because he had big crowds of people following him into his theatres. It is really a form of perverse aristocracy, the idea being that if everybody could understand something, it can't be good. Leftist aristocracy is more aristocratic than any writers' aristocracy, because the writers sometimes can bend to the peasant and appreciate the peasant's culture, but for these guys there is high culture and low culture, which is nonsense. There is culture or there isn't, but they were practitioners of the high culture, always. That is why a composer like Aaron Copeland always had trouble, because his work could be performed on a bandstand in a public park. Charles Yves, too, stuck popular music into the middle of symphonies and ordinary common Christian hymns. How could it be any good? But I tell you, I feel now as though I have weathered it.

BIGSBY: Can you recall when you yourself first became aware of the Holocaust?

MILLER: I think one of the intimations that something unheard of was happening was when [in 1939] a ship [the MS *St Louis*] arrived, filled with Jewish refugees, incidentally people of some means, because they had to have the fare to come over. They were forbidden to land in New York, so they went to Cuba, which, of course, was under a dictatorship, as it usually was, and they hung around the port for a couple of days, but they wouldn't accept them either, so they returned to Germany. Somehow, I don't remember now quite how, I learned that those people were killed. Up to that point, I think, one knew there were concentration camps, but we thought they were prisons. The idea of people being slaughtered, I think, first arrived in my head as a result of that ship. It was a very strong image. There was a German captain on that ship, and I think it was he who said to somebody that if they returned to Germany they would not live. These were not bedraggled-looking people. They looked like very bourgeois Germans, because the German Jews were more German than the Germans.

BIGSBY: Was it, however, just a human circumstance you were responding to, or did the fact that you came from a Jewish background intensify your response to it? Were you responding simply because this was a tragedy?

MILLER: No. I identified with those people. I had been through a lot of anti-Semitism in New York in the thirties, so, after all, this was not quite out of the blue. The problem was simply this: the reason that ship was turned back, and one realised it at the time, was that the Jewish establishment in New York, and in the States, had a policy of keeping a low profile. It is all forgotten now, but the largest audience for radio broadcasts, and there was no television, was for Father Coughlin. Father Coughlin was an outright anti-Semite. He was using Goebbels' texts, literally translated, about the Jews, on American radio, and it was frightful. This was the biggest audience for anything, including Jack Benny or any other comedian. So this did not come out of the blue as far as we were concerned. And, consequently, it was like a dark, dark, shadow over anybody here.

The Germans were thought to have the best civilisation in Europe, and if they could devolve into this kind of thing, then anybody could. It was a time when, after all, we had been through a thing called the America First Committee. That was probably the largest political organisation that has ever been in the US. They were opposed to us getting into a war against Germany. Lindberg came back, and he was quite clear that the whole war movement was based on Jews who were trying to get back at Hitler. And that incident simply confirmed what one's emotions had already registered, that is, that something extraordinary was in the air, something that nobody had ever dreamed could happen. As to when exactly I knew that the camps were killing people, it is funny I cannot recall an exact moment. Of course, one knew right after the war. We had film, army film, of the camps and the dead, but I must have known before then. I'm sure it was some time in 1943. [News of the Holocaust did not become public until 1942.]

BIGSBY: What trace elements do you see of the Holocaust in your own work?

MILLER: The whole idea of someone unable to awaken to reality is implicit in the Holocaust. Many of the Jews caught in the Holocaust had the opportunity to leave Germany and would not, could not, believe the evidence of their senses. They had been acculturated in such a way that it prepared them for this. And in a way it applies to the Germans themselves, who were transfixed by this dream, this image of themselves, which allowed for destroying people, women and children, in that way: the sleep of reason from which one cannot be awakened. This has a deep significance in my work.

Once it is let loose, there is a certain panic trigger in every human being. Once that is successfully pressed, I don't think there is any stopping it. We have done it here numerous times in this country. In small ways. It gets stopped because there is not just one civilisation in America, but several. If it were a smaller country, it could be much more dangerous. Everybody is screaming and yelling about something in New York, but in Texas they don't know what the hell you are talking about. So, there is a brake on catastrophic movements. Meanwhile the rest of the country is watching football, and they are not interested in that fanaticism. But imagine if the country was only the Midwest, Illinois, Ohio, Minnesota, maybe – boy, you could get something going good at any one moment. Sometimes on the East Coast people are going crazy while in the South they are hunting squirrels. It is what saves us. It is the uneven development of irrationality at any one moment.

BIGSBY: When I was looking into your background in Poland, I was reminded of something: the Nazis didn't just kill Jews, they wiped out the archives. In other words they destroyed history as well. In virtually all of your plays, history, either as a force in society or as individual lives, is absolutely central, and I wonder if that might, in some way, be in part a response to the Holocaust.

MILLER: I think you are right. What I got out of the reports of the Holocaust was that memory was being destroyed forever. If one looks at it from a distance the Holocaust, dreadful and terrible and significant as it was, was only one part of a wider phenomenon. Count the people who have been killed in wars this century, just the major wars. I'm not talking about Somalia or something. Think of the memory that has gone. I oftentimes think of that. After all, the Russians were supposed to have lost some 20 million. These numbers are meaningless. Maybe there were six people among the tens of millions who could have saved the world. That is a lot of people. Among them some handful may have had an idea which would have spared us so much of our agony about a reality which we don't understand. Some philosopher may have died among them who could have illuminated the whole universe. That is what gets me: this rampant destruction of memory. It is interesting you bring this up because I find, more and more, that whenever I'm talking to younger people, they don't remember anything either. Maybe one's function, a writer's function, in part anyway, is to remember, to be the rememberer. I talk to people my own age and they don't remember very much either. A lot of things pass through the mesh into the ether and are gone. I don't know what good it does to remember, excepting it anchors thought somehow.

BIGSBY: Maybe especially in a country like this one, that regards history as something you have to transcend.

MILLER: It is like a fever you pass through.

9

The Crucible

BIGSBY: Your next play, *The Crucible*, directly reflected the mood of the moment. But, in fact, the idea for it came long before that.

MILLER: I knew the witchcraft story when I was still a university student. It occurred to me to write about it, but I didn't know how. What was eerie about it was that it was too absurd. Nobody could be led to believe that in a small village in seventeenth-century Massachusetts people would start killing each other over whether one was a witch or not. It was so crazy that I simply shied away from it. It was only in the early fifties that there was a reminder that this whole interrogation we were going through in the United States, by a mountebank, a demagogue, had a long history behind it. There were trials taking place where I heard actual lines being spoken by American prosecutors which I vaguely remembered from reading about witchcraft in 1692.

At first it was simply unbelievable, but I went back into the history to research, and there it was. It was simply mind-boggling that the same matrix could have risen again 300 years later. I thought that maybe by doing a play genuinely about witchcraft we would achieve some kind of perspective on what was happening in the country at that time. It really does antedate McCarthyism, but the fact is that people seeing it later don't really have to make that connection because the process involved is, unfortunately, I am afraid, common to people. A tendency for human beings to panic, to lose their bearings, to put the law aside and simply act as a kind of religious mob, is still with us at various places in the world. Our civilisation is only a few inches deep anyway. So, the play has really outstripped its original context.

BIGSBY: To write the play, you travelled to Salem.

MILLER: I was not at all sure I could write *The Crucible* when I went to Salem because it presented formidable technical difficulties that I wasn't at all sure I could manage. For example, there must have been three or four hundred people directly involved in this whole thing. Clearly, I was going to have to symbolise enormous amounts of the story if it was to make any real sense, and I wasn't sure whether I was going to be able to do that without it seeming awkward and stilted. The other thing was the sheer language. It could not be written in contemporary English. At the same time the little of it that I had read would be difficult for an American or British audience to comprehend. It would be like writing a post-Elizabethan English, which I was not prepared to attempt. So there were big questions, and I thought the visit to Salem could help to solve them and make up my mind as to what to do.

I went up there and looked at whatever I could find of the original documents so that, first of all, I could study the language. Of course, the original language was not going to be the same as the way people spoke, but I knew that there was a primitive stenographic record up there somewhere, and I luckily found it in the courthouse. Indeed, they had the record of the interrogations by the ministers. It was not really in shorthand. They did not have a shorthand system. It was just abbreviations, but you could tell from the way they were writing it down more or less what it sounded like. The more I read it, and the more I immersed myself in it, the clearer it became that it was possible to do this, to write in this language. It also became clear that the condensation of events was possible through the story of John Proctor.

BIGSBY: Can you remember when you decided to make that relationship between Abigail and John Proctor crucial? After all, you bring his age down and you take her age up and create something by doing that.

MILLER: There was one note – I can't remember which document it was, it could have been in the Charles Upham's book on Salem witchcraft and Salem village – about a moment in the courthouse when Abigail put her arm over Elizabeth's shoulder. Now that was a very ambiguous gesture to me because, in fact, she had been fired by Elizabeth a year earlier. What did that represent, that gesture? Was it to disarm Elizabeth, or was it a genuine momentary feeling of pity for her? It was a loaded gesture, and it was out of that [that something was born]. They were not in the habit of making such gestures, and the testimony, at that moment, implicated Elizabeth, so I thought it represented a very astute little girl who was in effect saying, 'I am on your side, dear, and I am going to kill you later.' It was diabolical. That always stuck in my mind, and I always regretted that there was no moment, in the way the play is constructed, where you could see Abigail doing that.

BIGSBY: When you came to write *The Crucible* America, of course, was changing.

MILLER: *The Crucible* was written in the midst of one of the most frantic epics in American history, maybe in any country's history. We were in the midst of a hunt for dissident people. They were communists, or associated with the left. In some parts of the country you could be left if you didn't like to eat meat. Some of it was quite crazy. Some of it was less crazy. But in the middle of it all there was a kind of irrational sensation of overhanging fear that some unseen force had infiltrated society, that was busy boring holes in it to bring it down. There was no rational way to confront all of this, because every time you did so you could be accused of being part of that conspiracy. If in any way you opposed this hunt, they would ask, 'Why are you opposing this if you are not involved in it?'

It became impossible, after a year or two of McCarthyism, to have a simple conversation with anybody. You couldn't say anything like the truth about anything without endangering yourself. If you told them that anybody you knew had been a communist, or a left-winger, then you went home. If you said you weren't going to do that, and you didn't know that these people had committed any crimes, and I had known a lot of them in my day, in the thirties, the farce was too much to stomach. That was one of the reasons I started to write *The Crucible*. I had to find a means to address what I was convinced, by now, would end us up either in a lunatic asylum or in some kind of quasi-fascist system in which we were, in effect, censoring ourselves. Hence, *The Crucible,* which is about a social paranoia, at bottom, where a whole town was destroyed by a misconception, by an idea, a fear generated by self-interested people which permeated the whole society until it could no longer operate.

So I, in effect, was driven by desperation to reply to this. As I say, I felt that at some point we would end up in a kind of American-type fascism, where the most outrageously patriotic people would be running everything, and anybody who had anything negative to say about anything would have been simply destroyed, driven out of the social conversation. That included hundreds of teachers, who were either thrown out of their jobs or disciplined in some way or another. Universities were quietly reporting students who had some sort of left-wing opinion to the FBI. It was a madhouse as far as I was concerned, and I thought we were riding down that old road towards some kind of a dictatorship, because there was no way to contain this whole thing, since society requires a certain amount of good faith and trust. I remembered, as a student, reading about the Salem witchcraft, which at the time I thought of as a kind of local madness, but a book came my way called *The Devil in Massachusetts* [by Marion L. Starkey]. It was a left-wing view of the witch trials, but it gave a lot of interesting information. It aroused my interest, so, as I say, I went to Salem and read the original records. Having read these, I began to try to put together some scheme. It took half a year to do that until I finally came up with the script of *The Crucible*.

The reason I moved in that direction was that it was simply impossible any longer to discuss what was happening to us in contemporary terms. There had to be some distance given to the phenomenon. We were all going slightly crazy trying to be honest, trying to see straight, and trying to stay safe. The hysteria in Salem had a certain inner procedure, or several, which we were duplicating. Perhaps by revealing the nature of that procedure some light could be thrown on what we were doing to ourselves.

The Crucible

BIGSBY: You were putting your head on the block. Did you have any worries about the reception?

MILLER: I was not prepared, I have to tell you, for the depth of hostility the play generated. McCarthy was still alive, threatening a lot of people, including the president of the United States, who was scared to death of him. When the play opened, people didn't know what it was about half an hour into it. Then, gradually, they began to realise what this was really talking about, and the audience simply froze. It was like a thin crust of ice over that theatre. I knew we were sunk, but I hadn't believed we were that far along.

I was standing in the lobby at the back, and people I had known, a little bit or a lot, walked right past me and didn't say hello. I thought we needed this play badly because nobody wanted to believe that this had ever happened before. After all, there were communists, but there were never any witches. Of course, if you had stood up in Salem in 1692 and said there were never any witches, you would have had it. There were witches. They were as real as any communists were. They were out to subvert the society. They had secret members inside the society. They had a leadership avowed to bring down Christian civilisation. It was quite an exact analogy, a real parallel to what we were going through, and I feared we would come to the same end, and, indeed, soon after I wrote the play, the Rosenbergs were executed. To give you an idea of how outrageous that was, we have since had several people arrested, in one case for giving away the entire United States naval code to Russia [John Anthony Walker, arrested in 1985 and given a life sentence]. That means that every command given from a United States ship, or from Washington, was immediately legible to Russians. There have been three or four cases of this sort, really monstrous betrayals of the country, and got a tap on the wrist. Aldrich Ames gave the names of every CIA informant in the Soviet Union, who were promptly arrested and shot. He is in jail, but nobody is executing him. The idea of executing him would have been outrageous. But they executed two people for allegedly giving away the secret of the atom bomb. The point was that we had never executed people like that before. That happened after I had written the play. That gives you an idea of how severe this thing was.

Admittedly the production was quite cold and stiff, though not that cold. There were some wonderful actors: E. G. Marshall and Arthur Kennedy. But the fear on the part of some of the audience, and most of the critics of the play [was clear]. It took three or four years before a young group of actors, and a young director, did the same play in one of the earliest Off Broadway productions that I know of, in a hotel ballroom. It was a great success. And the same critics who had responded rather remotely to the original now thought I had completely revised the play, which I hadn't touched. They were now prepared to receive it, but McCarthy was dead and times had changed, so that they could contemplate something which before they did not dare to look at.

BIGSBY: In a play which is about a public betrayal, you begin with a very private one. What was the significance of that sexual betrayal? How was it linked to the greater political betrayal?

MILLER: You would be hard put, if you read the original transcripts, not to be aware of the profound sexuality of the whole business. First of all, it was an attack on women, by men. Women were carrying some awful, antisocial, explosive force. It had to be contained. It had to be suppressed. The girls were charged with dancing. It was a sexual activity, and was almost acknowledged as such. The suppression of sexuality in Puritan society was manifest. I don't think they would have denied it. Of course, it was not to be permitted. If it was permitted the whole structure would collapse. So, the sexual betrayal in the play is implicit in the whole story to start with. You couldn't tell that story without that. It seemed to me that they did it very well in the film [1996]. It was so manifest that these nubile girls were all exploding with a sexual energy, and that's what had to be contained. Part of the politics is the suppression of sexuality.

BIGSBY: At one stage there was an additional scene between Proctor and Abigail which was cut. Why was it cut?

MILLER: I cut this short scene in the forest, between Abigail and Proctor, which seemed at the time not to add very much and to hold up the progress of the story. It really doesn't. It's possible that I absorbed some of the anxiety about the play and tried to make it more compact. But as time went on it's been played numerous times with the scene, and we had the scene in a different form in the film.

BIGSBY: What is it that led Proctor and Elizabeth to marry? Proctor is very passionate, Elizabeth is not, or was that just after she learned of his adultery? What drew them together?

MILLER: What drew her to him would have been his enormous attractiveness as a man. As far as he was concerned, it was the fact that she could tame him, and he needed to be tamed, in his own view. He was too passionate. He wanted to be cooler, and a wife of that kind would help him to do that. Of course, this is unconscious.

BIGSBY: Yet you have said that in Proctor you wanted to create a conscious hero, as opposed to Willy Loman. What did you mean by a conscious hero?

MILLER: There are times when I watched the audience of *Death of a Salesman* when I felt they weren't getting the enormity of the society he was living in. They weren't thinking enough. I wanted them to see as much as they felt. *The Crucible* is attractive in that way because, with a hero like John Proctor, you could see that before you was an extraordinary opponent of the way things were. They could see a disciplined rebel. I felt the need of being far more objective about playwriting than I had been in *Salesman*. I was veering from one extreme to another.

BIGSBY: When Abigail and the girls accuse people of witchcraft, at first this is to distract attention from themselves. But there comes a moment when they offer people up to death. How is it that Abigail and the others can make that enormous step?

MILLER: It depends on how deeply you appreciate the hysteria of the time, because that's what it is. First of all, once they had begun to condemn people, even the first one, they were forced to go on. If they then said, 'We don't see anyone any more' they would have been pounded upon by the prosecution saying, 'You must see more people with the Devil. How could you not see them? You saw them before?' They are forced to do this. They are then self-convinced into thinking that they are doing something wonderful because the town is supporting this idea to the hilt. They are being blessed, as they walk down the street, for saving the village from the Devil, delivering the village from the cause of the Devil. How could they not condemn people from there on? Once they have done the first one, the story is over.

BIGSBY: Is there evil in the play, or is that just a way of not exploring the mechanism whereby people do things as they do? Is there such a thing as evil?

MILLER: I think there is such a thing as evil. But it is also a way of saying I don't know why people do these things. In Rwanda they killed, what, half a million people, and I am sure that if you talked to some of those guys who did this, you would get a blank stare as to why they needed to kill so many people. You have to say that there is such a thing as evil that gets into people. Of course, it is only because we don't understand it. Hannah Arendt tried to give it a different name, the banality of evil, the idea that anybody could do this if they are properly psychologically primed. I prefer to think that it is because we can't explain it.

BIGSBY: John Proctor is asked to name names, to offer up other people as part of his confession.

MILLER: The crucial thing about the prosecution in Salem was not only did you commit the crime of being involved with the Devil, but you must have seen others, and if you don't give us the names of the others it means you are still in that conspiracy. The proof that you are freed of the conspiracy is that you reveal the names of the others. It was the same procedure in the 1950s.

Some years later, in the seventies, I met a lady who was Chinese and had been arrested during the Cultural Revolution in China. She was put in jail for six years under terrible conditions. She got out, and I met her in New York. She told me the following story. When she got out of prison, a friend of hers, who was a theatre director, said, 'I've got a new production that I want you to see.' She went and saw this play called *The Crucible*. She knew nothing about me. When I met her, she had written a book published by my publisher, so I met her in his office. She burst into tears when she met me. I said, 'What's going on?' She said, 'First of all, I couldn't believe that a non-Chinese had written that play because the dialogue was exactly the same dialogue that we experienced with the Cultural Revolutionaries. I thought the Chinese director had fixed up this dialogue so that it would reflect the Cultural Revolution, but I went back to the original English, and it was the same thing.' So that will give you an idea of the farcical nature of this kind of persecution.

BIGSBY: The Cultural Revolution has gone. The House Un-American Activities Committee has gone. But the play is performed everywhere. What is it about *The Crucible* that makes it seem so relevant today?

MILLER: It's because we know, somewhere in our bones, that the impulses, the pressures that created that situation, still exist. It is a kind of a warning about the fact that the human being is still capable of that. I could always tell when a revolution was coming in South America when they started to produce *The Crucible*. It meant that something was going on there, or was about to break out. Or, that a dictatorship was over. That was when they produced the play too, to cast light on the previous dictatorship. So, it was before or after. I think the matrix lying behind the action of that play is immemorial. It will probably never disappear.

I believe that *The Crucible* is still relevant today because there is a general feeling, in the background, that these things are still possible, this kind of situation. It is also the ultimate challenge before us in this play, telling a lie in order to preserve one's life. While most of us would tell a lie, we want to believe that there are those that wouldn't, that there are exemplars in the world, people so true to their lives and their characters that they would refuse to do so. There is also the question of why Elizabeth throws this burden upon him, because she says it is his decision. That's a very Christian idea, that nobody can confess but yourself. She says, 'It's your soul. I can't make the decision for you.' She literally believes in that kind of salvation. It is a transaction with God, not with some judicial system. That is why she says what she says. She is a very religious woman. It is part of her code. It also makes perfect sense, because if she was given the burden, then what value would it have for him anyway? In a situation like that, he has got to make the decision.

I think *The Crucible* is always going to be relevant. The reason I say that is because there is paranoia in all of us. Every human being has a panic button. If somebody came in here and said the roof of this building is very weak and that at any moment is likely to be coming down on us, we would be heading for the exits, and those exits are very small. Before you know it, we would be trampling all over each other, and the roof might be as strong as it has ever been. So, in every society, especially societies that are full of conflicts, that situation is endemic.

The question arises immediately as to what recourse there is, and of course there is only one recourse, but it is difficult to take, and that is the law: proofs and documentation of charges. Finger-pointing becomes the immediate way of dealing with the sudden appearance of the Devil, and I don't see the possibility of it ever ending. All I can say is that we must keep our heads when it starts and keep asking the same old question to the finger-pointer: 'How do you know that?' 'What is the proof that you have of that?', whatever it is that he is charging anybody with. In other words, the law is finally the only hope of keeping civilised intercourse going, and as long as that is the case, I can't see an end to *The*

Crucible. In fact, that play is produced more each year, in more countries, than it ever has been in the past.

BIGSBY: What did you think of Sartre's adaptation of *The Crucible*?

MILLER: I thought it was Marxist in the worst sense, quite frankly. I thought that anybody who had the least sensitivity to history would be embarrassed by it. He has a crucifix hanging in a witch's house, which was exactly what they revolted against in Europe. You could not have a crucifix in one of their houses. It would be like showing a lot of Jews with a Buddhist statue in the middle of the room. It is that absurd. But they were imposing a simplistic class society upon this. In other words, the witch hunt was devised by the upper class against the lower class. Well, for God's sake, probably 30 per cent of the victims were people of property. Now that is more interesting. Rebecca Nurse was one of the largest landholders in the whole area.

BIGSBY: Sartre's script almost ends with a revolt.

MILLER: Well, there is some truth in that. I described it in the stage play. What had happened was that the community had gotten more and more alarmed because of the wildness of the accusations. When they actually hanged these people, that was a breaking point. When Rebecca Nurse was hanged, she had had an immaculate reputation in the town. She was a loved woman who had given away a lot of her worldly goods and helped people. She had a tremendous reputation. They were so hypnotised that they were willing to think that the Devil would hide himself in those who were least suspect, and so, on that reasoning, well maybe she was a witch, but when she stood up there and they put a rope around this ancient woman's neck and she said, 'I would not belie myself', there was a surge of people to get her down and the soldiers held them back. They hanged her, and that ended. There was just a revulsion. They did not want anything to do with it, though it was not the people in Salem so much as the people in the next town, Beverly, who stopped it.

When the court came in, the so-called court with the girls, they lined up in the road and would not let them into the town. They would not let them hold the court there. They said we do not want any part of this, and they turned around and went home. That was the end of it. It was not so much a revolt, it was just that they thought we are not having any more of it, we are not saying anybody is right or wrong, but do it somewhere else. This defiance spread. All the lawyers said, 'Well look, why don't we just forget this whole thing?' As usual in the United States, it sort of evaporated, as McCarthyism did. There is no date on which he fell. It just got boring, repetitive, and it lost its charge and its charm. People were onto something else.

BIGSBY: How far was *The Crucible* also about paralysis in the way that *The Golden Years* was?

MILLER: That play was written when everybody was terrified of this man, McCarthy, including people who knew perfectly well he was an idiot. With this silence – the paralysis, again, of decent people – I really began to wonder whether, with a little luck, he could take over the government. Wherever I looked, people were swept up by this great anti-communist crusade. As I say, I had known of the witchcraft hysteria back in college, but it had never meant very much to me, except as a strange event in our ancient history. It suddenly started to come back as a kind of metaphor for what we were going through. Because, as the play makes clear, it was more than your life was worth to so much as express any doubt or scepticism about these children being attacked by witches. After all, the greatest minds in the world confirmed the existence of witches and that the job of a Christian society was to combat them. So, what chance did anyone have to say, 'I don't believe in them?' He would be dead. That was how it was in 1952 with the anti-communist crusade. You would suddenly find yourself losing popularity, to put it lightly. Friends would be hard to find. If you were a teacher, or somebody on a payroll, you might find that you had lost your job, and it would take, as it turned out, something like twenty-five years before you were recognised as having been unfairly dealt with. So, I reached to the witchcraft as a way of illuminating the phenomenon as a national event, in the hope that people would get some insight into what was going on.

I never thought McCarthyism was unique. As soon as I started going into it, it was quite clear that this was coming out of the gut of the human being: the fear of the unknown, the sense that we were at the mercy of forces coming out of the centre of the earth. It goes back to our early childhood. I treated it with great respect as a human force that could be marshalled by unscrupulous people and turned into a tremendously destructive weapon. I am sure that the Serbs and the Croats and the rest of them believe that if they don't kill the other one, they are going to get killed. They demonise the other people, whoever they are. And we had successfully demonised anybody on the left by 1952, so that it became impossible to discuss anything without you being accused, implicitly or otherwise, of being an agent of that force. There was a paralysis of people like Dwight Eisenhower, who could not be brought to condemn McCarthy, who he privately regarded as the scum of the earth. They couldn't get him out on a platform simply to make some criticism. The best he could do was not be photographed with him. What chance did an ordinary citizen have? Not much. It was really a tremendous outburst of really primitive human terror.

BIGSBY: You said earlier that there were echoes of the Holocaust in *The Crucible*?

MILLER: I think that everything I have written has in some way or another, either directly or indirectly, been coloured by the Second World War and the Holocaust. It has been written at the edge of a cliff as a result. I don't really take much for granted as far as human beings are concerned, although I keep hoping I am wrong. Everything I have written has come out of that period in one way or another. There is a film I have written for Vanessa Redgrave, which is now a play, *Playing for Time* [based on Fania Fénelon's book about her time playing for the orchestra at Auschwitz-Birkenau]. It goes directly to that experience.

I personally think, though, and I hate to say this aloud, that in certain respects things are getting better. What do I mean by that? I mean that in my lifetime there has never been such a level of consciousness as exists today about certain social failings. We don't accept, as previous generations did, that, for instance, the water is poisoned. We may still have to drink it, but we don't like it. And we know that there is another way to do this. People are, I think, becoming less spiritually regimented than of old. They get restless in the face of inconveniences or dangers. Then there is the failure of the whole nuclear energy thing that dominated our lives. You can't sell a nuclear energy system any more. Why? People are scared of it. In past times I think they would have said, 'Well, what can you do about it?' Similarly, things like automobile emissions. I can remember when the first suggestion was made that the United States

Congress should pass some legislation to diminish the amount of carbon coming out of a car, the automobile industry said, 'You can't possibly do that. How will they control it?' Well, they passed a law, and they controlled it.

If we are going to be slaves to whatever it is, it diminishes us, and if we are going to resist, which I would suggest is the right thing to do, then our spirits change, and we begin to stand up straight again. In my lifetime, which is only a tiny historical moment, we were much more conformist than we are now. In fact, some people think we don't believe in anything any more, and that is the problem. Maybe that is the case, but I think there is an improvement in the political awareness people have. We elected George Bush, and old George had really never been on a sidewalk. He has been carried from place to place. But I still have the feeling that things are getting better.

10

A View from the Bridge

BIGSBY: What led to the writing of *A View from the Bridge*, beyond your seeing graffiti about Pete Panto?
MILLER: It came about for various reasons, social, aesthetic and personal. I wanted to write a play that had the clean line of some of the Greek tragedies, meaning that we would be confronted with a situation, and we would, in effect, be told what the ending of it was. The question was not what was going to happen, but how it was going to happen. The whole action was to be very overt. Instead of things slowly developing before us, there was a certain declarative tone. It declares itself in the way some of the Greek plays do. In *Oedipus*, for example, we know pretty damn well what this thing is going to get to. And that increases the tension, the fact that the end is not obscure. It is evident. I wanted that finally on stage. That was one side of it. Another side was that I knew of this story, or at least some of it. I had been told the story, which seemed to me absolutely a Greek story. Of course, they were Italians, but that was close enough. So, it wrote itself. I wrote it very quickly, in a matter of a couple of weeks. Part of the impulse behind it was somebody whose end you could not only imagine but were told.

The actual story came off the docks. It was substantially about immigrants who were betrayed. I never knew any of the people involved, but the story itself seemed so Greek it was something I could not avoid. I had a hell of a time writing it. The first production – originally it was a one-act play which, incidentally, the Greek plays are – was not successful on Broadway. It really belonged in a different environment. After the first production, Peter Brook did it in London, and I went over for that. We talked about it, and I realised that there was a large gap in the way I told that story in that the women were not really in it. So, I did some writing, and it got longer by fifteen minutes or something. And the role of the women is substantially what changed the length of the play. It became probably less Greek and more American as a result, but the story became more palpable.

BIGSBY: Why did you use a narrator?

MILLER: Alfieri's function in the play is that of the chorus. Interestingly, in the opera, which has now been written – I wrote the scenario with Arnold Weinstein, a professional opera man – we actually have a chorus which sings. I should add that the most successful American production also had a chorus, a chorus without lines. They simply acted on the stage as a neighbourhood. Peter Brook also had people on stage who were observing from on high and passing by because Eddie Carbone's conscience is made up of these people. They are the people who have the code he is violating. It is their protection he is violating. They are the society he has, in effect, wounded and which he knows he has wounded. In fact, he is killing himself by doing it. In the opera we have a chorus of which Alfieri is the leader. Here he has no background of people with lines but is the chorus.

BIGSBY: Isn't it curious that after *The Crucible* you write a play in which you give a sympathetic account of an informer?

MILLER: The informer in *A View from the Bridge* is an entirely different approach. It is being approached from his point of view. This poor guy is caught between the ethos of a small group of people, Italian immigrants, and his emotional needs. It is not as though he expected to become rich by his betrayal, or more powerful, or anything. He is just driven by subterranean forces in himself to keep a young man from taking his beloved niece away from him. I was sympathetic with him. I can't really say that I have been unsympathetic to any of the characters I have written about. I wouldn't know how to write a character if I didn't feel that, under certain circumstances, I might be him. If that kind of a person did not have a justification, he wouldn't exist. He is tragic. I was attempting to understand a man who does that, to simply treat it as a phenomenon rather than lowering a moral boom. It is a play about the relationship between individual need and, as I say, the ethos of the group. I think it relates to the Greek drama, which is inconceivable excepting in a small city where the welfare of everybody depends upon everybody upholding the moral law.

BIGSBY: Why did he react so strongly to one of the illegal immigrants, Rodolpho? Is it something about this man, or would he have acted similarly about any man?

MILLER: I think he would have reacted to any man. In fact, Catherine asks Eddie, 'Who would you think is okay for me? Everybody I ever went with, you disliked.' As it happens, Rodolpho opens himself to this kind of accusation because of his nature. He is, in effect, a kind of an artist.

There is an irresponsibility about him that Eddie can latch on to.

BIGSBY: Surely it is not unreasonable for Eddie to be suspicious of him.

MILLER: Absolutely. Sure. Had he not done what he could to involve this girl in his life, it would have been remarkable. Inevitably he would have done so.

BIGSBY: Is Rodolpho in love with Catherine or with America?

MILLER: I suppose it's a little of both, but I think it is Catherine first. It is also an opportunity to get his roots started in this country. Purposely, I think, we are left to wonder about that.

BIGSBY: And surely, Eddie is not wrong to look for something more for his niece.

MILLER: Absolutely. Sure. From his point of view, she is doing the wrong thing for her own self-interest. He has got a good case. That's what makes it so awful. It would make sense for Rodolpho to latch on to this girl in order to get a passport given the desperation of life in Italy at the time. People do this all the time. It is not in the play, but people get married simply to get the passport. This is an old story. So, he has a good case.

BIGSBY: Eddie is not a very articulate man. He can't allow his own motives to bubble to the surface of his mind. Was this a problem in writing the play?

MILLER: If he were a more educated person who could more easily summon up the speech that is required, he might well not have done what he did. He is left with his really profound, primitive emotions. I should tell you that after the first production downtown in a small theatre – a terrific production, the first part Robert Duvall ever had, who was marvellous as Eddie – Duvall had left, and an Italian American had taken over. He noticed that there was one man left in the audience who was in tears and who would wander out. A few days later he noticed him again, again devastated by the play. There was a third time, a week or so after. This time, the actor stepped off the stage and went up to him. He recognised that he was an Italian labourer. He could speak Italian, too. He asked, 'Why do you keep coming back here?' And he said, 'Well, I knew that family.' He said 'Really?' 'Yes, they lived in the Bronx.' Of course, I had never lived in the Bronx. He said, 'It is all true, except the ending was different.' The actor said 'Why? How did it end?' He said, 'It ended where Eddie was taking a nap one day and she came in and stabbed him right through the head.' I wish he had told me that before I wrote it. He said that all the details in the play were exactly as it had happened. Of course, I never knew that family.

BIGSBY: How far is Eddie's death at the end an act of denial, a way of not having to face the truth?

MILLER: He is not facing it, and he is facing it. The way it should be played is that by denying it verbally he is actually confessing it. He does know, and has experienced, the whole truth by the end of the play.

BIGSBY: When I was talking to the actors in a recent production, they wanted to know whether, when Catherine comes out of the room with Rodolpho, straightening her dress, they had been making love in that room, because in their view it would change the way they played the rest of the scene.

MILLER: Yes, they were making love in that room. They had heard Eddie and were quickly getting themselves ready to confront him.

BIGSBY: Why do you think we should care about the fate of Eddie Carbone? He is a man who has betrayed his own relatives, who has ambiguous sexual feelings for his own niece.

MILLER: The question is often asked about Willy Loman, who lies to everybody. I can only think that maybe these people are very involved with love. It may be the wrong love. It may be a crazy love. It may be a perverse love, but it is love in one aspect or another, and I suppose that's why we get so wound up in them. They are inconceivable as characters without an immense quantity of sheer love in them. It gets twisted, gets corrupted, but it is there and maybe most people in the world never demonstrated that enough, cared that much.

BIGSBY: There comes a moment when Eddie shouts out his name. Indeed, in a number of your plays your characters often shout out their names at the very moment they are betraying those names, or threatening to do so. What's in a name?

MILLER: It's true. In a number of the plays the characters do call out their names. It is an outcry against obliteration, against non-existence.

11

House Un-American Activities Committee

BIGSBY: How far did being called to testify before the House Un-American Activities Committee [HUAC] in the 1950s affect your work, and perhaps that of your contemporaries?

MILLER: I felt that the issue raised by that investigation was one's grasp of one's own past and whether one was going to betray it or not. That theme of betrayal is in *A View from the Bridge* as well as in *After the Fall* and most of the other plays I have written. I am not sure it wouldn't have been there if I had never been in front of the House Un-American Activities Committee, but it certainly was the emphatic theme of that hearing. What that Committee was trying to do was to force people to renounce the whole era of the thirties and forties in which certain social ideals were dominant and which were now, in the fifties, regarded as treasonous: the whole ideal of social equality and of one world, because we were now in the midst of the Cold War, which was a division of the world between Russia and the United States. So, I suppose it had an effect, but I cannot really be any more specific.

BIGSBY: Was there any move to suppress your work, to inhibit you from writing?

MILLER: Oh yes! *A View from the Bridge* and *The Crucible*, when they were made into films, had to be made in Europe. No American company would make them. As it happened, I was working in the theatre. In the Broadway theatre the financing is done by a lot of people. There is not one big company that provides the financing, so the blacklist which prevailed in Hollywood had some effect, but much less on Broadway, because there were too many entrepreneurs, and it was difficult to control. In Hollywood there were only four or five big corporations who could be brought together by the Committee and terrorised into creating a blacklist which would prohibit several people from working. But the reverberations of that period in the theatre, I think, remain to be investigated by scholars who are fair-minded.

I do not pretend to know all of them, but I think that [the Committee affected] a surprisingly large number of people, maybe numbering in the hundreds, and there were not a whole lot of people working in the American theatre at that time. Hundreds of people were knocked out of work, that is, they were quietly just not hired. They weren't fired, they just weren't given work. A large number were just forgotten, and the effects were tremendous on the spiritual life of the arts. I think they still, unbeknownst to most people, reverberate.

Those of us who lived through it know that the civilised skin of our relationships is very thin. It takes a matter of weeks of pounding on television and radio for people to start to avoid contamination with people who are accused of something. We have a tendency in America – I think it is probably true everywhere – to run in gangs. De Tocqueville, the great French commentator on American democracy back in the 1830s, wrote that Americans do not want interference from the government, but they also do not want to have a unique opinion. They want to be like each other. They want to be part of a crowd, and this tendency was evident in this period so that pariahs could easily be pointed out and few would come to their defence. I think it was a frightful time, and undoubtedly it affected me. *A View from the Bridge* has echoes of it. *After the Fall* is full of it. So it had a tremendous effect.

BIGSBY: When you were called before HUAC, in 1956, they flourished petitions and documents, and you remembered almost none of them. Was that because you literally did not remember them, or was that a ploy for the occasion?

MILLER: I probably didn't remember them any more than now I would remember, let's say, invitations to speak at various places, which I get every day of the week. In those days I got a petition every day of the week.

BIGSBY: They also, at one stage, produced an application form with your name typed on it. Is it plausible that you had filled in this form for membership of the Communist Party?

MILLER: Oh yes. But of course, I hadn't signed it, and that was their problem. So, really, I hadn't made an application.

BIGSBY: When we went to see your brother, Kermit, he said that he had been a card-carrying member of the Communist Party.

MILLER: That was news to me. I never knew that.

BIGSBY: So why did you not join when a lot of people were, including, it seems, your own brother?

MILLER: It was probably an aesthetic reason more than anything else. There were an awful lot of people in the theatre, mostly playwrights, whose work I really detested. I thought it was just propaganda. It was not very interesting, and I did not want to be in the same boat with those guys. I liked them all right, as people, but they were not really very good writers, and most of them were very quick to sell out, even to the advertising business. A lot of them became ad writers, while those who were luckier got Hollywood jobs. They did not hesitate for three minutes, because they were not really leaving anything, I think. Some of them became very good screenwriters.

BIGSBY: You may not have formally been a member of the party, but you shared the convictions of those who were.

MILLER: I thought that the system was basically a class system, which it is, and that the future lay in some vague way not with a revolution but a gradual change, so that the ordinary people and the workers would gain more control over what was done. The best of the actual communists I knew, and I knew a couple of them, were guys on the waterfront, two of them, both of whom became millionaires. One of them was Catholic and one was Jewish. It was a mafia kingdom, very dangerous.

BIGSBY: When you were asked at the HUAC meetings about the party meetings you attended, what were they about?

MILLER: There were some thirty people in someone's living room. I cannot remember what they were talking about. They lasted about two hours. I suppose they were talking about what they should be writing.

BIGSBY: They were writers.

MILLER: They were all writers.

BIGSBY: Was that in Brooklyn?

MILLER: No, it was Manhattan. I do remember one meeting. It was about a story that some writer had published about circumcision, and there was a discussion as to whether this was proper or whether this was creating anti-Semitism. I went to one of those meetings, and it was enough. The one thing I am unhappy with is the idea of anybody telling me what to do as a writer. That was simply intolerable.

BIGSBY: When you were asked by the Committee who was there, you wouldn't do it. Can you say who was there?

MILLER: You could talk yourself blue in the face about everything you thought about life, but if you had known someone in the Communist Party, or an affiliated group of people, and you refused to give them their names, even though they knew who those people were, this was a ritual. No information was really being asked for. They had had informants inside these organisations from day one. They knew everybody involved. It was to break the people who they were confronting. So, when they did that, it seemed to me like the actions of a dictatorship. It meant that you no longer had the privilege of association, political association. It meant that the government had the right to require of you the names of anybody you had had a discussion with. It was abhorrent. It was a horror. After all, I was living through a period when, in Nazi Germany, the same procedure was carried out. It was a breaking of faith, it seemed to me. So, I was fiercely opposed to that whole thing.

Anyway, they asked me who was in the room. They knew, of course, the whole story, because they had had information from the beginning. I said I wasn't going to talk about other people. I didn't know those people, excepting for a radio writer [Millard Lampell] who was sort of a friend. I would see him every few months around. These were screenwriters, playwrights. I didn't know them that well to tell the truth, but I could have named them.

BIGSBY: Kazan, of course, did name names.

MILLER: Kazan had only been active for about six months, six fatal months. The whole thing is a dream.

BIGSBY: But it lasts. When Kazan was given a lifetime achievement Academy Award, in 1999, it was still a live issue after all that time.

MILLER: It remains a live issue, I think, probably not for political as much as for moral reasons, the idea of getting other people in trouble, even though that was not strictly true either, because the Committee knew all the people. This was an inquisitional thing, a whitewash. The object was to cleanse the soul of the victim, and what they were asking him was, was he still a Jew, even though he had converted, and why is it that he wasn't working on Saturday. Was his little baby boy circumcised, etc. It was the humiliation of the person that was at stake, not any information about anything.

BIGSBY: It wasn't only Kazan who named names. So did Lee J. Cobb, who played Willy Loman, and so did Clifford Odets. Can you recall what you felt when you heard they had done that?

MILLER: It was rather like a dream, because, as I say, the people they were naming were all known to the government. They made a point of saying we know who all these people are. Then why did we have to name them? You had to name them in order to establish your credibility as a patriot. In other words, it was a ritual. It had no practical meaning. It was purely to feed the endless appetite of certain politicians, and to scare people. It just seemed so absurd and maddening that people were being torn apart, their loyalty to one another crushed, and that common decency was going down the drain. It is indescribable really, because you got the feeling that nothing was going to be sacred any more.

I understood their situations. They were very vulnerable people. Of course, I blamed them, but I have to say, for good or ill, it made me more despairing and more angry at the government. Why does everybody have to be strong in order to be an artist? Why do they have to go through this hell from their own government in a democratic society? I felt towards them probably as Czechs in Prague felt towards similar situations, that is, that it is necessary to see past the individual to the government, to the regime. I could not let myself be deflected from that.

I thought they were acting in panic rather than conviction. But it was a reminder of how vulnerable we are and that therefore we aren't safe. I felt at the time that the whole structure of human relations was falling to pieces, that nothing would hold any more as far as holding our commitments to one another together. I think it is now what still frightens people about *The Crucible* when they see it, because it is showing them how thin our security is with one another, and yet how strong it is when somebody decides he is going to keep it strong. My reaction to the whole thing was that it was a tragedy, a catastrophe, that was going to spread and spread and eat us all up, and that I might as well write about it and go down that way.

BIGSBY: When you were called before the Committee, was there ever a second in which you considered going along with what you were being asked to do?

MILLER: I had no conflict about that. I just felt contempt for that Committee. I thought they were simply using this whole Red hysteria to get elected. A lot of people felt that. I suppose it is partly because I wasn't an actor. I didn't depend on any organisation. Basically, I didn't want to hand power to this Committee. I felt it was undemocratic. It was destroying the democratic system. I didn't want to be on that side.

BIGSBY: Following your appearance before HUAC you suddenly found yourself sentenced to prison for Contempt of Congress.

MILLER: Yes. With a trial in a federal court normally these cases took a morning. Nobody ever mounted a strong defence against the charge. These cases were based on the government bringing in so-called experts on communism. They would say, 'I've examined the writings and speeches of the defendant and, as an expert on communism, I can tell you he is a communist, or under the control of the Communist Party.' In my case, for the first time, we brought in a counter-expert. He had read my plays and said, 'I don't see any sign of this guy being a communist.'

When we were preparing our defence, Joe Rauh, my lawyer, brilliantly got ahold of this former Red hunter who had realised the fraudulence behind a lot of the far-right activity. He had turned against them. Before he had turned against them, he had been a United States senator. By the time we got ahold of him, he had a television show down in Florida. His name was Harry P. Cain, a former Marine lieutenant from the Korean War, highly decorated. He was a very close friend of McCarthy. They used to play poker every evening. By the time I talked to him he was his opponent. He said something very interesting. He said, 'Joe isn't that bad.' I said, 'What the hell are you talking about?' He said, 'It's his wife.' I said, 'No.' He said, 'She is absolutely crazy. If some guy wrote something in a newspaper she would wake him up in the middle of the night and say, "You've got to get after this son of a bitch".' The least opposition to anything she would force him to run them down.

He said, 'Joe was an easy-going guy.' Isn't that wonderful? He latched on to the anti-communism thing purely out of political [expediency]. He had no convictions about this. He couldn't care less about the whole thing. But it was an issue that people grabbed on to, and he went with it. Alcoholics are very often frightened people, and he was a real alcoholic. He died of it. Cain said, 'He was scared of being discovered.' He was full of lies. He pretended he had been a tail gunner, and he never had been. He was afraid his lies were going to catch up with him. He said, 'He came out to help me get elected in the state of Washington.' They met at the American Legion hall. 'The place was packed. Joe made this violently anti-communist speech, and I made the same kind of speech. At the back of the hall, this guy stood up and started yelling embarrassing questions at Joe McCarthy. So, the fellows picked him up and threw him out into the street. They beat him up a little bit, and that was the end of that.' He said, 'I got into the Senate and, two or three years later, we were playing cards, and Joe looked up and said, "By the way, whatever happened to that guy?" It took me a minute to remember what he was talking about. I said, "I don't know." "What do you mean you don't know?" I said, "We just threw the guy out." He said, "You should have gone after him".' It was that mentality, because somebody always had to [plan] his ruin, and he was going to stamp him out before he could pop up with some dreadful news that would embarrass him.

He said, 'Apart from the anti-communism, he was a very sweet character.' But he had a sinister manner on television. That is what did him. Like Nixon, he always needed a shave. And he had a snigger. He made this funny noise, like a pig.

But he had the benefit of Roy Cohn [chief counsel to Senator Joseph McCarthy] sitting at his elbow. It was some period. I couldn't grasp it. I never wrote about it because I couldn't grasp it. The only way I could go after them was through *The Crucible*. At that time, a lot of liberal people were saying, well, he is dreadful, but there is a problem with Russia. That stunned everybody. Meanwhile, [President] Truman had to get on the wagon himself and make the same kind of noises. At the beginning he said this was all right-wing Republican garbage. Thank God that's over.

At the end I was pronounced guilty of contempt and was asked if I had anything to say for myself, and I said, 'No, not a thing. I've said all I wish to say.' And he said, 'Okay. You get a year in jail, a suspended sentence, and a $500 fine.' So we left the courtroom and were in the street when Joe said, 'Hey, wait a minute. You're a federal prisoner. We can't just walk out on the street.' I said, 'What do we do?' He said, 'We've got to go back.' It was five-thirty in the evening. 'We've got to go back and get you bail, so you can be bailed out of your prison sentence.' Well, we ran back in, but there was nobody in their offices any more, so, having been a dangerous menace to the United States we went in to find someone to arrest me. The farcical nature of this thing was beyond belief.

12

Mary and Marilyn

BIGSBY: Meanwhile, your relationship with Mary had been changing. In *Timebends* you seem to imply that the marriage began going wrong around 1947, but you have also said it was after the opening of *Death of a Salesman*.

MILLER: It is hard to pin it down because it was a very gradual thing. I would say there were two forces. One was that I was totally immersed in my work in a way, now that I look back at it, that I don't know how anybody could live with me at all. It was day and night, all day and all night. All I ever did was think about it. So I probably paid no attention to her, or very little, and at the same time she was feeling, no doubt, that she could be doing other things. She was very bright, well-organised and informed. She could have sat around waiting for me to pay attention to her, so I think both things were working against the marriage. Also at that time, to my basic surprise, I was becoming well-known as a writer, something I really didn't believe then. So my horizon suddenly opened up into all kinds of other ways of expressing my dominance. I felt I could do anything, and we kind of broke apart then, I think.

I would think it just wore out, the abrasion of time. She also disapproved of people more than I did, people who were disreputable, or had their own viewpoints towards life, or useless people to whom I gravitated, so that more and more my life had to be led by me. It was no longer a shared life. I think it was a desire, on my part, for a more varied life. We were blocking out a lot of life.

BIGSBY: In what way?

MILLER: Well, meeting all different kinds of people, which was very interesting to me but not her.

BIGSBY; You give the impression that it wasn't really a relationship that was founded on passion.

MILLER: It started out that way, but it ended up something else. It was more a meeting. We weren't on the same track. We were on parallel tracks, waving at each other.

BIGSBY: What happened, politically? Did she change her political views?

MILLER: No, she stayed very correct politically.

BIGSBY: You both retained your faith in the Soviet Union together.

MILLER: Anybody who lived in that time, people like us especially, understood that but for the Soviet Union Hitler would have won the war. It would have been a shambles if there had been a less obdurate resistance. When the whole thing began to change – and it changed with a rapidity which was breathtaking in a matter of weeks – the whole thing was turned around. One couldn't easily make that adjustment, in all honesty. People who were never really Marxists couldn't do it.

BIGSBY: So how did Mary feel when you went off to those few party meetings and later to the Waldorf Conference? Was she fully supportive of that?

MILLER: Oh yes, more than I was.

BIGSBY: Would she ever go to meetings?

MILLER: Sure.
BIGSBY: So she went to Communist Party meetings herself. Just as well that HUAC didn't track that route down.
MILLER: Had the thing continued, they would probably have gotten after her.
BIGSBY: Did she go to the same meeting with you?
MILLER: No.
BIGSBY: Who was more passionately concerned with going to those, you or her?
MILLER: She, by that time, was.
BIGSBY: Really? Was she ever a party member?
MILLER: Not that I know of. I don't think so. Anyway, it was a period when everything was out in the open. There was no big secret about anything. It wasn't that big a deal at all.
BIGSBY: Was there a sense in which it was ultimately your success which helped to undermine your relationship?
MILLER: Oh, no doubt about it, sure, because, put it this way, had I not succeeded, had I remained, say, a radio writer, which is what most people of that generation became, or they went to Hollywood and became screenwriters, had I gone in that direction, I probably would have remained married. What happens is that you get another mistress, and that is your career. And in the absolutely obsessive crazy concentration on the work, you don't hear anything any more. In all justice to her, she was going to the wall. I was really obsessed with developing new kinds of plays, and I didn't know how to do that and function in any other way.
BIGSBY: And would that have consisted of you locking yourself away in a room?
MILLER: Yes, I worked in a room. I was doing that my whole waking life. I was obsessed with writing or getting ready to write.

BIGSBY: So, there has been a human price to be paid for your success as a writer.

MILLER: Sure, I think you do pay a terrible price. It is a total engagement with this art, as opposed to being a technically apt playwright who knows how to put together two hours of entertainment.

BIGSBY: At first, Mary was a stenographer, and you were beginning to be successful as a radio writer, on the edge of a radio-plays career. There was a kind of equality between you.

MILLER: Yes, and of course she had a steady job. She went to work every day. I worked earning spasmodically by writing a radio play. It was two kinds of lives. They were not in step. Had I gone to an office, and gone to work, then we would have met.

BIGSBY: She becomes a support apparatus, and then you are successful, and she is in a subordinate role suddenly, invited to celebrate your success.

MILLER: That's right, and basically the work occupies your whole brain. It is indescribable. It is there all the time. I equated it with my father, who had to get out a new spring line. One day I thought to myself, I have to get a play ready for autumn. I was talking to somebody, and I thought this sounds like I'm in some business. Then gradually, when I missed this whole season, which I more and more frequently did, I shook that off. But there was that impulse, to do that.

BIGSBY: Your father valued success. As a student, and a radicalised student, you were suspicious of all that, and yet you went on to replicate that in some way.

MILLER: The usual story. It was more likely than not if you can do it. Tom Haden [a one-time editor of the

Michigan Daily who went on to be an anti-Vietnam War activist] became a representative congressman.

BIGSBY: There is another thing about success, though, and that is that there can be a kind of sensuousness to it. It lifts you into a different realm.

MILLER: I was very naive about it. I was not at all sophisticated about it. I remember being shocked, for example – well, not shocked, but taken aback a bit – when I heard that Marlon Brando had a business manager. An actor, having a business manager, an artist? That is the kind of mind I had. An artist was somehow treading on different soil to other people. Fame is a form of power which is sexual, or implicitly sexual. But I was pretty faithful.

BIGSBY: You say pretty.

MILLER: Well, I was totally faithful to Mary until the end of our relationship, practically.

BIGSBY: But not to the end of the marriage.

MILLER: Well, the marriage ended. It was a pro forma ending by that time.

BIGSBY: There is a hint, in *Timebends*, that your new fame potentially opened up sexual possibilities.

MILLER: Well, I didn't fool around, though I wanted to.

BIGSBY: You seem to have told your wife that you were tempted to stray but had not. This was surely not news she wished to be given.

MILLER: She was outraged. I didn't understand why she would be outraged. I was just telling her the facts. So, in a way she didn't exist as an ego, as another ego.

BIGSBY: What strikes me about your 1964 play *After the Fall* is that while everyone was concentrating on Marilyn, in fact it seems to offer a portrait of Mary, the very thing you just talked about, the accusation of ignoring her, not opening the door for her, as though she didn't exist. Isn't that Mary?

MILLER: Sure.

BIGSBY: You underwent analysis.

MILLER: We tried to hold the marriage together.

BIGSBY: You both underwent analysis.

MILLER: Yes. I was in analysis for a couple of years.

BIGSBY: How many sessions? How often?

MILLER: Every day.

BIGSBY: For a couple of years?

MILLER: Yes.

BIGSBY: That's money.

MILLER: It cost $25 a shot.

BIGSBY: Did you learn anything?

MILLER: I learnt a lot, but I would never advise anybody to do that.

BIGSBY: Why?

MILLER: Because about 80 per cent of it is repetition. What there is to learn you can learn very quickly. The whole process of laying it on the analyst doesn't work.

BIGSBY: So what did you learn?

MILLER: I learnt the whole process of the way one feels and thinks, basically. I learned, very quickly, a lot of stuff which I really knew about and had written about. Most of it was a waste.

BIGSBY: And it didn't accomplish what it was supposed to.

MILLER: No, of course not. A friend of mine, Jimmy Proctor, was a publicity guy. He did publicity on two or three of my plays and wrote a novel. I have never read the novel but in it this awful man went for self-analysis and after six

Mary and Marilyn

months says to somebody, 'You know what I have found out?' And he said, 'What?' He said, ' I am basically a very nice man.'

BIGSBY: Your analyst was a Freudian?

MILLER: Rudolph Loewenstein was quite famous inside the profession. He was regarded as a great analyst, and a very serious guy. He was himself a man of some wisdom. One of my disillusions with the whole procedure came when I was invited to the New York Psychoanalytic Society to listen to a speech by Gregory Zilboorg, who was then the most famous psychoanalyst. It was about a play. He was Lillian Hellman's psychoanalyst. He was the horse's mouth.
I thought it would be interesting to see what they would make of this. I knew very little about anything then. I went there, and what Zilboorg did was to tell the story of a play, reading little scenes, pieces of scenes, and I thought, what is he going to say about this? He never said anything. He was just up there having a wonderful time reading these scenes. I looked around at the audience. The place was packed with analysts, and they were fascinated. I thought, what are they fascinated by? That was a shocker.

BIGSBY: So, when was your marriage finally over in your view, in fact, if not legally?

MILLER: I would say maybe 1954, something like that.

BIGSBY: Did she sense that kind of sensuality that went with the success that now surrounded you?

MILLER: Oh yes. She felt locked out, long before, I think. As I said, I was not paying the kind of attention to her she wanted for a long time before that. I could have been a monk in a cell for all my relationships mattered.

BIGSBY: And presumably you had no self-awareness about this at the time.

MILLER: Oh no. I remember getting angry at her once, because Leonard Bernstein asked me to have dinner with him, and both of us went. I had met him before, so I knew him a little bit. He wanted me to write a play he could musicalise. I was not about to do that, because I felt I was more important than he was. Mary was there, and it was around the time I was writing, or had just finished, *A View from the Bridge*, and she went on to tell him the play's story. I was very resentful that she presumed to do that, which was beastly of me, because she was being proud of it, but such was my absolute need to control my work that I didn't want anybody talking about it, because the play wasn't quite finished yet. That will give you an idea of how violent my self-absorption was. She had a tough row to hoe. Imagine living with a guy like that. I wouldn't want to be a woman in that position, or anybody.

BIGSBY: By this time, you had known Marilyn for several years and presumably she was in your mind.

MILLER: Oh yes, she represented a kind of agreeable support rather than this censorious strict viewpoint. Of course, she was like anybody else, but one didn't know it then.

BIGSBY: I am struck by the fact that, when you first met her, she seemed to accept everything in a kind of naive and open way, and that must have seemed a contrast with your marriage. She also represented the sensuality you talked about that success lifted you into. There was Mary, meanwhile, still in the same world. How long did she go on working as a stenographer?

MILLER: Oh, she was not working. She took care of the children. She had two young babies, so she had enough to do from about 1946.

BIGSBY: What were the grounds for the divorce, because divorce was still not that usual?
MILLER: I never even thought of that. They are so spurious you don't pay any attention to them.
BIGSBY: What was the impact of the divorce on the children?
MILLER: I am sure it must have been terrific. But we then got a very good relationship with each other.
BIGSBY: With the children or with Mary?
MILLER: No, with the children. I haven't seen Mary for years.
BIGSBY: What about after the divorce? What happened about the children? Did you have visitation rights?
MILLER: Yes, I saw them at least once, and sometimes twice a week.
BIGSBY: Were you both living in Brooklyn?
MILLER: No, after the divorce Marilyn and I had an apartment on East 57th Street, and that is where I lived when I wasn't in Roxbury.
BIGSBY: And when you went to see the children?
MILLER: I went home to the house and went in, and they were ready and eager to go somewhere. I would take them back to the other apartment, or we would do something together.
BIGSBY: What was the relationship now with Mary?
MILLER: It closed down, because she totally disapproved of everything. I haven't seen her for twenty-five years, something like that. Actually, I saw her once and didn't recognise her for a moment until she spoke. That was way back in the mid sixties. She had really changed, and now I regret not having made any attempt. I did make one

attempt to sit down with her, but she wouldn't stand for it. I just thought we ought to, but you couldn't do it.

BIGSBY: You mean you phoned her.

MILLER: Yes, but she didn't want to see me.

BIGSBY: She didn't remarry.

MILLER: No, she never remarried. However, she had a very active, interesting life apart from that with her profession. She worked with disturbed children for many years and became very good at it, I am told. She was a psychological counsellor to children in the public school system. Apparently, she did a lot of travelling. The children grew up into a cool era, psychologically cool era. Unlike my generation, by the time they were in their teens people were getting divorced all the time, especially at the level of society they were in, so I really think the impact was less than it might have been earlier. It was much more of a shock to my generation than it was to them.

BIGSBY: Was the divorce a bitter one, or by then had you both decided there was no other way?

MILLER: I think I probably wouldn't readily admit that I walked out on her, but she was ready to go herself. It just collapsed, the whole arrangement, because of me, basically, and the fact that I was involved with Marilyn. It would have happened anyway. There was no question in my mind. No doubt about it.

BIGSBY: Was there a sharp contrast between what Mary had been and what Marilyn was?

MILLER: Well, instead of a judgemental woman, Marilyn lacked any to the point of being indiscriminate. She just took each moment for what it was, or seemed to be, at that point. As she matured, of course, she became quite the opposite, because a kind of paranoia took over which had nothing to do with me. It was part of her mental problem. She began to suspect everybody of exploiting or damaging her.

BIGSBY: When, during the HUAC hearing, you said you were going to England with the person you were going to marry, Marilyn is quoted as saying that this was news to her, that this was the first she had heard of an implied proposal of marriage. Is that right?

MILLER: I think she was carrying out a programme we had cooked up together that we wouldn't announce this marriage because of the publicity. She may have been out of step there. We had already arranged to go to England together.

BIGSBY: Did she know you were going to make that announcement in the hearing?

MILLER: No, I didn't know myself.

BIGSBY: You must be aware how intriguing, and I suppose in a sense how baffling, that marriage with Marilyn seemed to people.

MILLER: There is something baffling about all my relationships. I cannot say I understand more than a fraction of them, quite frankly. I seem to drift through life touching whatever comes up and trying to find what it is made of. So, I cannot say that I really understand what happened.

BIGSBY: My impression is that you realised that that marriage was a mistake quite early on, in fact very early on. Two weeks after getting married you were in England and already seeing things that you hadn't really expected to see.

MILLER: The fundamental problem I had with the marriage was that it became clear that she needed constant help all the time.

BIGSBY: And you had not seen that before.

MILLER: We hadn't been together that much. Someone else might well have been able to say, 'You'll have to do something about your problem. I have got something else I have to do.' But I wasn't able to do that.

BIGSBY: Do you think that part of the attraction of your relationship may have lain in the fact that it was covert, the excitement of nobody knowing?

MILLER: Actually, we couldn't take a deep breath. The press was on her the whole time. If we went for a walk, we had to disguise ourselves. She did, anyway.

BIGSBY: When you were in England, she claimed to have read a note you had written saying that the only person you could really love was your daughter. There is a scene in *After the Fall* to that effect.

MILLER: Actually, I invented it.

BIGSBY: So there never was such an occasion as that?

MILLER: I was not really prepared for what I should have been prepared for, which was that she had literally no inner resources. She sensed that Laurence Olivier [who directed and starred in *The Prince and the Showgirl*] had some underlying contempt for her. I denied it at the time, because I was trying to keep things happy, but she was right. Once she would sense something like that in a person, or hostility in a person, it was as though they had actually taken out a weapon and threatened her. You couldn't say to her that everybody has hostile feelings of one kind or another, or has envious feelings, or anxious feelings, or whatever their feelings are, but that all that counts is what they act out, otherwise you would be in a constant state of suspicion about everything and everyone. That is not the way she could operate. As soon as there was any sign that she detected – sometimes real, sometimes not – it was as though somebody had actually attacked her, or was on the verge of attacking her. This led to a life that was full of suspicion, and it got to be very difficult very early on.

BIGSBY: How soon did you think that you had made a mistake? After all, you had only just come out of another painful marriage. Now the new one was seemingly flawed.

MILLER: Some months. But I expected it would change. I figured it was temporary. I expected these problems would disappear.

BIGSBY: They did at times, didn't they?

MILLER: They did at times, yes. It wasn't as though all hope was lost just because of that. My tendency was to diminish any feelings of my own that this was a dangerous situation, figuring that it wouldn't last, that her real nature was cheerful and optimistic. After all, we were together for four years. It wasn't really until we began to approach *The Misfits* that I really thought there was no hope for us, or for her. I began to think that she couldn't go on indefinitely this way.

BIGSBY: But there were good moments, and they surfaced, for example, in some of your short stories. What comes through is a kind of naivety, on her part, an innocence in particular about natural things. In fact, she seems sometimes to have gone over the top in her sensitivity with respect to animals.

MILLER: She was always over the top about animals, about children, old people. She could get fierce about protecting these things. She would identify with them in a way that was total. She became a fish. She would get absolutely outraged that somebody had killed a fish, even though she ate fish.

BIGSBY: How much of a blow was it to have miscarriages?

MILLER: She only had one while we were married. She had an ectopic pregnancy, which is not a miscarriage because no foetus was formed. [Cambridge University Press note: this historical conversation may not reflect current understanding of pregnancy stages and outcomes.][1] We tried with a very good doctor in New York, but he finally couldn't help. In a way, I am not sure how good it would have been for her to have a child. It would have been an additional problem.

BIGSBY: But there was a part of her that wanted a family, to be in a family.

MILLER: In an ideal sort of a way, but I am not sure how it would have worked out in practice. The pathology set in fairly soon. In England she had to be under terrific pressure, more than most actors, because she was performing with the fabulous Olivier, who at that time, to Americans anyway, represented the ultimate acting talent. And here she was trying to prove herself as a performer. So she was scared, and she needed all the reassurance she could get, and there wasn't enough in the world to do that. Unfortunately, it was right after our marriage, practically.

BIGSBY: Because you hadn't had very much relaxed time together before you got married.

MILLER: That's right. It happened to work out that it was a terribly tense era in her life, and in my life, and it would have been a miracle, I guess, for any marriage to survive that.

---

[1] Alternative definitions are, for example, found on the NHS's website miscarriage page: 'Sometimes, miscarriages happen because the pregnancy develops outside the womb. This is known as an ectopic pregnancy', https://www.nhs.uk/conditions/miscarriage/symptoms/ (accessed 10 April 2025).

We could relax a little bit in Roxbury. That was the saving grace of the farm at that time. It was much more remote then than it is now, when it is practically a suburb. We were the only non-farmers in the whole valley, and nobody bothered her. Of course, the echoes were always coming at you through the telephone. It is true we were in a pressure cooker.

BIGSBY: And so what happened in England took you by surprise. You weren't prepared for that, were you?

MILLER: No, totally unprepared. I realised that when, in a desperate attempt to normalise life, she wanted to go shopping in a department store, a store she had heard of. I guess it was Harrods. They had to close the store. I don't know if the queen of England would cause such a situation.

BIGSBY: But when things so quickly began to go wrong, how did you feel? Out of the frying pan into the fire?

MILLER: I felt defeated, but I was also determined, and I believed that it was possible that we could make a life together once this was over. But it kept getting more and more dense with difficulties, and of course it played right into her main problem, which was that she was abandoned, and the least criticism, the most remote kind of criticism, she immediately picked up on as being a prelude to another abandonment, because that was the pattern she understood. I felt, and I think she did too, that we could build an open kind of existence, open in the sense that it was both spiritual and physical and even intellectual, because Marilyn was a very smart woman. She would have been capable, had her psychological problems been reduced, though I don't think they could ever have been solved.

BIGSBY: I remember you saying that she never really finished a book. She would sum it up quickly and abandon it.

Yet a lot of other people have talked about how she was a voracious reader of books.

MILLER: Well, they saw it. I never did. She would get the sense of a book and that was enough. She was too distracted.

BIGSBY: Did she read your plays?

MILLER: She read two or three of them. I think she read *Salesman*. She read *The Crucible*. She saw *A View from the Bridge*.

BIGSBY: You were writing throughout this period and, did, of course, create *The Misfits*, but there is a sense in which you seem to have put your career on hold in a way that you presumably never thought you would have to.

MILLER: I spent four years doing nothing basically, excepting *The Misfits*.

BIGSBY: That must have built additional tensions in you, and potentially bitterness.

MILLER: In all situations of that kind there is no ground to them. After all, I wrote *The Misfits*, and it was by way of a gift. It was going to be a great part that showed she really was an actress, which almost everybody questioned, to say the least, and it ended up where it just increased her contempt.

BIGSBY: Why do you think it did?

MILLER: Because all of her relationships ended that way. I was with her longer than anybody in her life. Nobody had withstood it anywhere near as long as me.

BIGSBY: The shooting of *The Misfits* must have been extremely painful.

MILLER: There are times when it was agony for her, especially, but of course for everybody around her.

BIGSBY: Even though the relationship was over, and there was a lot of bitterness and regret, you hadn't emotionally entirely let her go. You still cared about her even when the divorce was over.

MILLER: Oh, certainly. I had the illusion, and it turned out to be an illusion, that if I didn't care for her, take care of her life, she would come to a catastrophic end, because she was living on the edge of her acceptance of life. Death was always on her shoulder, always; it was always there. After all she had tried suicide several times before we ever met.

BIGSBY: And she tried in your presence.

MILLER: One time I brought doctors to pump her out because she had swallowed enough stuff to kill her. So, I felt she was in a very delicate psychological position. As it turned out, it took some years, but it happened. It was beyond my powers or anybody else's to hold her back.

The self-destruction was terrifying. It was certainly beyond me to master it. I could never do it. I doubt that anybody could have.

BIGSBY: There was a twelve-year difference in age between you and Marilyn. You are enough of a Freudian to pick up on the fact that she used to refer to you at times as 'Papa'. Does that imply that she was looking for a husband and a father simultaneously?

MILLER: Oh yes. It is a common thing with everybody. Men are looking for mama.

She wanted a father, a lover, friend, agent, above all someone who would never criticise her for anything, or else she would lose confidence in herself. I don't know if that human being exists. But she could be delightful to be with. She had a terrific sense of humour, of irony and generosity. I had had a Black cleaning lady from Waterbury for some years before Marilyn, and I kept her on when Marilyn was here. Marilyn kept giving her clothes. She was a tiny woman, so Marilyn gave her a black fur piece and black stockings and black shoes and a little black cape, and one day we came in and there she was. Her name was Della. She was a sweet little woman, lying on a bed with her head propped up on one hand and dressed in all this clothing. And Marilyn said, 'Oh, you look wonderful, Della.' Della said, 'Too black.' She could be wonderfully kind and generous and gave away everything.

BIGSBY: How do you reconcile that kindness with her cruelty, because she could also be very cruel?

MILLER: Well, it is in all of us, isn't it? It depends on the situation; it depends on the frame of mind you are in at any one moment. If she felt threatened, she could be very cruel. It was a matter of interpreting some action. Of course, psychologically she had a right to feel threatened because she had been threatened. So, any sign of disagreement raised a spectre of expulsion and attack.

BIGSBY: During the shooting of *The Misfits*, she supposedly saw Yves Montand. Was that true?

MILLER: No, no, that's a myth. She was on the set in Reno. She was in no position to do that. The only flight out she took was when Huston had arranged a hospital in LA where she went for a week, because she couldn't be photographed any more, because the stuff she was taking was making her eyes look funny. She had to be in a hospital where they could supervise her intake, and that was the only time she ever left that set.

BIGSBY: The relationship was obviously collapsing and had collapsed by the time of *The Misfits*.

MILLER: Well, it hadn't collapsed as far as I was concerned, not when the picture started. When the picture started, I thought it would be easier. She could really start to function in the way she had always wanted to function, with the director she wanted, with a cast that she loved. Clark Gable, after all, was in essence her father, and Monty Clift was just lovely. She loved him, and Eli Wallach. The conditions were absolutely perfect. I had brought in Frank Taylor, who had been an old friend of mine, as the producer, so she wouldn't have any problem with the producer. It was an independent picture, really. United Artists weren't going to interfere. The conditions were perfect, and I thought we were going to now function the way I imagined we should.

BIGSBY: So it came to you as a shock when things unwound.

MILLER: When I realised that she could not accept this good fortune, that is when it started to disintegrate.

BIGSBY: What was it that made her behave the way she did?

MILLER: You know, there is a pattern in people's lives which gets repeated, and if it doesn't get repeated, they are at a loss. It didn't matter whether it was with Billy Wilder or John Huston, she had to feel that, when she was making a film, they were persecuting her. I think it derives from the very nature of there being a director. He has to correct her. He has got to say, 'No, that's not good', or whatever, and that relationship already raises the spectre of expulsion. She did it with Olivier, with Wilder, with Huston, though with Huston she had a hard time adopting that stance because he simply backed off. I suppose he instinctively knew it was hopeless for him to try to exert authority. He knew her from the past and realised he would have to wait her out, which he did. Therefore, the picture took months more than it was supposed to. I think it was a pattern she was simply helpless to change.

George Cukor directed her in that stupid movie *Let's Make Love*. He had the same problem. George couldn't have been a milder director. I just came across an interview Billy Wilder gave right after the making of *Some Like It Hot*, which is a masterpiece, incidentally. She was simply fantastic, though her suffering in making that film made her feel she was being crucified. Billy was asked by the interviewer, 'Would you work with her again?' He said, 'I certainly would, but my psychiatrist tells me I mustn't.'

BIGSBY: You say you turned up in Reno not really knowing the marriage was going to disintegrate. What was the moment when you realised it had gone the other way?

MILLER: There was no moment. It was just a daily growing awareness that this was beyond her control. There was no way for me, or anybody else for that matter, to break through that pattern. She was simply bound to feel victimised. It wasn't just me. We had a cinematographer. He was unique, in the sense that he never had more than one or two grips helping him. As he said, 'You need one light.' He never delayed a shot for two seconds, because he never believed in anything except the camera rolling, and he was quite right. He didn't have to fool around with enormous equipment. All he ever had was one or two lights at most, and a film in the camera. But she felt he was not treating her right. She said all he was interested in was how some oil well he had invested in in Oklahoma was going. It became apparent that it was beyond reason. There was no way that anybody could penetrate this.

BIGSBY: Would you, though, have carried on with the marriage?

MILLER: At that point I thought I might, but I became increasingly aware that she was genuinely hostile to me.

BIGSBY: Did you ever have a face to face in which she explained why?

MILLER: Well, the only one was in England when we got into an argument about whether Olivier was persecuting her. I thought, mistakenly, that I ought to reinforce Olivier's standing with her because, after all, he had to direct her, he had to play scenes with her. She couldn't trash him too much or where would she be? She would be left with nobody on that set, so I found myself defending him, and that was the worst possible thing I could have done. But I don't think any other course would have mattered either.

BIGSBY: The marriage came to an end in 1961.

MILLER: It came to an end much earlier than that.

BIGSBY: But when you left the set of *The Misfits* the marriage was effectively over.

MILLER: Oh yes, we weren't speaking. There was no way to approach her.

BIGSBY: But were she to have changed at that moment, would you have wanted to continue the marriage?

MILLER: Not really. I couldn't have gone on. It would have killed me. I couldn't work any more. I couldn't possibly have gone on. It was out of the question. If I hung on during *The Misfits*, it was purely seeing the project through, because Huston wanted me there in case there were any changes in the script. Apart from that, he wanted my reaction to what he was doing, and I felt obliged to be there. After all, I had spent a lot of time putting that movie together. Had it not been that way I would have been gone long before that.

BIGSBY: There are two different accounts of Marilyn's last visit to Roxbury after the divorce. In your account she comes up with her sister and has a coffee. Marilyn offered an account of what appears to be the same visit in which you are not present.

MILLER: She was wrong, because I helped load a few of the things she had left in her car. There were a few nicknacks in the place that belonged to her. I remember her sister. I had my Land Rover, which was then new, in the garage, and she had never seen it. In those days very few people had seen Land Rovers anyway. They were very distinctive, with the tyre mounted on the hood of the engine, and it was very interesting to her to see this. Indeed, she wondered why I had gone to England to buy a jeep. We had a little talk about that, and I was there, most definitely.

BIGSBY: What, fundamentally, led to her end?

MILLER: It was impossible for her to live, let alone with anybody. You couldn't go on with that intensity of life, and those drugs, and manage to survive.

BIGSBY: Do you resent the fact that people who interview you have this concern about that relationship which, after all, was a very small part of your life?

MILLER: Well, it's a distortion, of course. But I can understand it. I don't have to contribute to it very much. I have never gone on about it. She is in my autobiography because she was in my life.

BIGSBY: From 1955 to '64, though you were writing *The Misfits*, no new Miller play appeared in America. Why that hiatus?

MILLER: I have led a long, invisible life that is not published. I actually started writing plays on a regular basis in 1937. I wrote for ten years before *All My Sons* was produced. I think I wrote eight or ten full-length plays, and probably twenty-five radio plays in those ten years, none of which have ever appeared, except the radio plays were done on radio. So that by the time I arrived with *All My Sons* I had a long history of writing for the desk drawer. At the beginning of that nine-year period [between *A View from the Bridge* and *After the Fall*], I had been writing for a hundred years. Most of it was never published or produced. Then, of course, I had a bad marriage, which can take up a lot of your time, and I was just out of synch with the whole country, I think. That would have been true whether I married Marilyn or not. I simply could not find a way into the country any more. This was the great American century, so declared by Henry Luce, what somebody called the twenty-year century. I never believed it would last. I did not believe in the values they were espousing. I did not think it had a future, and I felt we would pay for it in one way or another, which we did in Vietnam. I could not begin to speak of it. It was as though I was living in a different world. I certainly could not speak of it as an artist. I did not know how to do it.

BIGSBY: Did you feel that there was an audience still there to address?

MILLER: I think the audience in the American theatre began to dissipate sometime in the sixties with the rise of the so-called avant-garde theatre. We lost a big audience in that period, but no new audience came to be, and now we have neither of them effectively. The people who come to a Broadway play are basically interested in seeing a personal appearance of the star, of an actor.

The decay of a theatre is marked, in my opinion, by the loss of the leadership of the playwrights. Where the playwrights are not the major attraction, the theatre is in decline. It becomes a show-shop for personal appearances, and it hardly matters what those stars perform in. The theatre as a tribune of what the people are feeling, what they are thinking, what society is doing, becomes diminished and far less interesting, and that is where we are now. I think that is partly due to circumstances in New York, and maybe they will be reproduced in Britain. I do not know. The costs of producing plays are immense, so the risks of producing a play with any new approach are going to be taken with far less alacrity. Also, the power of the critic becomes immensely greater as the power of the playwright recedes.

In New York we have, of course, as you know, a situation where there is one morning newspaper, and the greatest critic in the world can't be right all the time, and I don't think we have the greatest critic in the world. I have seen plays that are not great plays, but pretty good, and they should be in the theatre. There is no reason why not. They are entertaining, some of them are instructive, people are interested in them, but the very elegant ex-librarian who has the job of writing a review compares them to masterpieces, and of course they are not going to stand up. The truth of the matter is, we do not get great plays because we do not allow medium plays. They are not permitted to survive, and when that happens, gradually playwrights get the message that this is not a place to try to make a career. Therefore, they drift off into the movies, television, etc., and that is where we are now.

13

Inge

BIGSBY: When your relationship with Marilyn was over, and the shooting of *The Misfits* was finished, you were in some distress, but, within days, you re-encountered Inge Morath [a Magnum photographer], and a romance was born.

MILLER: Inge had an element that was very attractive. She was also an artist, so did not expect logic in human relations. She was a great relief, as you can imagine, because she didn't need anybody nourishing her along.

BIGSBY: Inge told me that you invited her to a meal and that she was very doubtful, because you had just come out of this relationship with Marilyn, and she did not want to get involved with someone who was just coming out of something. It must have been odd for you after the pain of the break-up. Did you both have doubts about getting married, her second marriage, your third?

MILLER: I did, only because the whole idea of marrying seemed a little doubtful. But the idea of getting out of her life, or her getting out of my life, was worse. Put it that way. We were hitting it off very comfortably quite quickly. I was sure I would never get married again, and anyway she would leave New York from time to time after we got together because she had jobs. She was still photographing all over the world. Marriage wasn't the idea. It was fear of losing her. I went in it with very grave doubts, as I told her. I told her I was probably not the person to be married to anybody. Gradually she wore me down.

BIGSBY: Because you weren't going to change, in the sense of work being the centre of what you did, and you were saying earlier that that was a contributory factor to the breakdown of your first marriage. In fact, if anything, you had rushed back to work after Marilyn, because you had had to put work on one side. So now it must have become even more important to you to get back to work.

MILLER: Oh, absolutely, but she was a great one to be around when you were working.

BIGSBY: And, of course, the difference is she wasn't in a subordinate role, as Mary had been.

MILLER: Not at all, and also she had her own independence, which was terrific. She wasn't waiting for me to come out of the room. She was busy doing something herself, which is, I think, a very positive thing for people in general, in this age.

BIGSBY: Is there a sense in which marriage to Inge made you more of an internationalist, because you went with her to Russia, to China, all over the world?

MILLER: It was so. There was no programme. I didn't know what I was doing, as usual, but that is the way it worked out, sure. I never thought that I wanted to be in so many different places, quite frankly, but it turns out I was.

BIGSBY: After you came back from Italy in that post-war period you said you really didn't want to go back to Europe again. You had been there. It was wrecked. America became your subject.

Inge

MILLER: I thought Europe was finished. I didn't know what was going to happen to it, but I thought its civilisation could never recover. I thought it was like after about the sixth century, and the Roman Empire, when the aqueducts ceased to carry water and the roads were getting overgrown. I thought that is where they were heading. I wouldn't know where to begin to revive the civilisation, and therefore this country became the last bastion of any kind of operating society. Whether it was good, bad, or indifferent, it was operating. You picked up the phone and it rang someplace, and the phone bill came. When I was in Italy you sat in a room with a nice middle-class family with one twenty-watt bulb hanging from the ceiling of a not inconsiderable apartment, and a brazier of charcoal on the floor where people sat around holding their hands over the charcoal. The radiators were there for internal heat, but they were ice cold. There was no heat, and I thought that is the way it ends.

BIGSBY: Inge brought with her a personal history as well as a public history. Hence your visit to a concentration camp.

MILLER: Sure, though she, like most of them, really didn't know how bad it was. They knew people disappeared. Jews disappeared from the neighbourhood. Where did they go? Well, they went east to re-colonise, or some such story, and when the truth began to come out, it was as horrifying as it would be if it happened in England. They regarded themselves as civilised people. They regarded the Nazis as being simply right-wing, but nevertheless a civilised group of people.

BIGSBY: Inge told me that her father joined the party in the spring of 1945 and tried to persuade her to join when the game was over for everyone to see.

MILLER: I tell you, the political stupidity of Germans is unique. It is so stupid. They are so in the embrace of authority, regardless of what it is. Someone said they made the best fascists and the best communists, and that attitude of obedience to authority has betrayed them time after time. They ennoble it. It is noble in their minds, and it is inconceivable to other people, but it is quite ordinary. It must go back into the mists and fogs of history.

If I have learnt one thing, it is that some people are blessed with a so-called good past, some are cursed with a bad past. The Balkans, for example, had a very bad past. It is full of conflict between clans, which is all it is, because they are all worshipping the same alleged deity and many of them speak similar, or the same, languages. The United States were lucky in one respect, because the original matrix was set up by people who had a democratic, progressive idea of life, so when things got very bad you could always revert to that. That remains a default mechanism. When everything else fails you go back to that, time after time.

BIGSBY: How did you get to stay in the Chelsea Hotel?

MILLER: Inge was the one who recommended it because she had stayed there. And Mary McCarthy had led her to it in the early fifties, so that she would spend a week or two there, and I was trying to avoid the perversity that was surrounding my breakup with Marilyn. So that seemed a good place to go, but we found out that they were spreading the news far and wide. In the end I was there for six years. That was our home, though we were back and forth, but at the Chelsea more than in Roxbury, until [our daughter] Rebecca had to go to school. That was 1968. When I went there, I had never heard of the Chelsea. I didn't know anything about it at all. But it became a hang-out for sixties people, including Andy Warhol. We had a lovely apartment there, two bedrooms, a big living room, a separate kitchen.

We decided to move to Roxbury because of Rebecca. The sixties were very rough in New York. In the Chelsea especially there was a lot of dope. It was not a good place to bring up a kid. They were lying out in the halls. It was a terrible atmosphere. So, we decided to get out and move up to Roxbury. We would come down, and I would need a hotel. But it got to be very difficult, because New York became very popular. Often, you couldn't get a hotel overnight, so we decided to buy an apartment on East 68th Street. When I was married to Marilyn, we rented an apartment on 57th Street. It was a beautiful apartment.

BIGSBY: Where did you find it easiest to work?

MILLER: I occasionally work in our apartment, but I would rather work in Roxbury.

BIGSBY: Once Rebecca had gone off to university, you could have moved back into New York.

MILLER: One thing was that Inge had all her stuff at Roxbury, truckloads of it that she had stored in New York. But I just loved the country, especially in decent weather. We spent a lot of time in New York, but are mostly always in Roxbury, especially when Rebecca was going to school.

BIGSBY: Is there a sense that you are closer, in some respects, to democracy, living in Roxbury? A town meeting makes no sense in Manhattan.

MILLER: Very definitely. Oh yes. We've got a problem right now. Later this month, there's going to be a meeting. A big gas line is being moved down from Canada through all of New England to end up servicing Long Island to the South, which is a long way from Roxbury. They want to come right through my property with a 500-foot right of way on both sides of that line. There are some people in this town who own three acres of land. They've put their whole lives into three acres of land. If that pipe passes through their land, they can't sell that land any more, because you cannot build on top of the pipe. It is buried under the ground. With one blow, some ex-schoolteacher, or somebody who has managed to save up enough money to buy three acres, is simply wiped out. Now we are going to have a big fight.

I was instrumental in stopping a power line, a high-tension wire that was supposed to come right over my house. It turned out it was totally unnecessary. We did studies, we hired people, and it turned out they didn't need it at all. It never will be built. I now have to make a decision about what I think of this pipeline, because I know they are all going to be looking to me to see what I think. I have another idea already. We have an old railroad that hasn't been used in fifty years. They could come down that railroad bed. I wonder whether they know it's there in the woods. [Speaking later, he said] I was one of those who organised a resistance to it and drove them out of here. So we had a big town meeting, and people got up and said, 'I've been living here for eleven years.' Then others got up and said, 'I've been living here four years or five years.' And it turned out that I had been living there almost longer than anybody. Then one girl got up – she was wonderful – and said, 'My family came here in 1684.' There was clearly a kind of continuity.

BIGSBY: So the public and private are much closer in Roxbury.

MILLER: Absolutely. You can't have a conversation without bringing in society, because all these people have to make decisions all the time, whether to pave a road if it is not used, whether to close it, how much money to put into schools, all that stuff. But things have changed over the years, because now the place is occupied, for the most part, by people who are not indigenous here. Actors and writers gradually discovered this place, because before nobody within ten miles knew where this place was. But they found it, and a lot of them moved in here. Now I am probably the oldest inhabitant, and I have been for years. Of course, I also love to make stuff, and I have this wonderful workshop to make furniture, and there are working-class guys around who are helpful and come by and shoot the breeze.

BIGSBY: The thing that has come home to me is how important that relationship with Inge would turn out to be, and not just in personal terms. I wonder if you had not met her whether *After the Fall* would have been the same play. *Incident at Vichy* wouldn't have come along, *Playing for Time* might not, *Broken Glass* might not. She brought something new into your life.

MILLER: I could easily have slipped into a kind of complete negativism. As a writer I would probably have gone on writing, because I have always written, but I think it would have been a different kind of writing. It would probably have been a more defeated kind of writing. Who knows if it would have been better or worse, I don't know; it would have been different.

BIGSBY: Not long after first meeting her she took you to Mauthausen concentration camp. It obviously had a profound effect on Inge. What impact did it have on you?

MILLER: At that time there were no tourists around. There was nobody there. We had to rouse a keeper, who was sleeping in some shack, to get him to open the gate for us and let us in. Mauthausen was unlike the other concentration camps in one respect. It was obviously permanent. It had a stone wall that was several feet thick, and probably 20 feet high. This was no barbed wire. It had big iron gates. They intended to go on killing people for a long time, and once they had eliminated all the Jews it would not have taken very long before they would have wanted to put all the Poles in there. I think they were going to kill the Poles as a nation, totally, and maybe some of the other East Europeans. We had been saved from a kind of permanent feudalism. That was the idea.

BIGSBY: Why did you think Inge took you there?

MILLER: I think she wanted to confront herself there. After all, her father was a flier in World War I and World War II. He flew stuff into Stalingrad. He was too old to be a fighter pilot, but he could fly. I am almost certain he was sold on National Socialism, although, ironically, he had no anti-Semitism in him. He didn't know what that was about. It seems impossible. There was a Jewish scientist who he had been working with for some time, right into the Nazi period, and the guy came in one day and said he had to get out of the country because he was afraid for himself. He did not know how to do that, because he was afraid he would be picked up if he went on a train. He had no car, so Edgar, Inge's father, put him in the trunk of his own car and drove him over the Swiss border. He never made the connection.

I remember him sitting in the living room here when Nixon was explaining some of his shenanigans, and there he was, 3 feet away from the television, nodding approval of Nixon. One finds it hard to believe, but he respected authority, no matter of what kind. Once, I think in the 1940s, before World War II, the Russians were inviting a lot of German scientists to come to Russia to work, because they needed these people, and they invited him. He was a forestry expert, and that is what they were doing. He knew how to make plywood and paper and the rest of it, and they offered a good salary. His wife put her foot down and said he wasn't to go, because she feared he would be arrested at some point and come to harm. When the war ended, he was practically psychologically inert, as he found out what was going on in the camps. Inge had to get straightened out about all this for herself.

BIGSBY: She was going round the camp with someone who was Jewish.

MILLER: It was a way of expunging all this.

BIGSBY: But it must have been significant to you as well. You knew all about the camps, but from a distance. When you went to Italy in 1947 you saw camp survivors but seem not really to notice them. Now, suddenly, here you were. You were with a woman from Europe whose roots in the past were vital to what she was, and suddenly you were inside one of these camps which, to you, had only been an idea before.

MILLER: On meeting Inge, I suddenly got a human view of the whole thing. It was not simply a Jewish view of it. It was human, in the sense that the wholeness of that tragedy began to seep in on me. The tragedy of it became very poignant, because she suffered in the course of the war by virtue of her sensitivity, and I hadn't suffered at all. She had suffered far more, and here I am, the Jew, who came through without a scratch while she damn-near starved to death and was abused, and everything else, by cannibals.

This was before the Holocaust had become the coinage it later became. If you had asked almost anybody at that time whether anyone was going to remember any of this in ten years, they would have told you no. Already there were signs. The German educational system had obliterated the whole thing. It never happened. So, a whole generation had gone through school knowing nothing, and here is this monstrous building standing there deserted. I could easily put myself in the position of walking through that gate, or being driven through that gate, into that place. There were rooms in there that were obviously torture rooms. There was a stone square with a drain which was clearly for blood to be drained out. What they were doing was, first of all, knocking all the gold out of people's teeth, and I think they were probably operating on people alive, all kind of medical things. They were ghouls, ghouls in charge of a country.

BIGSBY: Did all this really enter into your sensibility then in a way that it had not done before by virtue of being there and seeing it?

MILLER: It made me certain that I had to write about this, in one way or another. The use of those images in themselves was not interesting to me. All that was interesting to me was to describe the death of love, people who were incapable any more of the human connection. I was not just concerned with the victims, but with our relations with each other, or anybody.

BIGSBY: Then you went to the trial of a number of Auschwitz guards in Frankfurt. Why, after going to the concentration camp, did you then want to go there?

MILLER: I had never seen a Nazi. When I read that the trials were happening, I thought I will go there just for a day and see what is going on, see some of these guys, see the horns on their heads. But there weren't any. They were just insignificant little jerks, such as we have everywhere except, when they were killing, they had the power of life and death over people. That was the strength of National Socialism. You take an idiot, give him power of life and death over people, and you have got a system.

14

―◇―

After the Fall and Daniel

BIGSBY: In 1964, you staged *After the Fall*. What brought you to that play, at that time, a play which touches on personal, political and a profound moral failure, the last represented by the tower of a concentration camp which looms over the stage?

MILLER: It is always difficult to know the answer to that question. I think that in part theatre had become private, insulated, and I just thought I would like to open it up and try and throw something on the stage that I thought was at the centre of our moral and political problems of the period. The play is really about the question of survival, how one spiritually survives a wreckage and still sustains some grip on life. The play is really about the death of love, and how one walks away from that and still feels some grip on existence. To be sure, you wouldn't know that from the way the play was handled in the press. But that is what it is about.

Why then? I remember one day going to the American Psychological Association. They asked me to join in a discussion. Someone raised a question about the scientific nature of Nazi experiments on concentration camp inmates. They used people as guinea pigs. For example, they would throw people into a swimming pool with instrumentation on them and drown them. The question someone asked was, why wasn't that science? I was surprised, because this was an audience of scientists. I looked around for someone to get up and tell us why it wasn't science. As I was talking, I realised that these people really didn't know why it wasn't science. They were all PhDs and doctors, and I thought, if we had a government which was especially crazy, run by essentially insane people, who had decided to make a test of what the human being could withstand, and had thrown people into a body of water connected by instrumentation to gauges, some of these people would find a rationale to do that.

I made some kind of an outraged statement to them and told them that they really ought to question their brains and their training if they could sit there and listen to the posing of that question without emotion. A couple got up and said that unfortunately it was science. Incidentally, it turns out that there was a long report by American scientists, who were finally given access, by the German government, to the Nazi records, which said that the science was simply absurd, that those who conducted the experiments were simply sadists, that they anyway knew nothing about how to conduct experiments. The material they got was totally worthless.

BIGSBY: For all that, it is a play which works its way towards some kind of grace. It is your first play in which you don't kill off a central character.

MILLER: I thought it was too late to kill anybody. I'd better start thinking of how to prevent people jumping off a bridge. It is true, I tried to explain why one lives after living through half or more of the twentieth century. That is what that play is trying to do.

BIGSBY: In *After the Fall*, the central character looks back over failed marriages in his personal life, but also over a century of failed values, and that work seems to have been a very important one to you, almost as though it came at a personal and historical balancing point in some way.

MILLER: It did, it certainly did, and the last production I saw of it was directed by my daughter in Cincinnati, with a group of actors of whom only one or two were professionals. The set was a house that had burned down, and they were moving around in this burnt house. It was terrific.

BIGSBY: How did Kazan come to be the director of *After the Fall*?

MILLER: That happened because he was the director of the Lincoln Center, and I would have to admit, in all honesty, that they could not have found a better one. Robert Whitehead had been a co-producer of *A View from the Bridge*, and I had always admired and liked him, and finally, after a lifetime of my saying how about having a repertory company, he got the public theatre which I had been looking for. They had not done anything yet, did not have a building or anything, and he came to me and asked if I would write a play for them. I was in the middle of that play then, and Gadge was the director of the theatre; that is literally how it happened.

They had already begun to collect a company some months before I got involved with it, and I felt that I was in a situation where I would have to perpetuate a blacklist, quite frankly, if I did not use Kazan. To my mind nobody was better prepared than he to run a theatre of this kind. It was not possible to deny that. I had not even seen him in all those years, and I thought, well, do I feel that somebody has a right to his artistic life or not, though I still do not approve of what he did and never have. I had written the play before I knew who or where or what was going to produce it. In fact, I was still working on it when I finally agreed that we would do it there in the theatre. But it was a weird situation.

BIGSBY: The central character is moving from one marriage to another. You yourself were in that position, having been married to Marilyn before marrying Inge Morath. It was a personal play in that sense.

MILLER: Yes, it was. Now it is an impersonal play by this time.

BIGSBY: If I turn back to your personal life, your daughter, Rebecca, was born and then your son, Daniel, who had Down syndrome. What were the circumstances of his birth?

MILLER: We didn't plan for a child. It just happened, and at that time we were not able to detect his condition in the womb. You can now.

BIGSBY: Were you there for the delivery?

MILLER: Yes, I knew immediately. The doctor kept denying it. I knew it from his hands. They have one crease across the palm, a whole line.

BIGSBY: And how was a decision made as to what to do?

MILLER: I had a cousin who was similarly afflicted, and he had two sisters who were older than him. One never got married. The other did and spent half her life taking care of him. She never had any children of her own, and I was brought up in the next street, so I knew how they reacted to him. He was miserable, this boy. We could all play ball. He was my age. He could do nothing, but wanted to. He wanted to be like everybody else, but that was impossible. He didn't have the coordination. He couldn't see that well. So,

I thought the best thing would be if we could find a way of bringing him up among people who he could possibly not compete with [and with whom] he wouldn't feel different. [In fact the advice given to the Millers and others in their circumstances at that time, both in the United States and the UK, was to hand the child over to professionals who were better placed to provide the necessary support.]

BIGSBY: How quickly did you make that decision?

MILLER: Very early on, because as soon as I saw him I thought of my cousin.

BIGSBY: So, actually in the hospital, at that moment?

MILLER: I said we mustn't start in the wrong way, because we would end up with everybody miserable. In fact, it ended up quite well. He works. He has got a job. He gets paid. He worked for a long time at the synagogue, moving chairs around and helping out. Then he worked in a restaurant. They loved him. He is a very sweet, hard-working guy. He gets on with people beautifully, all kinds of people. He has to take a bus to go to his job, and the bus drivers know him. They make the change for him. It is a small town. Today [in 2001], he has a job and lives semi-independently within a family setting.

BIGSBY: So you never regretted that.

MILLER: No, on the contrary. He lives in an apartment with another wonderful guy like him.

BIGSBY: He is supported in the community.

MILLER: Yes. They look in every day. They see what needs doing, what he needs, and we visit him frequently.

BIGSBY: That must have been a real trauma for you both.

MILLER: You accept these things as fate.

BIGSBY: But you came back from the hospital without a child.

MILLER: Yes, that was difficult for Rebecca. She wanted to know where he was, as she had been expecting him. It took a lot of explaining.
BIGSBY: What did you say to her?
MILLER: We told her the truth.

15

The Price and Vietnam

BIGSBY: You had a very successful play in 1968, *The Price*, in which two brothers, Victor and Walter, and Victor's wife, Esther, come together to sell the furniture left by their dead father. What did you learn from working on it with actors many years later?

MILLER: There was one concrete thing. I haven't seen that play in God knows how long. It is done all the time, but I was never near a production. It occurred to me, in watching a rehearsal [at the Young Vic, 1990], that there are two offstage characters, the mother and the father. I had always assumed that it was the father who was the vital centre of everything and, three or four days ago, began telling an actor who was playing Esther that I thought she ought to be standing in relation to a harp, which the dead mother used to play. Suddenly, it occurred to me that the unbidden guest was the mother, that she really formed Victor rather than the father. She, in effect, betrayed the father, when he lost his money. She devalued him right then and there, with one gesture. She vomited on him when he told her he was bankrupt. Victor's allegiance sprang immediately to the father.

Also, I never really understood the line that Solomon [the antique dealer buying the brothers' furniture] says. He is willing to part with any piece of furniture in that room, but not the harp. The harp is the heart and soul of the deal. I was telling an actor, Marjorie Yates, how to do something and I said, 'You are the surrogate mother here. You are the one that prevents this play from ending really early. They have got to fight it out for you, whose approbation they want. They both keep looking at you for whether you approve, or disapprove, of what they are saying.' When he said that it was the heart and soul of the deal I thought, yes, that is right. It is that mother who is the heart and soul of that deal. The reason they are tearing each other apart is their relationship with her. The father is only there for them to identify with, or not, but she is the prize. I never thought of it.

BIGSBY: So, your own plays still have the capacity to surprise you?

MILLER: Occasionally, yes. For example, I saw a production of *All My Sons* and it brought up something I had never thought of. Aidan Quinn did a fantastic job playing the son, Chris. His relationship with Ann was so intense and so romantic. It had never been played that way. It was very moving. It had never moved me before. You do get surprised. Actors are very, very important for telling you what you wrote.

BIGSBY: The major political issue of the 1960s was the Vietnam War. How did you first become involved in the anti-war movement?

MILLER: I can tell you exactly. It was quite early on. There was a teach-in at the University of Michigan which started that whole movement. They invited me to come out, and I did and made a speech in Hill Auditorium, along with the head of the United Autoworkers Union. I spent several days there, and it was a continuous discussion going into the night from 10 o'clock in the morning. Then, the Reverend Coffin, who had been in the CIA, called me from Yale, where he was the chaplain of the university, and asked me to come down, because they were going to have a meeting on the Green against the war. I went, and he made a hell of a speech. He was great. He was a great talker, and I made a speech and probably a couple of other people. So they were the first interventions that I was actually engaged in.

BIGSBY: Did you get any response to this?

MILLER: Abuse, mostly. For example, the local high school in Torrington, which is a neighbouring town here, invited me to come and talk to the students, and the local American Legion erupted and threatened all kinds of recriminations. They threatened the students. They threatened the teachers. It was really rough. I went down there, and I spoke about the war, and I saw several adults taking notes, to send to the government no doubt because they were very right-wing there. It was a Catholic area, and this was before there was any disillusionment about the war. They thought the war was going to be over in a few months and everybody would be coming home, like after World War II. People still had the illusion that this was good against evil. There were a lot of religious objections to what I was doing, and total ignorance. They didn't know where Vietnam was. It was pitiful, terrible. It took 56,000 men dead to teach them what it was, as well as dislocating the whole country permanently.

BIGSBY: Did you feel any inhibition about appearing on public platforms?

MILLER: I hated it. I have always hated it. The alternative, though, was to sit there silently when you knew there were certain things that could be said. That seemed to me a kind of imperative. I suppose I have always had, in the back of my mind, the conviction that repression was always possible in any society, and that if that ever happened, and I didn't say what I could have said, it would be hard to live with myself. I sometimes think that if I had put a different name on my plays, I could have lived anonymously, and this guy who wrote the plays could have answered his mail, and then I would have had a much more placid and productive life, because you take a lot of crap from people if you get out there in front. It takes up a lot of psychic time. You don't just stand up and make a speech: it reverberates for days afterwards. On the other hand, I suppose it is a kind of engagement which is productive in its own way.

BIGSBY: Yet the writer in this country, unlike the writer in France, has never really been thought to be that kind of public conscience of the nation.

MILLER: A writer here, I think, is probably basically an entertainer. People don't think of him as being some kind of instructor or moral conscience, or whatever you want to call it. He is basically like an actor. He is an actor who writes. There is an Anglo-Saxon aversion to connecting art with anything else but art.

BIGSBY: Look at Pinter. It is as though he were being asked what kind of business it is of his to be having an opinion on this.

MILLER: What does he know about it? I wonder where that came from? It is the Anglo-Saxons. That is why they loved Reagan. Reagan would never bother you with an idea.

The Price *and Vietnam*

BIGSBY: When you travelled to Cambodia you went really just to explore the culture. It wasn't a political trip. But you happened to be there at a critical moment.

MILLER: That was Inge's idea. She wanted to photograph there.

BIGSBY: What happened? How did you discover what was going on?

MILLER: I knew there was trouble, but I was totally vague about it because there was no real reportage coming out of there that I knew of. After a day or two there we were riding through the countryside on a little dirt road in a motor-driven, three-wheel vehicle. The Vietnam War was on, of course, and I said to Inge, 'It would be funny if a guy popped out of this foliage with a rifle in his hand and stopped us.' I was joking, of course. Well, it didn't take long before that was happening, and I remember asking our guide, who was a very polite, even-tempered, beautifully neat, nicely uniformed guy, who worked for the government as a guide, whether there was any feeling about the Vietnam War here in this country. He erupted in an amazing kind of anger, saying, 'We are not that kind of people. We do not believe in struggle of this kind.' And that convinced me that there was a real problem in the country, and of course in short order Pol Pot was running around killing 7 million people.

BIGSBY: And then the American bombing began while you were there.

MILLER: Mr Kissinger had decided to bomb western Cambodia, which was indeed a passageway for the North Vietnamese to come into the South, and we didn't know that. There was no declaration of war. There was nothing. All we knew was that one morning, in the little hotel we were in, the French arrived, let's say on a Tuesday morning, filled up the dining room, and then suddenly the next morning they were leaving, which was unusual, because it took at least two days to go through those temples. They had endless sculptures, gorgeous sculptures, when they weren't torn away and sold.

Anyway, an English family named Foxton – he had been the head of Shell Oil in the Philippines – was there on a vacation, and he knew this part of the world a little bit. His daughter, Penny, was the same age as Rebecca, and they were playing around with their dolls out of sight while we were sitting there having lunch, I guess, and these French were leaving the ship like rats. They were getting into all these vehicles and taking off. I said, 'Isn't it odd that they only stayed a few hours, hardly overnight?' Foxton began to smell something funny when our daughters arrived and said the swimming pool was full of soap. I said, 'What are you talking about?' They said, 'Yes, it is all full of soap. You can't swim in there.' We just dismissed this as some kind of aberration. We went on eating, and then they came back in and said, 'The swimming pool is empty. It has been emptied.' 'Oh well, then, they must have washed out the swimming pool.' Foxton said, 'We had better enquire about all this.' So we asked the manager, and he said, 'No, no, there is nothing wrong. Just stay where you are and enjoy your vacation.' But the French were leaving with a kind of manic determination. They knew something we didn't know, I figured.

So I called the American consulate, or embassy, in Phnom Penh, and some guy got on the blower and said, 'No, no. Nothing is happening. It is perfectly okay. Enjoy your vacation. We know you are there.' 'But what is happening?' 'Nothing, nothing.' Of course, they had already closed

Phnom Penh airport during this conversation. The bombing was going on in eastern Cambodia. The French knew the real story, that at any moment this war was going to be overwhelming the area, and this son of a bitch was telling us to stay there because they wouldn't admit that Mr Kissinger had done what he was doing, namely, ordering this bombing. Foxton had buddies in Phnom Penh, people he knew, and he made some calls and said, 'We've got to get out.'

By this time the French had commandeered all the vehicles, naturally, but there was one bus, a ten- or twelve-passenger bus, so we, in effect, bought that bus. It cost a couple of hundred bucks, and he would drive us to the border with Thailand, which was an American colony. It was four and a half hours over no roads, a bunch of fallen rock. So, we got in that bus at 4.30 the next morning and took off. But before we took off Foxton said, 'Do you mind? I have a friend in Phnom Penh who is going to go with us.' I said, 'Sure.' Well, this guy arrived, a very good-looking young man, and he jumped on board, and we took off, and ten miles out of town we were stopped by troops, and they were looking under the seats and luggage racks, and this British guy began talking to them in Cambodian, and that was a relief. I was happy to hear that. It turned out he worked for a big British training company. It is the most famous in the world, and he could speak Cambodian; he could speak Thai. He was probably a British spy. I was very happy to have him on board, and we arrived at the Thai border but couldn't go into Thailand, so stopped at a gorge which had a wooden bridge which was just collapsing. The gorge was about nine miles deep, and that bridge was really on its last legs, but we managed to walk across with our luggage on board with the little girls. We got to this Thai army post where, indeed, there were all these French who had left us, and the question was, where do we go from here?

There was no transport to go to Bangkok, and Foxton came over and said, 'How much money have you got?' I said, 'Well, I have got about two to three hundred dollars in my wallet.' He said, 'Let me have it, because I'll put in what I've got, and we could get a car. There's a Thai captain who will arrange that, but we mustn't make any sound about it.' He said, 'Come with me', and we walked behind a counter where people go with passports, opened the door and went in. There was a captain. We had got our money, and he was going to get us, I guess, an army vehicle. The door opened, and some Frenchman stuck his head in, and the captain said, 'I can't do it because he saw this happening.' So, we were stuck. Finally, Foxton, God knows how – he was a very resourceful guy – produced this Fiat. There was Foxton, his wife and daughter, Rebecca, Inge and I, and a driver and baggage in this car that was as big as a small desk. Before we got in, a woman came over and said to me, 'This is our car.' I said, 'I don't think so. I think this is ours.' She said, 'Well, my husband has heart trouble.' I said, 'We have these two young children. I'm sure there will be something along. You are not going to stay here forever.' And she said, 'You're calling yourself a humanitarian.' I said, 'Not today.'

Anyway, we did get to Bangkok, and that was where I saw the tragedy of it all. I met a man named Paul Garrison, who was a descendant of Garrison the great abolitionist. He was a marvellous man who was in Bangkok, I think, on vacation, but maybe he had some special secret business. He was a very close friend of our consulate representing the American government in Vietnam and was a major player in that whole thing. We started talking about the Vietnam War, and I was telling him what a corrupt thing this was from day one.

One day during the war, when we got back from Cambodia, within weeks I got a letter from a Colonel Miller at West Point. He was on the faculty and was inviting me there. The officers who had fought there and had come back to West Point to teach were desperate for me to tell the world that this war had to stop. These were all young, mostly infantry colonels. They took the real shit for however long they were there, and they still remember that visit.

BIGSBY: In the 1970s you wrote a play called *The Archbishop's Ceiling* in which writers in an unnamed Eastern Europe gather in an old archbishop's palace in which there may or may not be microphones concealed in the ceiling.

MILLER: I had spent some time in Eastern Europe, and it had occurred to me many times in Czechoslovakia, and in Russia as a matter of fact, that when I was talking to people, indoors especially, sometimes in automobiles, we were being taped, and that in some very subtle way the people with whom I was speaking, dissident people who hated the system, were editing what they were saying to protect themselves against that tape or people they might mention. This seemed to replicate to me what was happening in free societies, where we were also doing some editing, and that the total truth about what we felt was being distorted or suppressed, sometimes for conscientious reasons, sometimes for political reasons. So, I wanted to illuminate that process of self-editing. Basically, that is why the play was written, but the metaphor of it seemed to me the strongest in a country where they knew that most conversations were being edited, but they were never sure.

BIGSBY: Insofar as it touches on a dissident writer, it has another significance. As a past president of PEN International presumably you must feel acutely about the position of writers around the world, including Salman Rushdie.

MILLER: Yes, that is a scandal that won't go away, I do not suppose, for a long time. I cannot imagine now why they are going to lift that fatwa; I do not see what the impulse would be, unless the whole government of Iran should change. It is a scandal, nothing less.

16

The Eighties

BIGSBY: The connection between the private and the public is central to your work, certainly in your 1980 play, *The American Clock*.

MILLER: I could not get anybody's attention with that, really, and it failed. Now they are all excited about it; some of the biggest companies are involved in making a film of it. They have discovered that we had a Depression in the 1930s which nearly ended America as we know it. We came very close to a revolution of a sort, and many of the syndromes were repeated in the nineties. People lost their positions and are losing them now. One big corporation after another is closing down, and 25, 35, 40,000 jobs go in a morning. So these people understand what *The American Clock* is all about, but in the eighties that was not happening. There was expansion and prosperity. The impulse behind that play, it seemed to me at the time, was that there was no history any more. The so-called abstract theatre eliminated the past. No character had a root in any experience of the past. Human beings were seen as blips on a screen which appear and disappear. *The American Clock* was to warn audiences, and tell them, that two cars in every garage was not the beginning of the world. There was a time when getting a loaf of bread was a great triumph for middle-class people. The roots of much of what we have turned into were to be found in surprising places. It was really to create a history in the minds of the audience. In fact, where it has been done it has had that effect.

BIGSBY: *The American Clock* came out at the beginning of the 1980s, and that decade was an example of a materialism seemingly severed from history.

MILLER: I knew that was happening, that it was going to happen, that it was getting worse. We ended up with a Reagan who was a reassurance of the value of greed, that it was a social value, that greed is what makes the world go around. Goodness, and camaraderie, drop out of it. It is unspeakable.

The American Clock is devised as a mural, which means it is a large picture of a society with the details being individual portraits that are seen up close. But from a distance it should show a vast movement of a whole society. Part of my impulse was not only to deal with the Depression itself, but with the idea of survival. The fact of the matter is these were the same people who fought World War II, who went on to create a new age, with all its faults and its hopes. They were not defeated.

BIGSBY: Are you surprised your plays have found an international audience, and not just those of the forties and fifties?

MILLER: I look at my plays with such a special viewpoint I can't imagine that anybody else would connect with them. It reassures me somehow – it probably shouldn't, but it does – that there's a universal human being, because if we are not profoundly all that different then maybe there's hope for us if we last another thousand years, that there is such a thing as a human culture rather than a tribal one. That means we have some means of creating a permanent peace, that we have common interests, a common characteristic, because when I went to China the experts were all telling me they are never going to understand this play [*Death of a Salesman*]. The mistake they made is what we generally make. They said there hasn't been a salesman in China since, the latest, 1949, and even then they were gone. Of course, it doesn't depend on a salesman. It depends on a father, a mother and children. That's what it is about. The salesman part is relatively incidental, because it is his social side. It is what he does to stay alive. He could be a peasant.

BIGSBY: Do you think the same thing would apply to *The American Clock*, which is set during the Depression?

MILLER: Well, if you think about it for a moment, any catastrophe that a country has gone through, whether it be a war or a depression, that shakes it up so that the structure of a society is questionable, there would probably be a similar thing, I should think, because *The American Clock* is preoccupied, a lot more than my other plays, with the social side of man, how he relates as a citizen. If it is humanly valid, it probably would have an audience.

BIGSBY: Virtually all your plays make that connection between the public world and the private world, but here it is part of the structure of the play.

MILLER: Yes. Also, it is avowedly about people whose social trouble is not an incidental part of their lives. It is at the centre of their lives, because the one thing about the Depression was that society was in the bedroom, in the living room. You could no longer talk about a private life in the normal sense of the word. Seventy per cent of the people on the block had lost their jobs. What the hell else are you going to talk about? Then the petty mother-in-law jokes, the problems with sex, become, relatively speaking, boring. The interesting thing is what is going to happen tomorrow, what is Roosevelt going to say tomorrow? People woke up in the morning and got the newspaper to see whether he had invented something. Maybe he got a new idea, because it was all being improvised. We weren't Russians who had a five-year plan which some heavy thinkers had worked out. We were Americans. Sometimes a problem would go on for six months and you'd say, well that didn't work. I don't know what got into me to start that. Let's scrap it and start something else. The place was full of initials – WPA, CCC, NIRA. It became a joke after a while. So, *The American Clock* is preoccupied with the common fate of people caught in a national dilemma. It's really about the survival of that country. After all, the British were in the Depression just as much, if not worse, than we were.

BIGSBY: It's not hard to see elements of your own personal history appearing in that play. Are you in a way not merely tackling a public and a social issue, but laying to rest ghosts from your own past?

MILLER: Oh, definitely. I made no real attempt to disguise that. I was looking at a very young man mainly a little more warmly than I ought to when I was writing it. I suppose I am looking at it as a survivor. It didn't kill me. I managed to get myself through it. It did injure a lot of people, permanently. It dented their sense of security about the world. But, as I say, their children put it out of their minds completely. They didn't want any part of it. Or they make as though they don't want any part of it. They now criticise the New Deal, for example, and say that it was too socialistic. But they all survived because of the New Deal. Now, when the stock market drops in one day, that's more than it dropped in any one day in 1929, nobody goes screaming around, because there are seven or eight regulations put in by the New Deal which prevent that from unravelling. There are some guarantees which automatically come into play when this structure begins to shake. We have had bank failures on a scale, in some cases, greater than in 1929–30. The Continental Illinois Bank failed. I think it was the third-largest bank in the United States. Within about three days it was taken over by other banks. The depositors hardly knew there was a ripple. Why did this happen? Because of the New Deal legislation that guaranteed the depositors, so that everybody didn't show up Monday morning demanding their money. They went right on about their business thinking that we'll get paid one way or another.

I have been trying to get up an outline of *The American Clock* for television. It would be a good idea to do it, just to tell people how it was. It would be admirable on television. They have the budgets wherewith to do it properly. You could really re-stage the Ford strike, which involved thousands of people. It could be a real epic. But to get it into the form they require is not easy. I'm giving it another few days to see if I can crack it finally. Meanwhile, I've got two plays in January that I'm looking forward to. And I have another big play which is almost done [*The Ride Down Mount Morgan*?]. It deals with the parallel nature of our desires, two contradictory things at the same time. On this we are supposed to build a society. This totally contradictory individual on Tuesday wants exactly what he despises on Wednesday. That's part of it.

BIGSBY: In the 1970s, and thereafter, there came a series of plays which were going to do extremely well in Europe, especially in Britain, but not so in America. *The Archbishop's Ceiling*, *The American Clock*, *Broken Glass*, The *Last Yankee*, all did badly in America. What was your sense in that period? Did it not matter to you, because you had such a corpus of work that was being done all the time?

MILLER: I think that in the 1970s the talk, not from me but in general, was that we had come to the end of a theatrical period. People were quite correct in saying this. The time was over when any professional theatre would be doing straight plays, though I could not accept it. That is why it was a very discouraging period for me. In one sense there was no interest any more. My impression is that whereas before, the Sunday paper featured theatre on the front page of the arts section, this was no longer true. They were talking about television and movies. Whatever news there was of the theatre was inside.

BIGSBY: Did that decrease your confidence in your own work?

MILLER: I never really felt that I was part of that system. I always felt I was an interloper. I don't know why, but I never made any real long-term friends among theatre people. I knew them and was happy to see them, but wasn't involved, personally. It is probably because there seemed to be no society. There really wasn't. There was a production, the production would disperse, and that was the end of that. If I had had a Group Theatre, or something like that, it would probably have been different. There was nothing to get involved in. There really wasn't. The whole thing consisted of people raising money for a play, and then the whole thing vanished.

BIGSBY: But, happily for you, and certainly from the eighties through the nineties, there was another theatre, except it wasn't in America.

MILLER: Yes, right. But in this country, the old system has never recovered. It has gone, probably permanently.
BIGSBY: But they do seem to have rediscovered you in the last few years.
MILLER: It is because a new generation came.
BIGSBY: The Signature Theatre season, in the late nineties, seemed to me to do something to turn things around. There were some very good revivals of some of the earlier plays, and suddenly there was a spark there again in that theatre.
MILLER: Something got stabilised. In the Broadway theatre at the moment there is a lot of vitality. There are a lot of productions, a lot of straight plays, and I think there seem to be more playwrights now than ever in my lifetime. At a luncheon the other day in New York, they brought on a line of playwrights. They were in their twenties, maybe a couple of them a little older. There must have been about forty of them got up on the stage. I thought, when I was coming up there wouldn't have been forty people who would call themselves playwrights. Certainly not.
BIGSBY: In 1987 you published your autobiography, *Timebends*. What made you write it?
MILLER: I had a practical reason, which was that several scholars were threatening to write biographies of me, and I thought, before they did, that I would write my own version. Another thing was that I like to tell stories about things that happened to me, to my family and friends, and gradually began to feel that what I have lived through had been largely, as it always is, forgotten by a younger generation, and that it might be useful for them to see what it was like to be young thirty, forty or fifty years ago. There is a large degree of repetitiousness in existence, and it might

reveal a pattern to life that otherwise they wouldn't have. There are a lot of terrific stories that happened to me that I would not put in any other kind of work because, despite what people think, I don't write in a nakedly autobiographical way. My real autobiography is embedded in my plays but is not really *in* my plays as such. So here was a chance to do it.

Anyway, I accumulated probably 150 pages over the years, and I realised I had no form for it and that they probably would remain fragments, but my former editor, Aaron Asher of Grove Press, kept leaning on me to do this. So I thought if I could find a form for it, it might be worth doing, and if I could find some pleasure in doing it, because the idea of writing it day by day or year by year was boring. So I started to fool around with it and arrived at this form which has the advantage of expanding to wherever I wanted to expand and contracting to wherever I needed to contract, meaning that I could follow themes and people instead of following chronology.

BIGSBY: *Timebends* is an extended piece of prose. Are you tempted to turn back to the novel?

MILLER: I do enjoy writing them, but they get harder to write as I get older because I have become aware how tricky that form is. But I am so interested in theatre, basically, because it presents such a tremendous challenge. I know how to write a play, and I like to see it come alive in the theatre, when it does come alive. Maybe it is a question of power. You create a thing in a manuscript and pretty soon there are thirty-five people backstage working who you didn't even know existed, and all these strange actors walking around memorising your lines. When you write fiction, it is safer, because people don't pay as much attention to it. You are not as exposed as you are on the stage, but it is also less of a kick for me. I think everybody wants to be a playwright, because they get close to actors.

The world we live in is not a world that admits of easy description. It is really chaos. The internal life of people is in a state of tremendous flux, and it is hard to grab on to it truthfully. If I were writing some kind of formula, I could go on forever doing the same thing, but I could never get up the energy to do that. If I don't have anything special to say, I shut up. If I feel I do, I speak, and if sometimes it appeals to many millions of people, that is great. If sometimes it appeals to a few hundred or a few thousand, I cannot control it.

BIGSBY: Have your attitudes to your own characters changed with the years?

MILLER: I guess they must have. When I was writing earlier on, I was writing as a young man about older people. Now I am older than the older people. I don't think one attitude is truer than the other; it is just different. I am now more tolerant of Willy Loman or Eddie Carbone, because I guess I have too many things to atone for myself. I wouldn't know whether to call it tolerance, or just exhaustion.

17

The Nineties

BIGSBY: Why is *The Ride Down Mount Morgan* [1991] having its first production in London and not New York, or even one of the regional theatres of America?

MILLER: There are several reasons. One is that the director, who I particularly admire, Michael Blakemore, is British, and he had just spent many months in New York directing two plays, and he preferred not to have to be away from his home again after such a long time – he has got two young children. That is one reason. Initially I was going to give *The Ride Down Mount Morgan* to the National Theatre, but their schedule was such that they could not do it for about seven months, and I did not want to wait that long. I love the National Theatre. I think it is terrific, and that led me gradually towards London, where Blakemore directed it at Wyndham's Theatre. The other thing, though, is that in New York, on Broadway anyway, it is very difficult to find actors who will stay with a play for more than a few months. You are lucky to get two months. That means a director is constantly having to direct a play, to put in replacements, because actors are off to the movies and television, and this play requires mature actors. It cannot be done by neophytes or young actors, who would be more likely to want to stay with a play.

There is still a tradition in England – which I hope remains, but I think will probably be weakened in the future – of people who are basically theatre actors; they, of course, will do a movie because the money is there and the fame is there, but they are excited by the theatre. We do not really have that any more. Our theatre is basically a stepping-stone to the movies. It is in a desperate condition, and worse than that there is a great pessimism there, and I just did not want to throw my play into that kind of environment. As I said earlier, we have one newspaper in New York, the *New York Times*. There are at least a dozen in England whose reviews mean something, and one does not like to think that one reviewer can kill or make a play. It just seems undemocratic, and it seems cruel and stupid, which it is. So, for all those reasons I decided, well, why do we have to do it in New York? New York, London, Paris, these are all provinces of one great human empire now. One is no more central, really, than the other any more. That is one thing that has happened since World War II.

Another reason is that New York theatre at the present time is pretty depressing. At the moment there is one play on in the so-called professional theatre, and that's Neil Simon's *Lost in Yonkers*. The others are all musicals, many of which are imported, none of which started on Broadway. I just felt an atmosphere of discouragement and depression there. I had the feeling that while an audience certainly does exist for straight plays, nobody seems able to find it. Even when a play gets enthusiastic reviews, people don't come any more. As a producer friend of mine said to me, we've managed to drive that audience away from the theatre. So, rather than struggle against that negative feeling, Michael Blakemore suggested we should do it in England. So, for those reasons it is in London. Like all important decisions, it was really made because it had gotten to be five o'clock.

BIGSBY: Tell me a little about the play.

MILLER: Like all my plays, I find it hard to summarise. I guess if I could summarise them I wouldn't have written them. Mount Morgan is a non-existent mountain, in upper New York State, or rather it exists in my mind, down which the main character of the play comes in a heavy blizzard and crashes his car. He ends up in a hospital and, in effect, falls into his life. He is married to two women at the same time, unbeknown to one another. The point of the exercise is to investigate some of the qualities and meanings of truthfulness and deception. I think he is a very typical figure in our world now. He was probably always there but is especially evident now. It is a play in many scenes, set in different places, but it is very fluent; it moves in and out of his memory a little bit like *Death of a Salesman*. Some of it is in the present, some of it is in his past. It involves a very fluid use of the stage, so that scenes pop up whenever they need to. It is quite exciting, for me anyway.

You put it very well the other day, saying that it's basically about a man who has high integrity but no values. I think that describes the twentieth century from where I'm sitting. There are some terrific people, but they don't know right from wrong. This guy doesn't, either. He is another salesman, but this one is extremely successful and very rich. He is very intent on living a truthful life – 'truthful' meaning that his own impulses are expressed and not suppressed and hidden, the way most people's are. This naturally leads him into conflict with his own conscience because, as he puts it, the truth is you can be faithful to yourself or to other people, but not to both. This is the dilemma of the play.

It's very comical, as you can imagine from my description! In fact, we're trying to make it less so. It is a human comedy, a tragicomedy in a way, because the man fundamentally destroys himself, though not physically. We are left with, I think, a panorama of why a code exists even though it is rarely observed. I mean by that why we insist that it is morally better to keep one's word as opposed to not, and at the same time why we credit people who are outspoken and forthright and look down on people who are concealing themselves. This man does not conceal himself. I don't know what the audience is going to make of it, because it is too truthful. I haven't pared anything away from the dilemma. The dilemma is in our laps at the end of the play, and I am not sure that is where you want it to be. We would much rather have it resolved. I don't know how to resolve this dilemma, so I left it. I took it as far as I knew how to take it.

BIGSBY: I was interested to hear you evoke *Death of a Salesman*, which is about a man called Loman. The man in this play is called Lyman. The structure of the play is somewhat similar. We move around in time, go in and out of the sensibility of that individual. In a way, time, both in *Death of a Salesman* and in this play, is fluid. The past is never quite the past.

MILLER: The idea behind the structure of the play was that in the human mind there is no past. Everything is now. If you think of something that happened years ago, as you are thinking of it, it is happening now. The attempt in *Salesman*, as it is in this play, is to make everything concurrent. It is hard to explain to people that there are no flashbacks either in this play or in *Death of a Salesman*. It is just the past keeps rushing forward. That is a different feeling. My autobiography, I remind you, is called *Timebends*, which is time bending. I have been bending time for about forty years now. It is the way we think. It is one of the reasons we get tense and one of the sources of our wisdom, when we have wisdom, that we learn something from the past because it keeps rushing up into the present.

BIGSBY: It is, as you say, a blend of comedy and a sense almost of the tragic.

MILLER: It is fairly idiotic at times, almost farcical, but this is riding all the time over a tragic tide. I hope it all comes together in the audience's feeling at the end. It is an attempt to investigate the immensity of contradictions in the human animal and also to look at man's limitless capacity for self-deception and for integrity. Lyman is terrible, he is ghastly, but he does create, for example, a very socially responsible corporation. He works himself up from nothing to being a very important chief executive of an immense insurance company which has very progressive liberal policies towards minorities. He has a lot of terrific qualities. He has also got an immense appetite for life, for women, for everything. So, he is a kind of Faustian character, and, like our civilisation, is capable of enormous construction and destruction. I have just let it fall as it is. The play does not really condemn him particularly, it simply leaves him standing to one side of himself, trying to find himself. I don't know how further to characterise him.

BIGSBY: Lyman is bigamously married and regards this as a sign of integrity, because he could be married to one and simply keep a lover. Instead of that, he remains committed to both of them. It means, though, that, as you have said, betrayal is one of the themes and concerns of the play, as it has been from the your earliest plays onwards.

MILLER: I think the concept of betrayal, which is with us from the first page of the Bible, must be deep in the human animal. It is the ego against society, the wishes of the individual against his obligations as a citizen. It is no accident that, as one of the characters in the play says [and as he had remarked in the past], the Bible opens with the story of Cain and Abel. Without that story there need not be any Bible. If brothers would desist from murdering each other, which is a form of betrayal, the world would be safe. As it is, we can't rely on that, so we need a religion. I think that theological efforts begin from the idea of the fallen man. What is a fallen man? A man who betrayed his possibilities, or betrayed God. To paraphrase a line in *After the Fall*, why is betrayal the only truth that sticks? Why is it that our betrayals are the things we remember best? I could hazard a guess that those are the acts that can bring war about and destroy a group. In some little way our nervous energy tells us that that is the truth. But, as adult humans, we are doing it all the time. This play is partly about that, and it is also about another of my themes, which is guilt. In this case the man is quite conscious, quite sophisticated, and his object is to conquer his guilt and become free. We see what happens when he tries to do that. The truth is you can't have everything. You can't.

In the beginning God is beneficent, full of affection for his creature. After he rebels, God becomes quite angry with him, which is the traditional way of looking at the Old Testament and Genesis. What that play is really trying to do is detect what I think of as the biology of morals. It is about the underpinnings of the moral code, why it is necessary, and the reason it is necessary is that we are killers and are competing for the same goals, the same rewards. In some part of the human brain there is no limit to what we will do to get what we want. Lyman is intent on expressing himself and not suppressing his instinctual life, on living fully in every way possible, and that is his integrity. He will confront the worst about himself and proceed from it. The question is, what about other people? As he says in the play, what we all know is that a man can be faithful to himself or to other people – but not both. And this is the dilemma of the play.

He manages to convince himself and, I believe, some part of the audience, that there is a higher value than other people, and that value is the psychic survival of the individual. So it is a dilemma. The play has no solution to it. If I did, I could probably cure a lot of people. But it is laid out in front of us. I had a lot of fun writing it because it is very funny to me. It may not be funny to other people. It is not politically correct. The women don't kill him. They are toyed with by him.

BIGSBY: Are you drawn now to have your plays produced Off Broadway?

MILLER: I have done this musical – *Up From Paradise* – which is really an experiment. I don't know if it will ever work. I think it does, but it is not like any musical I know of, and probably that is why it will end up in some small place, which is okay with me. It has been put together over the years. The composer [Stanley Silverman] is a very good one, and in fact I was just changing a lyric on the telephone. As I said to him the other day, 'We are growing old together.' It will get on. I think it will be charming. It is a lovely thing, but undoubtedly it is not a Broadway show, except by some fluke. God knows what a Broadway show is any more, but I cannot imagine it being.

A play can get terrific notices now, a straight play, and not run. This used not to be the case. The public was far more likely to obey the critical reception of a play. I do not know of cases where critics have condemned a play and it ran. It could have happened, but not to my knowledge, but I know several plays with good reviews that did not run. Olivier said some years ago, when he was playing Strindberg in Canada in *The Father*, that he would not perform in it in New York because he did not want to act on a stage before an ignorant audience. He said, 'They won't know what I am doing in this play.' I think he was quite right. It is an unremitting play. It is not a barrel of laughs. It never lets you off the hook, and our audience is not likely to respond to that. It did once upon a time, but their attention span has become shorter and shorter. I really do believe that they cannot stay with it. I do not know whether it is television or just the frenetic life we lead. The actors tell me that they have to do all sorts of things to keep the flagging attention alive.

BIGSBY: So you may not go back to Broadway.

MILLER: I do not think it is any different Off Broadway, quite frankly. Maybe we will have to do what the Chinese do and ring cowbells. They do that. It is quite marvellous. The Chinese audience never stops talking: there is a hum of conversation from the beginning to the end. I don't know what they are talking about, but they are talking, and I think that this is why they rather depend upon the cowbells and those knockers to tell them when they should really be paying attention. Maybe we will have to do that. We will have to set off firecrackers or blink the lights to tell them 'It is time to listen, folks.'

BIGSBY: In 1993 you staged *The Last Yankee*, a play which appears to have the most private of subjects, but which nonetheless addresses public issues.

MILLER: It does. I have always felt that the real public issues are the ones that are most private, provided you see through the privacy to their roots. In this case the depressions that are being suffered by the women [in the play] have some resonance in the lives they lead in the world they live in. After all, as somebody says in the play, depression is the single largest cause of hospitalisation in the United States ['There's more people in hospital because of depression than any other disease'], and in the world, incidentally, in Western Europe. If there were hospitals in the rest of the world that could take these people, it would be true there too, so this becomes something quite a bit larger than a private dilemma.

BIGSBY: In 1994 came *Broken Glass*. It is set at the time of Kristallnacht in Germany, when all the Jewish homes and stores were being wrecked.

MILLER: In 1938 I graduated from the university, and I was already an anti-fascist, but I have to say that I was not prepared for this kind of obscenity. I don't think many people were. We had been through the Spanish Civil War, when people were out with their children, walking about in the street, and that airplane dropped a couple of bombs right in the middle of the city. By '38 you were more or less prepared for some horrors. But this was particularly obscene, because the people they were hounding on the streets, at least in the photographs one got in the New York press, were very dignified gentlemen, on their knees on the streets, cleaning the sidewalk with toothbrushes, while they were surrounded by crowds of people laughing at them. That was of course the introduction to our dear century. But we were not yet prepared for what was to come, though, as I have said, anti-Semitism was a very dense thing in

New York, a very powerful political fact. Inside the United States, the Jews were afraid to say very much for fear that they would exacerbate the anti-Semitism in the country. Roosevelt didn't do very much about it, because he needed to get elected again. The paralysis of this woman in the play [Sylvia Gellburg's legs suddenly become paralysed] is a metaphor for the paralysis of millions of people.

I remember Kristallnacht very clearly, because neither I nor anybody else knew where this was going to end. It just seemed to be alarming, like a society going crazy.

Of course, we were, in 1938, in the last year of a deep depression in this country. Despite later mythology, the country was in a state of deep spiritual disorganisation. There was a real struggle going on between people who were spiritually alert to fascism and those who weren't. The largest part of the Midwest, I am convinced, was on the wrong side. It was a combination of isolationism and the feeling that they knew nothing about Europe. They couldn't see why we should ever get involved. Furthermore, nobody was making the point that this was not just about Jews: it was about France, it was about England, it was about Europe, it was, indeed, about the world. But, at the moment, it appeared to be some argument with Jews in Europe. I knew better even at that time. It seemed perfectly clear to me what it was about. It was a new imperialism that was going to crush everything around it.

BIGSBY: So you weren't like one of the characters in the play, the Doctor, who is confident it will go away?

MILLER: No, but I would say that his was the most common attitude on the part of people who knew anything about Germany at all. He studied medicine in Germany, spent four years there. People who did that had a high opinion of the Germans, which I never had. But I was just a kid then. *Life* magazine at the time ran some pictures of what was going on in Germany, and the text read that, despite what one saw, there was a general feeling that this was a temporary aberration and that the good sense of the German people would prevail. That was a common notion.

BIGSBY: What were the origins of the play?

MILLER: It actually goes back fifty years or more. I have known that image of a woman who has lost the use of her legs and nobody can diagnose the reason for that, many years, since, I would say, 1940. I thought about writing it many times, but I could never find a way in. And there is another image that is as old as that, that of her husband, who was a very curious fellow. He was curious because he always dressed in black. The first title of this play was *Man in Black*, but it didn't mean anything, except to me.

BIGSBY: What were the circumstances of the real person who you knew fifty years ago?

MILLER: A lot like those of the character in the play. But, of course, I have had to invent a character, create a character, because all I really had was a visual image. I could have made a movie out of it without going any further, but on stage there has to be some depth, and so it becomes part of my own psyche.

BIGSBY: Was this just an image, or was this a woman who had reacted to the same events as the woman in this play?

MILLER: This is my conflation of two things. You know, I only recently found out the other day [in January 1994] that there was, in the 1930s especially, an unusual amount of physical paralysis among some Jews in America. The weirdest thing. I never knew that. There was an article in the paper about Cambodian women. After the Khmer Rouge got finished with them, and they supposedly murdered several million Cambodians in the most brutal fashion, there is a lot of hysterical blindness among them. They can see, but they seem not to register what they are seeing. All this seemed to come up after I had written my play. Just the other day, my daughter was telling me about a woman who she knows, a concert pianist, divorced, with one child, who sat down to play one day and could not feel her hands. She was never again able to play the piano. They cannot find any physical reason for this. I don't know much about the circumstances, but it is fascinating. It seems to be a matter of the brain or the spirit controlling the physiological function of the body. In my play this process is associated with the terror which reached the United States in relation to the rise of fascism in Europe, though, in truth, this was felt by very few people.

BIGSBY: This idea, or image, has been in your mind for fifty years. Why has it coalesced now into a play?

MILLER: Those people come alive, and it becomes possible to write about them. It is fundamentally that. You feel them, begin to hear them, and, for one reason or another, I hadn't heard them before. I think that is basically the reason.

BIGSBY: The characters in the play are virtually all Jewish. This is the first play, maybe since the first one you wrote back at university, of which that is true. Has your Jewish background become more or less important to you?

MILLER: Both. It has become more important in the sense that I see that a lot of my own attitudes come out of that tradition, which I wasn't aware of for most of my life, really, because there are other traditions that contain the same attitudes. I am speaking mainly of American democracy, which, to me, is the political experience of Judaism.

BIGSBY: That would come as news to the Founding Fathers.

MILLER: Yes, but of course, let's face it, when they opened the Bible, they opened it at the Old Testament. When I wrote *The Crucible*, about the antecedents of the Founding Fathers, any reference to the Bible was an Old Testament reference. It always struck me that these were a lot of Jews running around going crazy about things. I only later realised my connection with that. It was far from political; it was ethnic, among other things. But what are you saying when you say that? You are not saying very much. Another person had the same feeling from a totally different vantage point, a completely Christian point of view, or even a Muslim one.

BIGSBY: Philip Gellberg, who is at the centre of this play, resents his Jewish identity almost as though it were a kind of unfair burden that has been put on him. As he says, 'Why is it so hard to be a Jew? Why must we be different? Being Jewish is a full-time job.' Were you ever made to feel guilty for not making it a full-time job?

MILLER: I didn't know how to do that. From the very beginning I was weaned away from the idea that certain things were particularly Jewish. My first mother-in-law, who lived in Ohio, was of Catholic, German and French background. We were having breakfast, and the paper arrived and there had been a particularly vile bank robbery the night before, during which somebody had got beaten up, and she saw the headline. She said, as she handed me the paper, 'I hope he is not a Catholic', meaning the robber. This is exactly what the Jews would say. I am sure anybody would say that who feels a minority status, though you would hardly think the Catholics would, because they were running the state of Ohio, along with Illinois and Michigan, but they still had that feeling that they were on the edge of the abyss for historical reasons. The Blacks feel it when an African American is caught doing something bad. I am sure, in certain circumstances, God help us, even the English would. This is an anxiety that comes with feeling that you are not running the place, that you are there on the sufferance of others.

BIGSBY: The play is set in 1938, which is also still the time of the Depression.

MILLER: Sure, it is. It is in the atmosphere of the play. It is said of the protagonist that he never knew any Depression. He worked for a big bank and his position seems very secure, and always has been.

BIGSBY: Yet his job is foreclosing on other people.

MILLER: Yes, he gives loans, but he also forecloses; he giveth and he receiveth.

BIGSBY: In fact, there is a relationship, is there not, between some of the lessons that came out of the Depression and some of the lessons that came out of the events in Europe. There is more than glass being broken – there are human contracts and promises.

MILLER: Civilisation is being broken. The social contract is being torn up. To me one of the basic threats posed by the fascists was that here was a movement that was going to literally tear up all the underlying web of obligations that keeps society in place. As I said earlier, a key image, for me, of that whole period, was the time one Nazi bomber flew over Guernica. Picasso later did a painting about this. In broad daylight it sailed above the town and dropped a bomb right in the middle of the square where all the people were shopping, sitting on benches in the sun and so on. I can't tell you what an effect that had on me. I could understand artillery bombardments from a distance during the First World War which destroyed one village and town after another, but that guy doesn't see where the missile goes, so he can snuggle into his irresponsibility by saying, 'Well, I am just a soldier. I am in danger myself.' But this was something else. This was a guy looking down at this peaceful square and dropping high explosives on it, and I can't tell you what a concatenation that made in my head.

The largest radio audience in the United States at the time, bigger than that for Jack Benny or any other comedian, was for Father Coughlin, who every Sunday was literally reading Joseph Goebbels' speeches. Goebbels was the propaganda minister of the Nazi regime. This was the largest audience in America, and the speeches were as anti-Semitic as Goebbels could get. It was a pretty heavy thing, in those days. It was touch and go. You didn't know, particularly after France fell, whether the English were going to make a deal with the Germans. And if they did, sooner or later you had the right to suspect that we would. I would not allow myself to think of it as theoretical. These things have always had consequences in terms of people, and I think that has probably infiltrated my plays – the idea that the individual is always in the midst of a social situation. His social identity, the work he does, his public attitudes, are quite as important as his private relationships. I wrote once [in his 'Introduction' to *The Collected Plays*], speaking of individuals in society, that the fish is in the water, but the water is in the fish. It is inseparable. *We* are inseparable. I cannot understand anyone who does not see himself as a social being as well as a private psychological unit.

BIGSBY: What led you to write *Broken Glass* when you did?

The Nineties

MILLER: One was a purely personal thing. As I say, I began thinking about this woman who I knew back in the thirties or early forties, and it remained a mystery in my mind. She was a very sweet, intelligent, energetic woman who lived in my neighbourhood who suddenly and inexplicably could not walk. She suddenly could not get up, and they had all kinds of doctors looking at her. Nobody could figure it out, and she went through her life and died unable to walk. It is one of those mysteries that I suppose medical people nowadays could diagnose, but I could not. They had some pretty good doctors in those days, and they could not either. It suddenly appeared to me to be a wonderful kind of analogy of where we are now. We have all the equipment to understand everything, and we cannot move, we just cannot move. Everybody agrees it is a catastrophe and, if I am any judge of it, if my emotions are similar to others, I cannot get onto that horse. I think maybe we have had too much catastrophe. If you stick an electrode into any kind of an organism, after a while it doesn't react to it, and I think we have maybe been numbed for a long time by the brutality in our natures, and something is telling us that the whole thing is hopeless in a deeper way than we are willing to admit.

So that was one of the impulses to write about that woman, because she was one of the few people I knew who fairly early on got excited about the Holocaust, not the Holocaust as a lot of crazy Germans running around after some Jews, 3,000 miles away. She was not a political woman. She read probably two or three newspapers a week, which was unusual for a woman in her position in those times, but there was no political ideology of any kind. Nonetheless, it reached across the ocean. Some bug flew across 3,000 miles of water and stung her, and she became aware that this was a catastrophe that was bigger than anything anybody had ever known. She caught this thing, and it was a mystery to me and probably still is. How did she manage to do that? That is really why I got so fascinated with her and wrote a play about it.

BIGSBY: At the heart of that, as you are hinting, is a private story, and yet there is a crucial arc that connects it to the public world as though they are, as you say, not separate from one another.

MILLER: I have always felt that my upbringing would indicate that I have never been a private man, in the sense that I thought there were no public consequences to what I did. I guess that is a biblical idea, that God recognises the just man, and that the world will not be destroyed while there is one just man still alive. I don't know where that comes from, but it is in the whole mix, and I have always felt that what we do privately has consequences outside of where we are, and I guess they do, but trying to trace that out in concrete terms is almost impossible. So, you are backed into metaphor and analogy in poetry, which is the only way you can handle it anyway.

BIGSBY: We are talking about this play as though it were purely about the 1930s but, as you suggest, it is a very 1990s play, not merely because of the revival of fascism in Germany, but also because of places like Sarajevo.

MILLER: They are bombing the hell out of that town, and we are all sitting here saying, 'Tut tut, isn't that terrible.' They blew up sixteen or more schoolchildren today, and did you see anybody pause on his way to lunch? I didn't. That is what it is about.

BIGSBY: Because buried in the play seems to be yet another question, which is why we behave as though we cannot do anything in the face of these events. We let them disable us in the same way that the character in the play allows it to disable her.

MILLER: You know, I think we are so helpless about it because in each of us, whether recognised or not, and it usually isn't recognised, is this same bloody ethnic nationalism. This is not coming from the moon. This is coming from us, and we haven't even come close to confronting this thing. All the patriotism and the ethnic nationalism, and the rest of it, is knocking on the door, and it is as dangerous as it ever was. Right after World War II I happened to meet Jean Monnet, who was the French originator of the Common Market, and he said, 'We are never going to have another war in Europe, because there is no such thing as a German coal mine any more, or a French railroad. The capital is so mixed, international cooperation is so overwhelmingly powerful now. Ford has plants in every country, including Germany, France and England. General Motors likewise. So they are not likely to bomb themselves.' Well, I took that very seriously for quite a while, although emotionally I found it hard to accept. I thought, well, maybe we are at the end of something here. I don't know about that any more. I don't know if that is strong enough to withstand the rush of emotion that comes with these ethnic feelings.

BIGSBY: That is because these things are not external to us. In this play the reason she has become momentarily disabled, unable to walk, is partly to do with an external public event, betrayal on a social scale, but it is in part to do with a betrayal on a private level.

MILLER: They are both the same thing. That paralysis could destroy the world now.

BIGSBY: There is a sense in which this play seems to me almost a companion piece to *The Last Yankee*. Certainly, some of the same concerns are there. In *The Last Yankee* there are two women who have retreated into mental instability in the face of a sense of distrust, horror, broken relationships. They have to work their way to the possibility of reconstructing their world, and the possibility of reconstructing is as important in *Broken Glass* as the analysis of the sickness, is it not?

MILLER: It certainly is. They are related. I guess I had never thought of it that way. Well, why wouldn't they be? I am the same writer, more or less. But what intrigued me in *Broken Glass* is the human animal's capacity to create a fantasy, based on reality to be sure, but so powerful as to paralyse an otherwise physically sound woman. She has made war against herself, and the trigger is what she reads in a newspaper, something she cannot possibly believe. She says, 'You mean I am sick because I read a newspaper?' ['I can't move my legs from reading a newspaper']. Well, yes, in a way. I don't propose to solve that dilemma in the play, of course. In real life it would probably be impossible to solve.

BIGSBY: No, but apart from anything else, it is concerned with something I find elsewhere in your work, namely a concern with survival, with finding some way of going on which involves more than mere resignation.

MILLER: Oh, certainly. In this play they are struggling with resignation all the time. Everybody in the play, including Gellburg, is trying to find their way out of it too.

BIGSBY: How do you see Philip Gellburg?

MILLER: He is a very conservative man, conservative in every sense of the word. He believes in the system as it was then and as it still is in most places now. He believes that the banks open in the morning and you take your money out. And most of the time that is how it is. Most of the time. He is a material person. He is also a snob, a snob not only about non-Jews, but about Jews, about everybody, to tell the truth. That is his defence against the feeling of emptiness that he has.

BIGSBY: Doesn't that emptiness come in part because he lives a life based on denial?

MILLER: He is denying everything. He is denying his ethnicity, his Jewishness, and he is denying his wife's love as well. As the Doctor's wife describes him, he is a miserable little pisser. He is also a pathetic one. But I think he is a significant one.

BIGSBY: Why does his wife stay with him?

MILLER: He adores her, for one thing, and she knows that. He is also a very good provider. He knows how to make money and has a good job for that period, that time when people often didn't have jobs.

BIGSBY: But he has been sexually withdrawn from her for over a quarter of a century.

MILLER: That is right, but people didn't rush to the divorce courts in those days. You got married for better or worse, especially in this class of people. They were not about to renounce this marriage. They might not be all that religious, but the customs were more important than the people. The custom was that you stayed married, unless there was some extreme problem, which in this case there is, but she is not about to appeal to it. Why? Because her mother would collapse, and though people did get divorces for just such a reason, her character is not such that she will do it.

BIGSBY: In fact, she has put her life on hold.

MILLER: She just stopped and, let me tell you, the Brooklyn neighbourhoods were full of them. I suspect the London ones were likewise. Just stop the organism. Psychologically speaking, it goes into a state of arrest. It is just pulsing, not moving any more.

BIGSBY: So, she also is a denier?

MILLER: Everybody in the play is. Including the Doctor.

BIGSBY: Who you describe as a scientific idealist.

MILLER: He is a great idealist. He is also a womaniser, when he can manage it, but not for some years now. He is telling the truth when he says he hasn't been with anybody for a number of years. He can't remember the last one.

BIGSBY: But he must have been with quite a few before, because his wife instantly assumes it is going to happen again.

MILLER: Yes. But that is partly because it amuses her too. The idea attracts her.

BIGSBY: Although the Doctor's wife, Margaret, is in a way a minor player, along with Sylvia Gellburg's sister, she plays a significant role.

MILLER: I do not regard them as minor at all. They bring the neighbourhood into the play, for one thing. They are the neighbourhood, a kind of secret chorus in the drama. They are carefully placed in the play so that they offer us a sense of normality, the average man's attitude towards this incredible set of events.

BIGSBY: There have been a series of drafts of the play with different titles. After the first read-through you were already typing new parts of the play. When does that process stop?

The Nineties

MILLER: I think it is going to stop right now. I cannot think of anything more now. This is not unusual for me, of course. I have done this before. But these changes are minor, a few words here, a sentence there. I might cut an exchange simply because it doesn't add sufficiently to warrant its presence in the play. The scene I wrote today [1994] was one I had had in my mind for weeks. I simply could not latch on to it until the read-through, when I suddenly saw where it belonged. You do learn, of course, but I try not to learn too much, because you begin scribbling when you shouldn't. In this case what is being bonded together is a public concern and a private neurosis. In my opinion this is always the case, but to try to find the juncture where it meets is not so easy. I knew it was central to this play, but I hadn't quite realised it. I was aware of that before we ever had the reading, but I thought, I'll wait till I hear it before I attempt to make the concrete juncture. I think I have now. That is what was bringing my director to tears a little while ago.

BIGSBY: The cast in this American production is almost entirely Jewish, but it is not a requirement of the play.

MILLER: No, no. As a matter of fact, in the course of trying to cast this play, I would say 90 per cent of the actors we talked to were not Jewish at all. We did not have this play cast two weeks ago, after, what, two years of fiddling around with it. Suddenly four actors showed up and we had a play cast; it was utterly amazing. If I had any hair, I would have lost it. It was terrible, but we have real problems in America. As I have said, let an actor, God forbid, give an especially striking performance in a play and he has immediate offers to go to the movies, where he is going to make a lot of money. He can't make any money to speak of in the theatre. So, when they get good, they go. What you are left with is people nobody happens to want at the moment. They may be perfectly good actors, but your choice is much more limited than it used to be, and this makes it tough. We get an actor who is perfect for it, and he says, 'Gee, I would love to do it, but I've got a TV thing they want me for, or they may want me for, and I've got to keep myself free.' It is the difference between making a few thousand dollars a week and making a hundred thousand dollars for half an hour's work. So, it is tough.

BIGSBY: Why didn't *Broken Glass* work in America while it won an accolade in England?

MILLER: I think partly it was the production. It had a very good actress [Amy Irving]. She seemed to be tough, and the fact is the woman was very vulnerable. She did not seem vulnerable; she seemed angry at her husband. She should be angry at him, but it is the anger of a vulnerable person and that wasn't there. So the sympathy for her was missing.

BIGSBY: The ending chopped and changed quite a bit, or at least it did in New Haven [Connecticut].

MILLER: You know, there is a curious question involved in the ending, whether it was Sylvia's capacity that enabled her to stand up [a paralysed woman, she rises from her wheelchair], whether it was a victory over him, or a discovery, on her part, that she had the strength. That is a difficult one, in view of the fact that he is dying. They did it well in England.

BIGSBY: What is it that makes you respond to British audiences and British audiences respond to your work?

MILLER: I don't know how to answer that, except that the audiences, not only in London but in various other cities, are presented with some terrific productions. Let's face it, there are wonderful theatres all over Britain that keep not just my plays but other people's plays alive. If you don't have those productions, the vitality of the whole enterprise begins to dissipate, and that is what has happened with us in the United States. We rely completely on the big hit play. Those were never very many, and now simply there are none.

BIGSBY: In 1997 came *Mr Peters' Connections*, as part of a series of plays produced by the Signature Theatre Company.

MILLER: I do not know how to describe it, because it is a kind of a crazy comedy. A man is confronting his own death and wrestling with the inconsequential nature of what he conceives his life to have been, because he can't find a meaning for the whole affair. So, it is a mixture of social history, on the one hand, and a personal quest for some kind of redemption in his own life. I think it is funny, I think it is sad, but how to describe it formally I wouldn't venture to say.

BIGSBY: Mr Peters summons into his mind people he has loved, members of his family, but he seems to meet them as strangers.

MILLER: Yes. I am not quite sure why that is, to tell you the truth, excepting that relatives are equivalent to strangers, and it is only through the course of the play that they become his relatives again, become his people. He meets them as humans, you might say, unnamed humans, and then they become recognisable to him as his family.

BIGSBY: What are the implications of the title to you?

MILLER: Well, his connections, literally speaking, are the connections that his mind continuously throws up, but they are also his connections to life. They are the connections he has made between his own experience and his demand for some meaning in his life.

BIGSBY: So, it is not only the connections between people, but between the past and the present, between events and their consequences.

MILLER: Right, exactly.

BIGSBY: In some senses it is a play about death, but perhaps thereby it also becomes a play about life.

MILLER: That is why it is a play about life, as crazy as that sounds. Yes, in confronting his end, which he has to do, all his livingness erupts in him, and it is necessary for him to confront death with his life intact, so to speak, armed with his life.

BIGSBY: This is a man who is on the verge of death. He is in a half-world between being asleep and being awake. In another sense, it seems almost like a limbo he has entered.

MILLER: I do not know how to define it, excepting that he is between sleeping and waking. It is a kind of limbo that you realistically, psychologically, sustain when you know you are dreaming, when you know you are asleep. Sometimes you try to climb out of that sleep into wakingness, and it is impossible, and you slump back into a deeper sleep, or you do wake up. Mr Peters is trying to come out of it, but it has got him, it is at him, and it has pulled him down into it.

BIGSBY: So, this is a man at or towards the end of his life who is looking back and trying to see what the meaning of that life has amounted to, what the subject of his life has been.

MILLER: He is looking, in his own words, for the subject, what is the pinion which connects all these events. There must be something that makes sense. In the end he does arrive at something approaching a satisfactory centre for his present existence.

BIGSBY: His revisiting of the past is summing up memories. It is also nostalgia. What is the distinction between nostalgia and a search for true meaning in the past?

MILLER: Well, it is nostalgia, but he is endlessly comparing an older America, a former America, to the contemporary one and trying to figure out how that can compete, the madhouse that it presently is. So that is the connection.

BIGSBY: He is looking at an America that seems to have lost the plot, lost its subject. Does that mean that you yourself believe there was a time when it had not lost its subject?

MILLER: Inevitably. I think everybody imagines that in his youth the world made more sense. I am not sure that it is only in our time that this explosion has occurred, but now it is more manifest, I think. It is manifest even in young people. They feel that there is simply a kind of moral and experiential chaos. Everything is possible, and consequently nothing is necessary.

I felt like writing that the ship had no keel. It's a great ship of state but is bumbling around in the ocean. It no longer has a direction that is under anybody's control. Everything is adventitious. Everything is compromised. It is expressed, to a certain degree, in the profound changes that occur in this society, which we are paying for in a way by the absence of continuity, so that you can't look back more than a week with any assurance that you are going to connect with whatever you are looking back on. I spent twenty years on the streets of Brooklyn. I don't recognise them. There are big stores, all sorts of things going on. The aspect of the place is completely strange to me. I could get lost in two minutes. I lived in three different buildings in Brooklyn Heights. I had an endless number of friends. I used to visit them all over the Heights. Now it would take me a little work finding my way around. It's symbolic of the fact that we're constantly ploughing up the field. So, as soon as anything grows, we plough it under.

BIGSBY: And does that lead us in the direction of metaphysics? Is it not simply a person who has lost a subject and a country, but in some way existence itself, which he once supposed had rendered a sense of meaning?

MILLER: That is right. That is the way I feel about it, and it is the way that he feels about it.

BIGSBY: At one stage he says that God is precisely what is not there when you need him. But that therefore puts an obligation back on the individual. Meaning is not inherent in existence: it has to be created.

MILLER: He has got to create it. And I think people who have not completely lost their wits are constantly trying to do that, trying to make sense of it.

BIGSBY: But isn't the notion that there was once an order, a structure, a purpose, that has now disappeared, simply a feature of getting older? When you are young, everything seems established and in place, unquestioned. It is only as time goes by that that order begins to disintegrate. Isn't that a natural process?

MILLER: Yes, it is probably a function of maturity that you see everything is made up and nothing is rooted. The world you thought you had entered, which seemed a rooted world, really wasn't. So, he is registering that now, excepting that now there is an objective correlative to the whole thing. Take almost any kind of phenomena in current life – take

The Nineties

suburbia, for example. Suburbia was once settled farms. It is hard to find that any more. It is more lucrative to sell your land for real estate than to farm it in most places, so you go from Canada down to Florida, and you go from one big metropolitan area to another. Basically, our country is a city, a city with suburbs. Well, that wasn't the case even twenty years ago.

BIGSBY: So it is not just that there is an absence of subject: there is an absence of place. Mr Peters is literally deracinated?

MILLER: Well, he says, 'I've never been in this neighbourhood before.'

BIGSBY: But it is not only a play about literal death, because it envisages other kinds of death, spiritual death, boredom, lethargy – in other words, not giving life true force.

MILLER: That is the atmosphere I feel we are in, and people like him, who are vital people, people who know a lot and have experienced a lot, have that feeling that nothing quite makes any sense at all. There are no values, in other words, that he can say are real. As he says, they have advertisements in the paper for enlarging or diminishing a woman's breasts for $4,400, and his father paid $5,000 for a house they lived in for thirty years. Where is the value? How can you speak of values any more in relation to those two equations?

BIGSBY: Is there also a sense that the people he summons into his mind – a former lover, his brother, both of whom are dead – in dying have taken something of him with them. That is to say, they have taken his past, part of his shared memories. They were the ones who corroborated his past, confirmed who he was and what his life was about, and as each one of them goes so they thin him to a kind of transparency.

MILLER: Yes. He needs others to corroborate himself, his own existence. As he says to his long-dead brother, 'You don't remember me – do I exist? Who the hell am I?' His daughter, though, is not dead, his daughter is quite alive.

BIGSBY: It is a play that has echoes of *Death of a Salesman*.

MILLER: It has got colours in it, although it is quite a different play.

BIGSBY: But once again it features somebody who is summoning memories into his present self to deal with an emotional state in which he finds himself. That was true of *Death of a Salesman*, and it is true again here.

MILLER: Yes, that is true. Well, so be it.

BIGSBY: And Willy Loman, too, was looking for some kind of meaning, but he was looking for it outside himself.

MILLER: Yes. This is now more than forty years later, and this man is a contemporary man. Willy was a much earlier generation than this guy. He is already acutely aware of the crumbling of what Willy was trying to prop up. As he says, he worked for Pan-American Airways as a pilot, and it was not so much an airline as a calling. They were princes of the air, and some idiot accountants came along and destroyed the whole thing.

BIGSBY: Pan American may only be a company, but it is one of those things that people thought would always be there. It was part of the definition of the culture, and then suddenly it wasn't.

MILLER: That's right, like the banks he describes. When you used to walk into a bank you felt they suspected you, and it gave him a certain reassurance that they suspected him. You felt that somebody was in charge there. Now he says it is like a salad bar, and they are all running around trying to get people to borrow money from them, whereas before it would be an outrage for a bank to go looking for borrowers that way.

BIGSBY: Is there a sense in which this play is a personal one, that it is Arthur Miller, in his eighties, looking back and asking questions not dissimilar to those that Mr Peters is asking?

MILLER: Yes, but there are a lot of them that are not mine. They are his because of the nature of his calling. However, of course anybody who gets as old as I am shares the feeling of someone who has seen a hell of a lot, and there would necessarily be a parallel feeling between myself and him.

BIGSBY: There are various lines there that seem to have echoes of Arthur Miller. One was Mr Peters' sense that the movies do not have a subject any more, and that television is just language. There is a good deal of you in Mr Peters, isn't there?

MILLER: I hope so. Yes, it is a very personal piece, but at the same time the audience knows exactly what is happening there in his head because these are very broadly shared reactions to our life, I think.

BIGSBY: The play has been in rehearsal for a long time and, as we are talking, is approaching preview. Have you learned anything about the play in the course of those rehearsals?

MILLER: I would say that what surprised me was that so often the actors had to stop to consider what level of consciousness they were in, because the character is talking to some people who are dead. But one does that in a dream. It is only at a certain point in the conversation when you say, 'My God, this is Harry, Harry is dead', but nobody ever dies in the human mind until the light pours in from some little open window in the skull and you say, 'Oh yes, of course, he is dead.' I would say that I learned something about the play because it is twisting around, in and out of certain levels of consciousness. It would seem to me to be perfectly natural when I was writing it, but, at some point, this character has decided to wake up. Anybody who has had a deep sleep, and knows he has got to make a train in some other part of his brain, and says 'I have got to get up at this point', but the dream isn't finished, knows that kind of paralysis. However, actors had to go down deep, then a little shallower, then almost conscious and so on in order to do the play, and that took a lot of work.

BIGSBY: It is also a comedy, and it is often very difficult to rehearse comedy.

MILLER: Yes, of course so much is in the timing, and that you do not get until everybody knows their lines. I assume as they get closer sheer terror will overcome them and they will pick it up. It is true that a comedy is tougher.

BIGSBY: The principal role is played by Peter Falk, who most people are going to know from Lieutenant Colombo on television, which is not entirely inappropriate, because there is a kind of mystery element to this story.

MILLER: I loved the idea of him, because he is always enquiring, and that is what he is doing in this play. He is enquiring about himself, he is tracking himself, but he is very inquisitive, and Peter Falk is wonderful at that. It is his natural manner of acting. I think he will do it brilliantly because he is that way himself.

BIGSBY: There is a mysterious character in the play, a Black bag woman. Is she there as a kind of chorus?

MILLER: She is like the dust in the air. She is part of the city. He is always aware of her, but nobody pays any attention to her. She makes remarks and nobody listens. They go right past her, right through her. Occasionally she takes the stage, but nobody is particularly listening, and that is really the way it is.

BIGSBY: And it is a play that recapitulates the history of New York. The building in which it takes place has been various things at different stages.

MILLER: It is the last hundred years.

BIGSBY: And it recapitulates the history of a culture and of an individual.

MILLER: Right, of how the people used to be and the way they are now.

BIGSBY: I remember George Bush Sr being challenged by a reporter because something he was saying contradicted something he had said a year before. His reply was, 'Oh, that's history. That doesn't mean anything.' How do you, as a writer who has always stressed the significance of the past in a country which Gore Vidal has called 'the United States of Amnesia', deal with that?

MILLER: To me, that is the hardest part of being a writer in this culture. It is like ploughing the sea, and behind you there is the wake for two seconds, and then it flattens out again and there is no sign of that ship ever going by. It is in everything. I'm working in the American theatre. It has a long history. If I threw at you the name of the dominant playwright of twenty-five years ago, or even more recently, I question whether you would recognise the name. They are gone, gone, gone. Sydney Howard, Robert Sherwood, Elmer Rice, most literate people would have no memory of these men, but they dominated the American theatre for several decades. I could dredge up another dozen. There is no past. Every day is today. I am often quite frankly amazed that I am still here, that anybody remembers anything I ever did.

I often wonder what is taught in schools about history, or whether it is a vital subject of any kind, quite frankly.

I occasionally talk to some people, and it is an oblong blur, the whole thing.

BIGSBY: You have written four plays in seven years. You have written more in this past decade than you have written in any decade.

MILLER: No wonder I am tired.

BIGSBY: Where has this suddenly come from?

MILLER: I don't know. I just give less of a damn about what is going to become of them really. They are written less for the public than for my own satisfaction. Nobody would write a crazy play like this who was eager to please the public. I do not know what they are going to make of it, whether it will hang in there or not. But if you were in the business of doing that, you would not be writing this kind of a play, and so the point is, I suppose, that what happens is you get more and more careless about that and more carefree about it.

BIGSBY: As we are talking, there are two Eugene O'Neill plays on in New York and there will be two Arthur Miller plays on in New York. It is quite like old times.

MILLER: Well, there is a lot of money around now, you know. That accounts for a lot of it. I do not think that *A View from the Bridge* would have been picked up on Broadway even two or three years ago, because money was not flooding the place the way it is now. People are desperately looking for a place to throw their money. That is the way it looks to me, and so they will invest half a million dollars to move

A View from the Bridge from a 500-seat theatre to a 1,300-seat theatre in the middle of Broadway. That is why plays are being done more.

BIGSBY: But does it also say something about what audiences are looking for?

MILLER: Look, I felt the audience was there. I have never really felt they were not there; there were just not as many of them with money to spend on theatre tickets as there are now. There is a boom going on here. There is a klondike, a lot of people with money to spend, and they do not apparently mind spending whatever it takes to get into a theatre now, more so than for probably twenty or thirty years, maybe more.

BIGSBY: This is very unlike you. Usually, you are offering a jeremiad on the state of the American theatre.

MILLER: Well, it is still hanging by a thread. This is a function of the booming economy more than anything else, I think.

BIGSBY: I remember you withdrew from the stock market just before the '87 crash. Are you pulling out again now?

MILLER: I never believed in it. I still do not believe now. I have my fingers in my ears waiting for it to explode again. It will come down with a bang. It has been doing that forever. The trick is to not be in it when it falls, but the fact that it is going to fall I do not think anybody really seriously doubts. Now they are repealing some of the New Deal legislation which was put in after the Crash in order to ensure that, in the event of an economic problem in the country, the banks would be left unaffected. They insulated the banks against a crash on the stock market, for example. How did they do it? They did it by a law forbidding banks to be in the insurance business, the brokerage business, this business, that business; banks were banks once more. Now they are removing all that, so that banks can once again speculate with your money on the stock market. They are just asking for the catastrophe again. It is as though they are once more hypnotised by this endless upward boom, and the banks want to get in on it, and apparently they are going to. If it slides, it will take everything with it. So have a good meal, enjoy the day. It is problematic, the whole situation.

18

Resurrection Blues

BIGSBY: In *Resurrection Blues* [2002] you create a play in which . . .
MILLER: The sublime and the ridiculous rub together, cheek by jowl.
BIGSBY: It is set in a Latin American country, and yet it is in large part about America. What aspect of America interested you?
MILLER: I guess it comes down to the use of language, for one thing. In the play there is a dictator who was fronting a revolutionary movement. There has been a war on, basically for the last thirty-five or thirty-six years, and it goes on, as he says, like a haemorrhage. It just continues. And this young man has appeared, up in the mountains, and the peasants, who are very uneducated and simple people, have come to believe he is the Messiah returned, and worship him. The dictator has arrested him and decided that shooting him won't work, because they see people shot on television every day of the week, and it makes no impression on anybody any more. But if he crucifies him, it will get their attention and will pacify the population for another few years. The thing is that an American advertising company is making an offer of $75 million for the rights to photograph the

crucifixion as it happens, to put it on television, and to sell advertising while it is happening. Because it takes about five or six hours for him to die, they would probably show it worldwide, attach ads to it, and make a real bundle out of this.

In the course of the play, it gets more and more reasonable that he should be doing it. The advertising man who represents the company comes down and says, 'We're only photographing it. There's no reason why not. It's not our responsibility. It's the way they do things down here.' It is a question of where the limits are. Are there any, when you get a lot of money involved in an event?

But it is also a question of language, because the way language is used and misused in the play is a lot like the way language is misused in our political life now. George Bush has just appeared in Maine [2004] to espouse his terrific record as a conservationist. He says that America's air is cleaner than it has ever been, which is true because the EPA's rules make it cleaner. But he doesn't add that they are gutting the EPA [Environmental Protection Agency] now. So from now on it is going to get much, much worse. That's the way it is in *Resurrection Blues*. It is one lie after another, which sounds marvellous. It sounds absolutely true. That's what it is about.

BIGSBY: Of course, you wrote this before Mel Gibson's *The Passion*, from which you emerged to buy replica nails from the crucifixion.

MILLER: Well, in my play, written two, three years ago, one of the characters, who is a beatnik, says of the Messiah, 'He must not come back down, because if he does, one of the things will be that they will be selling replicas of the nails' [in fact, fingernails].

BIGSBY: It is a play, it seems to me, about the disappearance of the idea of transcendence.
MILLER: Yes, that's a good way to put it.
BIGSBY: Because they have no faith. Even those who had ideologies have traded them in for something else.
MILLER: It is a curious thing. It goes along with a kind of criticism we generally have too, a reductionist attitude. Things are nothing but acts. You no sooner put out a work of fiction than these big flies start falling around it, digging in to find out where it comes from. Did this happen to you? In other words, they are trying to eviscerate the writer, whereas in the ancient time he was part of some zeitgeist. He was the voice of some mysterious spirit. Now it is directly the opposite. So they reduce everything to its biographical elements, if there are any. Where did you get this idea? And my answer usually is, if I knew, I would go there in a rocket.
BIGSBY: You grew up in an ideological age. Is there a sense that somehow the axle has disappeared from the car, that there is actually nothing particular driving experience? Experience is simply accumulating events.
MILLER: That is correct. I think so. The remnants of religion have been flattened out. Some acid dropped on the thing and it dissolved. It has gone. If you pick up a nineteenth-century novel, whether it is Dostoevsky or any British novelist or French, in the distance you hear the Bible somewhere, the spirit of the transcendent spirit. All we get now basically is the spirit of decay, the threat of dissolution. This is imminent. It is on the horizon. It is a different thing. I always read the Bible.
BIGSBY: Why?

MILLER: I love that language. It is terrific. I haven't read it in years now, but I used to read it a lot. I read Shakespeare too.

BIGSBY: Is it just the language or is it the idea of transcendence?

MILLER: I feel religion is a very dangerous game to put in the hands of ordinary people, because it makes them so manipulable by unscrupulous priests and rabbis. There is hardly a violent, catastrophically violent, conflict in the world today that is not led by religion. There would be no Northern Ireland or Israel and Palestinians, all the rest of it. After all, the leaders of the Israeli push to establish those settlements were religious people, Orthodox. They interpreted the Bible as giving a whole lot of land to Israel. The ignition of the Palestinian craziness derives from the idea that the Jews do not belong in Jerusalem. What they do with a thousand years of history is their business, but the capacity of the religion to lie is endless. There is no depth they won't sink to.

BIGSBY: Your version of God, however, whether it is in *The Creation of the World and Other Business* or *Resurrection Blues*, is of a very self-doubting deity.

MILLER: That is like every creator who is of any depth. He wants to smash whatever he has got before it is finished. I have never heard of a great painter or great architect who was not on the verge of destroying what he did. My impulse was to write about the possible origins of morality in the psychological make-up of the human family. There is a reason why something would be right or wrong, and if you don't pay attention to that, somebody is going to get killed. Out of that impulse to murder comes the impulse for [order]. Man created God in order to enforce this.

19

Theatre

BIGSBY: What, for you, is the essence of theatre?

MILLER: I suppose it is the direct communication from one human being to many with no screen in between, either metaphorical or real. It is the closest thing we have to an unmitigated contact with live human beings en masse, the mass with the individual. I guess that is coming down to the rudimentary bottom of it all, because the other media always have something in between, a camera lens, editing, etc.
I think playwriting is partly acting. In my case it is, anyway. Playwriting, for me, even Shakespeare, is not primarily a literary occupation, it is partly a performance in itself. Good dialogue, good dramatic speeches, practically speak themselves. Once the actor achieves the secret of them, they roll off. That is because the playwright has acted them out, either literally by speaking them or in his imagination, and it is a different operation completely.

BIGSBY: But it means that you can never know that what you hear when you sit in front of the typewriter or computer and speak the lines will be what an audience will hear.

MILLER: You can almost always be sure that it won't be, in my case. I found, for example, in my plays that the actors are perpetually discovering that I have not been writing realistic dialogue. About the third day of rehearsal, they realise that nobody really talks like this, and therefore people who are not talented enough, or do not have enough wit to understand, will never get to the bottom of these plays. They will be doing them on a level that is extremely superficial and has only a remote connection with what I intended.

BIGSBY: Does that mean that a playwright is fated to be frustrated?

MILLER: Always. That is the nature of the game. In the decades that went by after the Shakespearean era was over, they did not know what the hell to do with his work. Right through until relatively modern times it was an elocution lesson for most audiences. It was full of bombast, strange locutions, people talking some language they could not make much of. Certainly, they could not connect any emotional life with it. If it could happen to him, it could happen to anybody. This is a real risk, and it accounts, I think, for the rise and demise of many playwrights over the years. The interpretation is cockeyed, and it loses its tenuous connection with life.

BIGSBY: How can an audience tell with a new play whether it is the play or the production that is at fault?

MILLER: Very difficult, almost impossible. What you hear is the actor's voice. What you are listening to is his interpretation, mistaken or not, of the text, interfered with by all kinds of so-called production values that may or may not be adequate to the text, or even relevant to it. It is a real mess. But it is the nature of the beast. If you are a composer, and the notes look great on the page, and then some oaf picks it up and starts to play stupidly, you are dead. And everybody thinks the piece is no good. A hundred years passes and some really great player finds it, and people say, 'I wonder why nobody understood that this was such a good piece.' Likewise, of course, a piece can sound marvellous and then, twenty years later, they realise it wasn't any good. It was just a good player. Performance art is in the hands of the performer, to a large degree. There is no way around that. Of course, we are hearing language on the stage, so you know whether it is terrific or dull language, but without the performer you can't move. Therefore, you have to make your peace. The theatre is a libretto for a singer. It is exactly the same. If you write an opera, and you get musicians who really do not dig that kind of music, you are out the window. I remember there was a recording made years ago of Toscanini doing one of the Beethoven symphonies. I had heard other versions, but when Toscanini recorded it, you jumped out of your chair. It was the same notes. That is the way it goes with any kind of art that has to be performed, I am afraid.

I accept having to deal with the mechanics of the theatre, which are simply that you have got to find actors who are capable and hopefully talented and somehow fit the roles you have written. That is a big job, and it is worse today, more difficult than it ever was. Then there is the director, scene designer, all the rest, who mount that play and make it live. Otherwise, it is simply a score for an orchestra that never assembles to play anything. You do not resent it. It is just like a horse that pulls a wagon. A horse does not pull the wagon if nobody is going to feed him, so you pull the wagon, but I do not particularly look forward to, or enjoy, doing that. Some playwrights, however, do. They like to direct their work. I would do it if I could stand the boredom of hearing everything sixteen times. I can't bear that. After a while my mind goes dead, so I would much rather somebody else's mind went dead.

BIGSBY: Does that mean that, as a writer, you want to be present when a production is being put together, or would you rather keep out of it?

MILLER: The reason I would rather keep out of it is this. It is not very common that they can get the actors who belong in one of my plays. It is nobody's fault. It is just that George happens to be in California or South Africa at the moment and, with all the good will in the world, the temperament, the appearance, the age, the voice of an actor is wrong for that role, and there is nothing you can do about it. You can talk until you are blue in the face. He can be trying his best. He will give a version of it, but he won't give you the heart of it, the soul of it. So what are you going to do? What you get is an attitude of fatalism. I throw these crumbs on the water and hope somebody is going to find them to whom they belong.

BIGSBY: But all of this makes me come back to the question of why did you not stay with the novel, which does not bring any of those kinds of issues?

MILLER: Because you cannot see people applauding in the novel; you cannot witness the impact of a novel. But it is more than that. I find myself very impatient with descriptive writing. I enjoy it a lot, and many times I read a book for that reason. I found very early that I got attracted, for some accidental reason, to Dostoevsky. I was a teenager, and though this sounds insane I thought he was a mystery writer. The book was called *Crime and Punishment*, and it had a detective. But I found that the parts I enjoyed most was where they were talking. I would skim down pages and see the dialogue, and that was what I loved to read. The rest of it was okay, and I would go back over it and read those things rather dutifully, but it was the words, the speech, that intrigued me. Speech is the evidence of the person's being; the rest of it is commentary. When you are reading a text, and suddenly in any text, a journalistic text, a study of housing, a man who lives in one of these houses says, 'I think this house is beautiful, excepting that the toilets don't work', that tells you in one sentence what would probably take a lot more to do. I love the concision of it, the compression. It is harder to bull around with what people are saying. You have to have more evidence. It is a witness to an event. So you come to climaxes more cleanly. The dialectic is sharper.

Almost anything can be theatre, performed in front of an audience. A magic show is theatre, recitation of poems is theatre, or could be, or a demonstration of the absurdity of trying to get through a traffic jam, whatever. Drama is a different order of experience. Half the time we have lost the way of separating them. I used to know a very old friend of mine who was a policeman in New York. We grew up together, and I hadn't seen him for twenty years, then I saw him again. By that time, I was a playwright and he was a policeman, and he said, 'I don't go to the theatre.' I said, 'Why?' He said, 'I don't like it.' I said, 'What is there not to like?' He said, 'Just when it is getting really interesting, they pull the curtain down.' He wasn't onto the ritual. He had also been brought up on the movies, which estranged him from the ritualised acceptance that there is a crisis in a play which whets the appetite, and then you return from getting a smoke or breath of air and you head towards the climax, or resolution. He did not know how to listen to a play. He was not acculturated to it, that's all. It is not good or bad; that is the way it is. I think that is probably true of a lot of people who simply haven't been through the requisite cultivation, you might call it, of the theatre.

BIGSBY: An English playwright, Peter Nichols, once remarked that the problem with Broadway at the moment is a severely under-rehearsed audience.

MILLER: It is a very good thought, or very uneducated critics, you might say, or inexperienced ones, or ones that have only one kind of experience. The theatre is infinitely various. It is not just one kind of show. I guess the big question is whether it is going to be around for very long. Even when I go to anything in New York I wonder why they bother. It is so difficult to go to the damn thing. Maybe people like that. Maybe that is part of the attraction, that they have got to get there through this congested city. They have got to withstand the threat of being robbed, being banged over the head. They have got to pay an outlandish sum of money, $50 or $60, to sit there for two hours. It is insane, and yet, if there is a big enough excitement about something, they will tear the doors down to get in there. I think part of the thing is they want to feel that they are in on it. But, let's face it, we are talking about 1 per cent of the population. If there are 800 seats in a theatre, that means 6,400 people if it is packed every week. We are talking about a clique. The difficulty of going to the theatre, and the cost of the ticket, which I think is just prohibitive, has made a big difference. You naturally block out, for example, schoolteachers, who used to be a large part of the audience. You block out the young intellectual who is trying to find his way through the history of ideas and does not have all that much money.

BIGSBY: In the Greek theatre the notion was that drama was concerned with addressing the whole nation state. Has that ceased to be true?

MILLER: Yes, it has ceased to be true. I think what happened is an increasing domination by various cliques.

The theatres tend to want to preach to the converted. Maybe that is an inevitable thing, but we often get the domination of style, and it is as though the purpose of the theatre is to confirm that dominating style. The idea of using a style to transcend visible reality and arrive at some fundamental truth seems to me to have disappeared. The theatre does not take human beings all that seriously, does not take issues all that seriously. There is no life-and-death thing, and therefore cannot be any tragic story. Life is basically seen as a kind of unfunny comedy. We live in an ironic age, but that does not mean that you have to be ironic.

BIGSBY: When you started writing for the theatre, back in the 1930s, you said that you wanted to use theatre as a way of changing things. Presumably over the years that conviction has dulled.

MILLER: It has not gone, but it is close to being gone. There is a sigh of exhaustion going on all around on that score. However, it is not just the theatre. We are in the hands of gods that do not reveal their faces. They are probably blind and deaf and are just going about their business, and we have to wait to see what their work has turned out to be. So it is not just the theatre that has lost this feeling of the capacity to control events, because that is what it comes to.

BIGSBY: How protective are you of the text you have written? How willing to see actors change lines, directors make alterations?

MILLER: I would love them to do it if they did it better, but they generally do it embarrassingly worse, so I therefore protect the whole thing. I do not allow it if I can help it. There are occasions when a production idea occurs, as happened in London, when they did *A View from the Bridge* with Michael Gambon. I have never seen a production like that for one reason. They were not acting the syntax of the lines, but the rhythm, so that from time to time they speeded that thing up and, with the speed-up, moved with no realistic motivation. It was a kind of dance-like movement, a dance-like movement not just simply to be such, but to express some underlying anxiety or climax or awareness or realisation, and it simply swept up the whole audience, and myself. I was astonished by that production, and I could never dream of a production like that. It changed the way it is normally produced.

Why did it fit that play to do it in that way? I think because it was avowedly built on a Greek model. What came to me through all that was this marvellous stasis, this mobile immobility, this feeling that these gigantic figures are overwhelming you, or are about to overwhelm you and, in *A View from the Bridge*, Gambon got to the point where I got scared. In the last ten minutes of that play, I was physically frightened. I felt this guy is going to do something absolutely murderous. I knew what the text was. I knew what he had to do. It didn't matter. So therefore, I am perfectly overjoyed when something like that happens. As to changes in individual lines, I do not allow them if I can help it.

BIGSBY: The London production of *The American Clock* [1986] made various changes.

MILLER: Right. Peter Wood did make some changes and put in a few lines, which I did not object to because they were not very decisive lines. He stuck in something about the Vietnam War, but that was all right because we had both agreed that it had to be a kind of vaudeville show and, in a vaudeville show, you do improvise. So it did not really hurt anything. Altering lines is the problem, as I see it. If we had an actor here, he might differ. Actors, like the rest of us, don't like too much difficulty. They would rather find an easier way to do something. Very often in a play there is a speech, or a sequence of speeches, which are particularly difficult to do to elicit their meaning. Emphases, tempo, all sorts of things get involved. It is hard to keep all these balls in the air sometimes, so they like little short cuts which, they say, is essentially the same thing. 'Essentially' is about the longest word in the dictionary: you can stretch it out to circumscribe the world. This evasion complex is a problem we all have. Once they start fiddling, they are always making it easier when they should not make it easier. They should confront the difficulties and stretch themselves rather than the language. That is why I warn them to stay with it.

I have a story that happened the other night. They did *The Price* in New York with Eli Wallach playing the old Jew, Solomon. In the middle of one of his speeches a fly, a real fly, not an Actors' Equity fly, landed on his nose. He brushed it away and it came back again. He brushed it away and it kept bombing him, so the actor playing the policeman walked over. He had parked his pistol at the opening of the play in his holster on the table. He took the pistol out, walked back to Eli and started aiming at this fly. Eli described this to me on the phone. I did not see it, but he said the audience was simply dying of laughter, and the fly disappeared. Well, he said, we never got out of character. We played it like it was really happening. That could only happen in the theatre. So, I said, 'Why don't you keep it in?' He said, 'But where am I going to get a fly that will do that?' But I loved that idea. It became part of the life for that audience, that cast and that play at that moment.

There is a species of tension in a good performance of a good play that I do not find in a film, a specific kind of tension which has to do not with techniques, not with machinery, but with a human being and a concrete situation in a definite place where the actors have a personal connection with the audience. It is a miracle and that kind of miracle I don't see happening in a mechanical medium, I don't care what it is.

BIGSBY: What is the ideal relationship for you between writer and director?

MILLER: First of all, the director should be the servant of the play. He should not conceive of himself as being a co-author. There are some authors who want a co-author, perfectly legitimately. Hundreds of plays have been written by two or more people, but my concepts are mine and I don't want them to be messed with. So, for me, the best director is somebody who will plumb what I have done, come up with contradictions, perhaps, say, 'You can't say this if you are going to say that.' I want someone who will objectify what to me is still subjective. Then I will have to defend it, but I like to do that. I do not, though, like someone trying to use the play as something that reminds him of something else. You see a lot of directors who think they should use the play at hand as a skeleton for some other play that they have got in their minds. Maybe they could get some poor play that hasn't got any life of its own and make something interesting out of it. That is possible, but I don't want to be involved with that, because I think I would rather see my own stuff on the stage and sink or swim with it. In other words, the director should try to interpret the play, not create his own.

BIGSBY: Is there a gravitational pull towards realism in the American theatre?

MILLER: Right. They can't stand a metaphor. Metaphor is dangerous, ambiguous; it leaves people slightly mystified, and the conscience of the American theatre is that of an intelligent businessman. He is a realistic, intelligent, even sensitive person, but he ain't interested in metaphors. He wants to know who is on first, and this has made for a very strong realistic tradition, not just in the theatre but in the novel, the movies and so on. But as soon as you begin to stretch that into a metaphoric area, they get uneasy.

They are always trying to push you back into the old bucket. Plays are nothing but . . . whatever. This is not a play about America, like, let's say, *The Last Yankee*, it is a play about a neurotic woman and her stupid husband. It is remarkable, the absence of that kind of sensitivity. I suppose it is a part of the cultural strength of the country as well as a weakness, but to me it is destructive. They make allowances for it in other arts, like the ballet, which, of course, can't be realistic, or painting. But to make a juncture of some kind between a concept and an action is very difficult for some of them. I find the audiences are better than the critics in that respect. Critics are always trying to get to the bottom of things, when they are already at the bottom of things, if they only knew.

BIGSBY: In an age of multichannel television and virtual reality, does the theatre have a future?

MILLER: It depends what day it is. I think there are more people in the United States who are interested in the theatre, interested in being actors, actresses, writers, than I ever experienced in my life. They are all over the place. There are theatres in places I never thought there would ever be a theatre, places in Nebraska, in North Dakota, South Dakota, God knows where, that weren't around when I was coming up. On the other hand, the production process is crippled by the costs of it. I don't want to get into that terribly boring subject, but that has put the critic into an extremely important position, which he probably does not like. I do not know that many critics, but I am sure they would not appreciate the fact that they are not simply criticising the show but may be responsible for closing it. That was not in Aristotle. You weren't supposed to be closing *Oedipus Rex* because you did not like it. So those are the obvious difficulties.

But I think there may be a different dimension to it all, and that is that there is a sense of haste. I feel it myself. I turn on the television and if the damn thing doesn't jump at me and make me listen, I get rid of it, and I suspect that that is what is happening to people now. The people that do come to the theatre, at least the ones I know about, are not substantially different from the ones that used to come to the theatre. They seem, it appears to me, to be as patient and as attentive as they ever were, but I think there is a pressure on people now, that there used not to be, to dispose of stuff which does not make them die laughing or grovel on the floor weeping or send them home crazy. If it is just something quite touching, it probably is not going to have the effect it used to have. We have been jabbed too many times by too many sensations, and maybe the time has come when we are numb.

I find it difficult to pick up a book and finish it any more. I feel there is something else I should be doing. I used to read books that were mildly interesting. I cannot get myself to read a book like that any more. What can I say? Of course, there are probably more plays being written in the United States today than there are shoes being manufactured. Everybody writes a play after his mother has finished using the typewriter. I have never seen so many plays, and the people who receive these plays, and have to choose them, tell me that one is worse than the other, but that doesn't discourage anybody. Maybe it is all for the best. Maybe we are improving little by little, sideways instead of going forward. I am not entirely pessimistic, sort of medium pessimistic.

What I do not find, to tell you the truth, excepting for a very few writers, is the idea that they are writing a play for everybody. It is hard to explain this. When my generation was coming up, we had this cockeyed idea that in the audience would be the policeman, the man on welfare, the working man, the lawyer, the doctor, etc. The whole society would be out there. Strictly speaking, that was never the case. There were never any Blacks in the audience. There were hardly any poor people that I ever saw. It was a middle-class theatre, middle and upper class, but the illusion was powerful enough so that it affected the ways plays were written.

Tennessee Williams' plays and, I think, mine, can be played in front of any audience. You don't have to have gone to college to receive those plays, to appreciate them. There are not many literary references in them. There are not too many words that are difficult. The emotions are basic emotions. Something happened in the fifties, or maybe in the early sixties, that narrowed that audience down to the college-educated people, more sophisticated people, and the plays began to get narrower and appealed to a small recondite group of people who were basically talking to each other and made a point of not sharing the tastes of the great unwashed masses. And no excuses were made for this. In Siracusa they had 14,000 seats. Those gathered there weren't all intellectuals. It was the entire population of that area, and yet they could listen to some of the most pure philosophical work that has ever been written. So that, for me, is the fundamental difference.

We have a few writers who understand that their inheritance, going back two or three thousand years, has given them the right to address the whole population, but there are not that many. I think most of the writing has been secret writing for most people. I have friends who are uneducated people, and I would not know what show to take them to, because they would be at sea. They would be lost. They would not know what the hell to make of it, excepting for the musicals. The musicals are still aimed at most people. What they are aimed at is another story, but the target is the masses, and they have a certain vigour as a result. It has a kind of muscularity which is there, and which I think most of our theatre does not have.

BIGSBY: Looking back, how did you see your plays in relation to audiences?

MILLER: You were writing for the whole people. As I said, I never thought I was writing for intellectuals. However, I considered that intellectuals might be interested in these plays. I never thought that I was writing for hip people. I thought that I had to present, in dramatic terms, an argument which would draw in anyone with common sense, almost anybody who was alive in the United States at the same time as I was. You felt that you were embracing the whole city, and therefore the whole country. And for that reason, the nature of the plays we were writing had a story. Psychologically, they had some depth, but they were translatable into common experience.

The theatre as a whole began to dissipate. Tennessee Williams, who had a quite different orientation towards things, felt the same way about it, that people weren't caring much any more about the feelings we were dealing with. They were being ironical, rather cold, cool, unmoved about life.

What I was looking for back in 1956 was holding a broader audience by some kind of subsidy, or by lowering prices to a degree that anybody could get in. Mind you, at the time prices went anywhere from $4.40 to $6.60 to $8.80 or $10. It seemed to me a scandal. I didn't know anybody who could afford $10 to get into a theatre or would want to pay $10. We are now [1989] without an audience at all for what you could call a serious theatre. They have been driven out by habit. Now we've got to start from scratch. The implication, since I am speaking in Britain, is that if you go the way we went, you may well end up in the same place, that is, you ain't going to have a theatre. We have shows. That's not a theatre.

This country [England] was the one hope, as far as I was concerned, in the later years. It was because of the subsidised theatre. The theatre of the bottom line, meaning that what pays big goes, and what doesn't pay big doesn't deserve to live, is a catastrophe. There is an enormous amount of print in the *New York Times* every Sunday, billions of trees go down, and you will see 'Entertainment News' which will tell you what this star uses as a hair rinse, and how he or she started as a grocery clerk, but nobody discusses the question 'Where's the audience?' Nobody. There is nothing to discuss except that. Any discussion in this country which does not fasten on the question of subsidy is useless, because it is an art that cannot work on a commercial basis for very long. It won't go. The costs are too high. Society has to make a decision: do we want to have significant theatre? If we do, you've got to pay for it, as you do with symphony orchestras or opera. The ticket will not pay for it. On Broadway, the ticket does pay for the musical, and that is what you've got. You go from one musical to another. They are not even good musicals most of the time. If I sound hysterical it's because I can't get anybody to register the news. And that is where you are heading. You will be back where we are. Maybe, if that is the decision, then you will have to ask yourself whether there is a mass audience, or even anything remotely like it, possible any more. Then you will have to go into the corners of the towns, certainly not in the middle of London, New York or Paris, and find a little place to put on your play, but in that case you had better not write a play with more than four or five characters. You had better not write a play with twelve characters and, God forbid, with music. So it is going to narrow that play. It will be a strange little item on the tail of the shirt of history.

BIGSBY: Why, then, does theatre matter?

MILLER: I think it matters because it is the only form where you get a human being, as a human being, addressing you, instead of a machine. When you are looking at a movie you are looking at a machine. It is the difference between shaking hands with your friend and shaking hands with a camera. The intensity of the feelings is accordingly greater. You are far more intellectually active in the theatre than you can ever be with a film. As a consequence, because you put more into it, you get more out of it. The theatre will never go away for that reason. It is the simplest, most naked way of dramatising life.

BIGSBY: You did, eventually, turn *The Crucible* into a film, though not without ambiguous feelings about the medium.

MILLER: Until now I have never attempted to write a film of one of my plays, *Everybody Wins* [1990] aside. That was partly my adaptation and partly the invention of others. As a consequence, the unity of the whole thing suffers. You get a kind of bastardised vision. It sometimes works, it sometimes doesn't. The ideal thing for me is the director writing his own screenplay, or a screenplay writer directing what he has done. I let other people do it, and I have always regretted it. It is not that they are bad writers or directors, it is that a play is fundamentally based on words and a movie is based on images. I have often thought that the worst source of a movie is a play; a better source is a novel, because it doesn't rely on dialogue as much. After all, a novel is giving you pictures. It is describing events, which a film does. So I have not had the experience of being gratified by any movie made of any play of mine. I have written the screenplay of *The Crucible* because I always felt it has the possibility of being a great movie, but nobody, then, wanted to do it. It seemed to me that it can be transformed from a play into a succession of terrific images, and it need not rely, as it does on stage, basically on words. I think, I hope, I have succeeded in doing that. [It was subsequently successfully filmed in 1996, with Daniel Day-Lewis as John Proctor.]

20

Looking Back

BIGSBY: You said you are not really pessimistic. As you face the future, has that changed? [October, 1991]
MILLER: Pessimism to me is sentimentalism. I get very depressed when people raise serious subjects in the theatre or the movies and then sentimentalise them. That means that they really can't face the facts. That is saddening. That is pessimism. Beyond that, I am prepared for anything.

After all, had Saddam Hussein not been stopped, presumably he would have had an atom bomb. I do not question that he would have dropped it on Israel and, if he had, we would be confronting Armageddon. Half a dozen countries now have the weapon which they could float into New York Harbour, or up the Thames. If I were to say to myself that that is the whole truth, then I am a pessimist, but I do think there are forces working against that event. So, all I believe in is the dialectic, the conflict that will undoubtedly continue indefinitely. Parts of it get resolved, only for new conflicts to develop. I'll tell you something, though, when I cross the streets in London that have those arrows that say 'Look that way', I look both ways.
BIGSBY: And what of your earlier radicalism?

MILLER: We are in a different age, and the so-called radical part of the world is now in shambles. In my opinion it has been so for the past forty years. I have been going to Russia for at least twenty-five of those years, and I lost any hope for them four decades ago. That kind of radicalism has had no basis in reality for me for a very long time. I don't think you can talk in those terms any more. The radical centres of the world are now hungry for the old enemy to come in and buy up their produce. What do you say to that? You simply have to register the way the world moves, and it has moved. In a way I am glad it has moved. At least we now have a conceivable way of moving towards an equitable future if various problems are solved. But good and evil are not separable. They are intertwined. To try to separate them is to fall into what used to be called Manichaeism, which is simply the idea that there is a dark side of life and a light side of life, and the dark and the light never mix. I don't believe that. To describe the nature of existence with that kind of balance is not the easiest thing in the world. It is only really a symbolic work of art that can ever attempt to approximate it.

BIGSBY: Your diaries are laced through with self-doubt. But you have written all these plays.

MILLER: I figure my whole life has been a struggle with self-doubt. Everything I have ever done has always been to prove that I could make this stick to the wall. It wouldn't bounce off. But most of it did bounce off. I would write and write and write, and very little of the stuff would be published or produced. When you consider the bulk of the words, a minor percentage have ever seen the light of day.

BIGSBY: The world has obviously changed tremendously since you were born in Harlem in 1915. Was the world really any more innocent then than it is now, or does it just seem that way in retrospect?

MILLER: I think it was, quite frankly. I think, objectively speaking, there were certain expectations about human beings which were unrealistic, and which were commonly held, and you could say that that is a kind of naivety. I think that the two world wars did us in, and the concentration camps and the whole fascist interlude, which lasted something like twenty-five or thirty years, from Mussolini to the end of World War II, and the communist experience in Russia and Eastern Europe. However, that is not to say that we are not capable any longer of feeling hope for the future. I see [life] as a truly endless struggle. There is no time when we are going to arrive at a plateau where the whole thing gets solved. It is a struggle in the way that every plant has to find its way to stand up straight. The conditions of existence are pretty well fixed. Otherwise, we wouldn't, for example, be able to understand Shakespeare or the Greek plays. If you go beneath the surface half an inch, you know who these people are. All these plays are probably in one sense projections of that struggle and my attempt to assert a human victory over conditions, the conditions given both genetically and environmentally. A lot of the time it is a failure, but it is not a failure if there is some enlightenment that comes out of it.

BIGSBY: Have you suffered, as you seem to think, from not having had a relationship with an individual theatre, in the way that in Britain Wesker, Bond and Osborne did with the Royal Court and David Hare has with the National Theatre, David Edgar with the Royal Shakespeare Company?

MILLER: I am quite sure of it. I think had there been any theatre, in that sense, in the United States, in my career I would have written many more plays. I have no doubt about it. The commercial theatre has its advantages. It does some excellent work now and again. One of its disadvantages is that it is a very unfriendly place in which to work. In general it looks at an artist in terms of how much money can be made on him at all times, but there is a kind of art that can't make any money at any particular moment. It may later on, but it won't now, or it won't make as much money as another kind of art. So, consequently you get into a conflict which is simply irreconcilable. What I wanted was a place that would welcome whatever it was that I wanted to do, and I never found it. Lincoln Center, in recent years, has tried to reconstitute itself, and I hope it will.

BIGSBY: Can you really have a national theatre in a country the size of America?

MILLER: No. I think what you can have is far more activity of a creative sort in the local theatres. We have a lot of wonderful local groups, but they are scared to death now. They need the money, and they are not getting it. They are reverting to safe plays and safe ideas.

BIGSBY: Comedy seems to have become more central to you from, say, *The Price* onwards.

MILLER: I am not sure I know how to explain that except, as you get older, I guess it gets funnier. Partly I think it has got to do with the awareness that the human being is constantly rediscovering the same thing, and that is funny. I was very young when the Great Depression occurred, and we discovered radicalism. Then fifteen years passed by, and we discovered radicalism again. I thought, 'I've been here before.' Then it was discovered again about ten years later. You begin to wonder what's new. At the same time, things will change. It is not a dead repetition of the same thing, although the oriental religions are very often based on the wheel that simply keeps turning and turning. I do think we learn something. Sometimes we learn a lot, but there is a vast repetitiousness in life that is comical, and the pretensions of people, including one's own, become funny.

BIGSBY: Do you ever look back at your work and wonder how you wrote it?

MILLER: I always do that. I just rewrote a story that I found and thought, 'How the hell did I get myself to write this piece?' It is only fifteen or sixteen pages. It is like diving off a high building, and you hope you are going to land in a net. It is really the difference between a creative act and an imitative act, I suppose. The risk gives it its energy. It is winning out over a high obstacle, and with a lot of writers the obstacle is not very high. If you stop doing that habitually it can be harmful.

BIGSBY: Does it depress you that people tend to think of you in relation to your early plays?

MILLER: That is inevitable. I don't mind it really. I think it is pretty lucky to have come up with a couple of things that have become coin of the realm. Why not? What does a writer want? He wants to have left his thumbprint on the world.

BIGSBY: You have been in the theatre for most of your life. If you had been denied that line of work, for some reason or other, what would you have been happiest doing?

MILLER: I am not sure I would have been happy, but I probably would have written movies, I think, and ended up shooting myself.

BIGSBY: I had this vision of you becoming a carpenter.

MILLER: Well, it could have come to that, because the kind of movies that were being made when I was coming into the field were so inane that I probably could not have hung in there with it long enough to succeed. But I could have made a living as a carpenter, sure.

BIGSBY: You made the bed you sleep on.

MILLER: Our bed is made of cherry, and I get a great satisfaction from creating something out of nothing, which is really what a writer is doing anyway. We'd been sleeping on that bed for twenty-five years. Every time my wife laid down to go to sleep she said, 'I love this bed', because it is immensely comfortable. It's solid and ain't nothing going to happen to it. It will be there as long as anybody wants to use it. So, there is something immortal in that.

BIGSBY: What drives you back to the computer at a time when you could reasonably have packed it up and relaxed?

MILLER: What the hell do you do with yourself? I cannot just sit around all day. I have this itch which I suppose goes on to the end. Anyway, it is just fun. I enjoy it a lot, getting something to work. It is better than lying there on your back staring at the ceiling. So off I go into the blue yonder again. I also have a weakness for actors. When they are transformed, or seem to be, by something I wrote, it's a miracle. When they become somebody I imagined, it moves me very much. I guess the other thing is the wonder of it all, that I am still here, that so much of it did work, and that the people are so open. It gives me a glimpse of the idea that there is one humanity. There is just one homo sapiens. Underneath all the different etiquettes, and the incomprehensible languages, we are one. I think it is a sort of miracle.

I cannot imagine what I would do with myself if I wasn't writing. I don't write that much. I haven't got thirty plays or so by me. It takes me a long time to get a play from start to finish, several years usually. But I couldn't retire. I wouldn't know what to do. It would be like cutting my heart out. Why would you do that?

21

Arthur Miller at Eighty

[On the occasion of his eightieth birthday, after a public conversation at the local theatre, Miller was celebrated with a gala dinner attended by writers, directors, actors, critics and members of his family, along with the public, in the Sainsbury Centre for Visual Arts at the University of East Anglia, home to the Arthur Miller Centre for American Studies. The principal speeches were by the director of many of his plays, David Thacker, and Salman Rushdie, still under the fatwa declared in 1989. As Miller notes, it was a night complete with fireworks. What follows is the speech he delivered that night.]

MILLER: To say I am overwhelmed is an understatement. I never expected anything like this. In fact, I thought we would have six or seven wandering actors showing up. I'm glad I got to be eighty, I tell you that. When you ask me how it feels, I really have no idea, principally because I have a very defective grasp of the calendar, and I think I know why. When I was growing up, I had an older brother and a younger sister. We would be at dinner and my mother would suddenly say, 'It was your birthday last week.' So I never took it all that seriously. My father never knew when his birthday was. He adopted my sister's birthday for his, and I simply lost track of chronology. I was always a decade late trying to figure out how I felt. I had better hurry up.

Someone asked me in the theatre today why I thought my plays work in so many different cultures, and it made me think that I began writing basically with the idea that my father would understand what I was doing. He was all but illiterate; he could barely read and write to his dying day, but he was really wise, as such people sometimes are. They learn how to read lips, how to read intentions, what someone really means when he is saying those long words. If someone was telling a lie he would just sit there and listen, and then they would see that they hadn't made it with him, so they would elaborate a little bit. If that didn't work either, they would elaborate a little more. He would never say they were lying. He would just nod, but he had a look in his eyes that told you that you had better do better than that. Then they would come out with the truth, and he would say, 'In other words, that's it!' That is a lot like playwriting. There are many ways to write a character, but there is only one way to do it so that you say, 'That's it. That's him.' Sometimes it takes forever to arrive at that.

My father loved actors. He had two criticisms of them: one was, 'He puts it over' – that was good – or 'He's dry' – that meant he had not been affected by the guy. Actually, that's all there is to it. Sometimes he would ask me what I was writing, and here I was, trying to involve this heavy philosophy through my plays, but I could not talk to him on those terms, so I had to boil it down to human actions. I could see in his eyes whether I was making it or not, because, if I was not, they wandered a little, but if I was telling the story right, and the thing was true, he knew that it was the real goods. If you were just horsing around up there, he knew that too. So, I owe a lot to that semi-literate man. It got built into my subconscious that I had to be talking to people like him as well as people who were graduates of various universities. In fact, when you took all the covering off, they were people like him. I believe sincerely that if there is any validity to my work it is because I have always felt that we are basically all one humanity. There are differences in etiquette, and there are differences in the way we express ourselves, but underneath we are man and woman born of woman, and we share far more than separates us.

I cannot separate myself, or my work, from the United States. The fate of that country, and of its culture, has always been at the back of my head, I think, because I was born into an era of fascism. The greatest subject in the world was the rise of Mussolini, Hitler and the Japanese dictatorships. We were living in an era when there was a real question as to whether the democratic system could survive. A lot of very intelligent people thought it could not. I think that stuck in my mind, politically. I learned to detect a certain seed of charity in the drifts of political opinions. Perhaps I am particularly sensitive to that, but it has always been there, and that has given a certain form to my work. I have said before that *The Crucible* is produced in certain countries that are about to be dictatorships, and in countries where dictatorships have just been overthrown. The instinct in whatever I have done is to create a defence in mind and spirit against that fascism of the heart.

I have been asked a number of times why my work is so well received in England, and, believe me, it is as unexpected as it could possibly be. I believe that the answer is simpler than one would suppose. It is simply that the British have still got a theatrical tradition. The theatre, with all its difficulties – and there are plenty of them – does have a public, and they want good stuff. Enough of them want it to support it. I fear that, at the cutting-edge of the future, as the United States usually is, we may be showing the way to a different culture altogether, one in which film and television supplant the theatre, to a large degree. I hope I am wrong. I believe that in one way or another there will always be theatre, but the idea of a professional theatre, a theatre which creates long-term careers for actors, to train themselves and develop over a long span of time, and for writers, is on very shaky ground.

I used to write commercial radio plays for years in order to support myself while I was writing plays for the theatre. Nowadays, people write plays in order to get picked up by television, and that is a profound difference. It means, let's face it, that the play is going to be slanted towards the television attitude, which, with all due respect to the few wonderful things I have seen, tends towards the quick fix. It is an impatient form. It needs quick solutions to dramatic problems. Therefore, it cannot go terribly deep, and I have the feeling that the art is under siege. We don't like to admit it, but I have seen too many plays on stage that were really television plays, which is not to demean them, but it is a different spirit from the theatrical spirit. It has not got time for character development in depth. I talk to students now and then, and I have found them hoping for a television career because that is where you can make a living. But, beyond that, they think in terms of pictures, and the theatre thinks in terms of language. They are not the same.

However, as I speak, there are at least six geniuses working in dark corners of this country to write great plays. They will always be there, and they will always come forward and astonish us all, at least I hope so. I am just happy that I managed to speak into this corner of the theatrical universe, where there are actors and a flat place to play, and some light and people out there interested enough to come. I think many of the people here know what a tremendous door out into the universe theatre can be. It can tell us how we should have behaved, how we are behaving, where the hope is and where the despair is. It can tell us almost everything if we listen.

I want to thank everyone involved in this occasion, and especially these crazy actors who came all the way up from London to be here with me. I think that most of them are mentally defective, thank God, or why else would they be in this idiotic business, but they are the salt of the earth, and people like me depend upon them to make us look good when sometimes we are not. So, there you go. I am here and you are here, and I am very happy for it. And the fireworks we just enjoyed are my favourite entertainment anyway. In New York, once I watched from the shore across the Hudson River. They were Fourth of July fireworks, many years ago. The whole boat blew up!

22

Arthur Miller at Eighty-Five

[In 2000, Miller became a Freeman of the City of Norwich. The award was conferred in the medieval Guildhall, in the presence of writers, directors, actors and academics. Among the speeches was one by fellow playwright Arnold Wesker, who had once lived in the city. This was his response.]

MILLER: Sitting here, and looking at this place, and thinking of this beautiful city for some reason, which I will probably understand years from now, I began thinking of where I began, which was in a very middle-class neighbourhood in Brooklyn. My first audience was there. In those days there was no television, so young guys used to hang out on the corner. They entertained each other. One guy could do accents, another knew a joke. Another one could stand on his head. We were desperate for some diversion. I invented stories. I could tell when my audience was about to kill me by the looks in their faces, when their eyes went blank. I knew I had to start cutting. That I should be standing here, in this beautiful city, in my ancient gown, and being lauded is quite astonishing. I, of course, always wanted to succeed. Anybody who doesn't want to succeed I don't think writes. But to have made a friend of this city is beyond anything I could have dreamed of. So, I thank you.

I just hope that, in the years to come, I can come back again with the same feeling that I am in a place I can call home.

[That evening, again in the presence of his fellow theatre practitioners, and in the Sainsbury Centre for Visual Arts of the University of East Anglia, he was once again praised, this time by Warren Mitchell, who had played the role of Willy Loman at the National Theatre and around the world, and by Michael Blakemore, who had directed several Miller plays, including *All My Sons*, *After the Fall*, *The Ride Down Mount Morgan* and *Mr Peters' Connections*. This was his brief reply, on what turned out to be his final visit to the university.]

MILLER: This has been a great day for me. It is very moving, to think that a city so far away from where I usually am should have such touching feelings about my work and myself. I am a bit speechless, because it is something that is not supposed to happen any more in our techno world.
I hope I deserved it all and that I can go on a little more and pick up a few threads that are still lying around. It strengthens me, and it has for years now, that the English people have been such steadfast fans of my work. It has helped me to go on. I'll try to carry on.

[Plans were made for another gala to mark his ninetieth birthday in 2005, but he died on 10 February that year, the same day of the same month on which *Death of a Salesman* had opened on Broadway in 1949.]

For EU product safety concerns, contact us at Calle de José Abascal, 56–1°,
28003 Madrid, Spain or eugpsr@cambridge.org.

www.ingramcontent.com/pod-product-compliance
Lightning Source LLC
LaVergne TN
LVHW041954060526
838200LV00002B/16